The Representation of
the United States Abroad

The Representation of the United States Abroad

Edited by
VINCENT M. BARNETT, JR.

REVISED EDITION

Published for

THE AMERICAN ASSEMBLY
Columbia University

by

FREDERICK A. PRAEGER, *Publishers*
New York · Washington · London

Frederick A. Praeger, *Publishers*
111 Fourth Avenue, New York 3, N.Y., U.S.A.
77–79 Charlotte Street, London W. 1, England

Published in the United States of America in 1965
by Frederick A. Praeger, Inc., *Publishers*

This is the revised edition of the book first published
in 1956 by The American Assembly.

Foreword

The Representation of the United States Abroad was first published in 1956 as a collection of background papers for the Ninth American Assembly, which met at Arden House, on the Harriman campus of Columbia University, May, 1956. Now it has been revised with a more general readership in mind. The original volume aimed to provide an account of developments in the field of overseas representation as a basis for focusing specifically on certain policy questions to be discussed at Arden House and in subsequent regional Assemblies with Stanford University. Tulane University, Southwestern at Memphis, and the University of Illinois. The present edition does not address itself primarily to the formulation of questions for discussion and debate but rather to a description and analysis of the continuing problems in this field.

The Ninth American Assembly was originally financed by a grant from the Carnegie Corporation of New York. Both the Corporation, however, and The American Assembly have taken no official position on the views expressed in either edition of this volume.

The American Assembly
CLIFFORD C. NELSON
President

Preface

The authors of the original papers of this volume all found it possible to take part in the revision of them for this new edition. In the case of Professor Fox's paper on military representation, we had the good fortune to enlist the assistance of a collaborator, Professor Davis, who has made a major contribution to what is a substantially rewritten piece. Each of the other papers has been revised by the original authors, taking the opportunity to reflect more recent developments and in some cases substantially recasting the material.

I thought it well to reproduce the introduction to the earlier edition in its original form, with some minor deletions of passages dealing specifically with the working of the Ninth Assembly session. This is an effort to make clear the assumptions on which the papers were written.

A good deal has happened since 1956 that bears on these assumptions. Yet most of these developments have served to confirm the assumptions. The basic premise of a nuclear stalemate between the U.S. and the U.S.S.R. rendering large-scale war unlikely would probably be more widely accepted today than when the volume first appeared. The prospect of competitive coexistence embracing a wide variety of confrontations—economic, political, propagandistic, as well as relatively small scale "proxy wars"—continues to be a good guess as to the shape of things to come. At the same time, however, there seems to be increasing possibility of limited accommodation with Russia in specific areas, brought about by U.S. strength and resolution, by the Sino-Soviet split in the Communist world, and by increasing evidences of centrifugal pressure among the Soviet satellites. This prospect is not necessarily threatened by the growing importance of the underdeveloped countries and the rapid emergence of new nations on the world stage. This is, of course, another area of confrontation in which the challenge to U.S. policy and to U.S. effectiveness in executing policy is great. But it is probably fair to say that the ideological penetration of the new nations by Soviet doctrine—at least as represented by solid ties to Soviet diplomacy and international adventurism—has been less extensive than most informed observers were expecting a few years ago. U.S. efforts in these countries are no doubt partly responsible for this, and must be maintained and strengthened. Imaginative innovations, such as the Peace Corps, have had a substantial effect. The emergence of new non-governmental institutions into prominent roles has also characterized recent years. Universities, private foundations, private consulting firms, internationally-minded business enterprises— all play a much more significant role than before.

For those who are concerned with the most effective organization and staffing of U.S. representation abroad, all of this adds up to an increasingly pluralistic, varied, complex set of tasks requiring not only clear general policy outlines but more professional and sophisticated overseas effort staffed by the best people and coordinated effectively both abroad and at home.

These are essentially the same conclusions reached in 1956. The intervening events have served to sharpen both their soundness and the urgency of their achievement.

There is a surprisingly high degree of consensus in the scholarly community on the main outlines of the needed improvements, although of course there are differences in emphasis and detail. There seems not to be much consensus in the political community, or at least not enough to give the problem of an effective career service for "the new diplomacy" the degree of priority and urgency it deserves.

Since 1956 there have been two special reports which reaffirm the character of these goals and the importance of early action aimed at their accomplishment. One is the Report of the Committee on Foreign Affairs Personnel, entitled *Personnel for the New Diplomacy*, published by the Carnegie Endowment for International Peace in December, 1962. The Committee focused its attention on the State Department, AID, and USIA. The report emphasized the importance of *operations* abroad, as distinct from observing and reporting; it argued that the responsibilities of this country cannot be adequately met by "generalists" with only a superficial knowledge of relevant specialties; and it stressed the "need to achieve a greater degree of unity amid the diversity of talents, perspectives, and efforts required in foreign affairs." Its major proposals to reflect these needs had to do with strengthening the primacy of the State Department in foreign affairs, the creation of a National Foreign Affairs College at the graduate level, and the passage of legislation establishing a family of compatible professional career services encompassing the respective foreign services of the Department of State, USIA, and AID. The primacy of the State Department's role would include the strengthening of the ambassador's role as coordinator of all U.S. activities in the country to which he is assigned.

The second report mentioned above, in a somewhat narrower field, also stressed the need for increasing professionalization of our overseas representation. This was John Gardner's *AID and the Universities*, published in 1964 both by AID and by Education and World Affairs, Inc., which provided the staff support for the study. This report, addressing itself primarily to the problems of technical assistance and the role of the universities, also came to the conclusion that statutory and organizational changes were necessary in the interest of a more highly professionalized and better-coordinated overseas effort. It urged the creation of "a small, permanent professional service" in the field of technical aid offering a lifetime career in social, economic, and political development. Along with this would go the establishment of a larger, more diversified "reserve" of university professors, business experts, men drawn from foundations and other non-profit organizations, and experts from relevant governmental departments and agencies, with a commitment to serve abroad periodically and a corresponding "right of re-entry without prejudice" in their regular careers. The report also recommended the creation of a semi-autonomous Government institute, the National Institute for Educational and Technical Cooperation, which would supplement AID by devoting its attention to the long-range aspects of foreign technical aid.

These reports, as well as the other developments since the issuance of the first edition of the present volume, serve to highlight the importance of serious attention to these problems by all who are concerned about the effective performance of our overseas obligations. When President Eisenhower set up the USIA by Executive Order in 1953, he authorized the agency to establish a separate personnel system based on the provisions of the Foreign Service Act of 1946. This action was intended to facilitate any future merging of the two systems. The President, referring to these arrangements at the time, said, "I do not consider them permanently suitable. There is need for a critical analysis of the various systems of employment and compensation for United States Government overseas civilian personnel. I am directing that this entire matter be studied with a view toward recommending appropriate legislation." There have been several subsequent studies, but no such legislation has been forthcoming. Crises of policy have always seemed more important than the careful and difficult revision of administrative organization and practice necessary to give effect to policy. On the whole, our postwar activities overseas have been characterized by a considerable degree of stability in the goals and objectives of United States foreign policy and by a bewildering series of improvisations on the organizational side.

As we come more fully to see the shape of our continuing responsibilities in these areas, it becomes increasingly necessary to put our overseas machinery and our Washington policy-making process on a sounder and more permanent organizational footing. It is clear that we must adapt our overseas mechanism to the arduous and continuing global competition which seems to be the pattern of the future for the United States. It is in the hope that it may contribute to the understanding and resolution of these problems that this volume has been revised and reissued.

V. M. B., Jr.

Hamilton, New York
January, 1965

Contents

xi

*The Representation of
the United States Abroad*

Introduction:
Changing Aspects of the Conduct
of Public Business Overseas

VINCENT M. BARNETT, JR.

One of the vital problems facing American policy-makers, and crying for comprehension by the American public, is the conduct of our overseas public business. The events of this century have thrust America into a position of deep involvement in the political, economic, social and military developments in nations and areas all over the globe. This involvement is unprecedentedly broad in scope, costly in resources, perplexing as to policy, and complicated in administration. Yet it is no exaggeration to say that the successful handling of the issues flowing from it is crucial to the very survival of America and to the Western way of life. Nor is the weight of this burden likely to decline substantially in the foreseeable future. Even assuming the possibility of avoiding large-scale military conflict, the rising crescendo of competition with totalitarianism for the effective political and economic mobilization of vast populations and resources poses the most direct challenge to the energy, strength, and capacity for leadership of the American people.

We cannot withdraw from this contest. With the help of our allies, and with the imaginative use of the many advantages which lie with us, we can prevail. But we can do so only if we fully recognize the magnitude of the task, accept the burden it lays upon us, take the necessary policy decisions, and strengthen the administrative structure and processes necessary to carry them out.

The Broadening of American Participation

It requires little further argument to convince the American people that the comfortable days of "non-entanglement," even if only as a partially realizable ideal, are gone forever. In the light of the present world-wide struggle with Soviet expansionism, the famous words of Washington's Farewell Address seem wholly anachronistic:

> Europe has a set of primary interests, which to us have none, or a very remote relation. Hence she must be engaged in frequent controversies, the causes of which are essentially foreign to our concerns. Hence, therefore, it must be unwise in us to implicate ourselves, by artificial ties, in the ordinary vicissitudes of her politics, or the ordinary combinations or collisions of her friendships or enmities.

This was undoubtedly sound doctrine in the early years of our national existence. That it is essentially inapplicable today is some measure of the distance we have come. Even if we substitute Asia, Africa, Latin America, the Middle East, or the Far East for Europe in this statement, it can no longer provide a useful directive for our policy. The hard facts of life in the last half of the twentieth century, even though faced with regret and reluctance, make this clear. And the American people, at least in a general way, have accepted these facts.

The nineteenth-century security system which enabled America to approximate a policy of non-entanglement was shaken in the first quarter of the twentieth century and destroyed by the consequences of two world wars. "Minding our own business" could mean relative isolation in a world in which we were the beneficiaries of external facts making it possible. The maintenance of a balance of power in Europe, the extensiveness of the British Empire and of British naval supremacy, and physical remoteness from her potential enemies—all combined to cushion the United States from the immediate impact of events overseas. Two world wars, and the breath-taking progress in the arts of transportation, communication, and destruction, have decisively changed all three of these factors. The European balance of power is no longer the fundamental key to the world situation; the focus has shifted to two mighty superpowers, the U.S. and the U.S.S.R., towering above the other nations of the world and confronting each other in a contest that tends sooner or later to align the others, in sympathy at least, with one of the two camps. The military and political strength of the British Empire is much less significant than in the nineteenth century. And the startling technological changes have made the physical remoteness of the United States a thing of the nostalgic past.

In this kind of a world, "minding its own business" thrusts America squarely into the evolving political, economic, and military situation all over the globe. It is America's business to survive as a nation, to protect and promote the way of freedom against the way of totalitarianism, and to participate in the kind of leadership for the free world which will insure its ultimate victory.

From this point of view, American involvement is not just a matter of short-run commitments arising out of World War II —commitments which can be cleaned up with one eye on the prospect of an early withdrawal. Congressional action from time to time has tended to leave this impression, and it may indeed still be the view of a large segment of public opinion. Emphasis, in the early days of the economic-aid programs in particular, on recovery and restoration of something approximating the *status quo ante*, as major goals of policy, tended to reflect such a view. We need to face the fact that there is not going to be any *status quo ante*, and that the United States will be engaged for many years to come in a wide variety of operations overseas related to our unsolicited but unavoidable role in the strengthening of the free world.

The Increasing Complexity of Managing Public Business Overseas

Acceptance of this fact carries broad implications for the content of American foreign policy, and especially for the need to evolve methods for assuring long-range continuity and consistency in that policy. Much has been written and said on these questions, and the attention of some of the best minds of the country is being focused on them. Less consideration has been given to a vitally important companion problem—the necessary adaptation of machinery for the execution of policy and operations overseas to the prospect of an extensive and long-run load.

There is need for careful and constructive consideration of this problem. The machinery and the processes for the carrying out of overseas operations have tended, in these postwar years, to be characterized by *ad hoc* solutions, rapidly shifting and exuding the aroma of temporary or emergency devices. Studies of the organization and administration of foreign policy, such as those of the Hoover Commission, tended to emphasize the organization of the State Department and the coordination of policy in Washington rather than overseas. The well-known Wriston Report was limited by its frame of reference to the Foreign Service itself rather than to the over-all problem. But the range of problems far exceeds the question of the Foreign Service itself, as heretofore conceived, or the question of appropriate Washington organization for the formulation and coordination of policy. The wide range of increasingly important and in some cases novel operations that will continue to be carried on abroad makes the challenge of their effective organization and execution in the field too crucial to be underplayed. The ultimate test of our success in these areas is likely to be in how effectively they are administered. And their administration will be carried on by thousands of Americans in the field in day-to-day operations. There can be no more important problem than that of how to organize these far-flung activities on a stable, continuing, integrated, and efficient basis.

The Role of Specialized Operations

We need to focus attention on the kinds of things we are doing overseas, and will continue to be doing, as a result of our acceptance of new and decisive responsibilities in the pattern of world relationships. They entail functions and activities in which we were not extensively engaged prior to World War II. They involve a greatly increased emphasis on operations, as distinct from the more familiar overseas functions of reporting, negotiation, and representation. These operations are inseparable from the "cold war," or "competitive coexistence," or whatever phrase is used to describe the nature of the current contest with totalitarianism. That contest need not culminate in war, although the possibility that it may can never be prudently ignored. The issue may, in fact, be resolved—and resolved in our favor—by the vigorous and effective use of other measures to strengthen the free world and gain it new adherents. Translated into terms of operations, the strengthening of the free world will depend on economic, technical, and military assistance programs, and on an increasing ability to explain our purposes and to secure firm acceptance of common goals.

So long as the nuclear standoff is really a standoff, and so long as our military posture at home and abroad is such as to maintain it, we can contemplate a long period of coexistence characterized by competition with the Soviet Union for friends, allies, economic strength and world opinion. This means that an awesome responsibility for the future of the United States rests on the effective carrying out, in countries all over the world, of economic aid, technical assistance, information and cultural programs. Such programs have come into prominence in the postwar period. They promise to remain as a long-range feature, with implications for the structure and coordination of our overseas representation that have not yet been squarely faced.

Some Problems

The papers in this volume address themselves to these problems. Following a brief survey of the growth of coordination difficulties in the postwar years, by Professor Gordon, the papers deal with the several aspects of overseas representation that call for continuing attention. The prevention of military conflict depends in good measure on the effective administration overseas of our military assistance programs and of our military-diplomatic activities in general. The paper by Messrs. Fox and Davis deals with this set of problems. The strengthening of the economic bonds of the non-Soviet world requires the competent management of economic aid and technical-assistance programs. Mr. Lindeman's paper sets forth the distinguishing characteristics of this range of problems. None of these programs will be successful unless world opinion can be mobilized for our fundamental goals and for our methods of achieving them. Mr. Sargeant's paper deals with this problem in general and with its implications for overseas operations in particular. We shall continue to pursue all these goals at least partially—and perhaps increasingly—through international organizations reflecting a multilateral and regional approach to their achievement. The special aspects of these operations are treated in Mr. Moore's paper. Finally, overseas operations of all these types will fall far short of their potential unless they are appropriately coordinated in the field, and unless the Washington organization is such that this coordination can be effected. Professor Gordon's concluding paper explores the many-sided problem of coordination overseas.

From these papers emerge a conviction of the complexity of the challenge and a doubt that it is being met as squarely and effectively as it must. Are we sure that our organization of overseas representation has been adequately studied and properly adapted to the momentous challenge it faces? Are we sure that it does not still reflect a primary concern for the age-old functions of diplomacy, and only a reluctant and insufficient adaptation to the needs of newly important operating activities? Are we sure that the ambassador, as nominal head of what has become a many-faceted operating agency, has the authority or the organizational backstopping in Washington to enable him literally to act for the President in these matters? Are we sure that the accelerating trend since World War II toward personal crisis diplomacy by a roving Secretary of State augurs well for the long-run strength and effectiveness of our overseas missions?

These are only a few of the many questions raised by our emerging role in the world today, as viewed particularly from the angle of the *overseas* problem, and of the *functional* operations in which we are engaged. Broader problems of the shape of United States foreign policy have been much discussed, and are not the main subject here. Likewise, the problem of Washington organization has received much careful attention, and is relevant here only insofar as it affects overseas operations. Neither the Hoover Commission nor the Wriston Committee was able to give the total problem of overseas representation the attention it demands. The Brookings Institution study of 1951 was addressed more directly to this issue, but it tended to regard the bulk of these operational activities as temporary, arising out of a "defense emergency" of relatively short duration. The purpose of the papers in this volume is to focus attention on the longer-range problems of policy formulation, coordination, decentralization, and execution, and to provide constructive suggestions for dealing with them.

Some Assumptions

A useful discussion of these questions can perhaps best proceed if the underlying assumptions are specified:

1. Extensive United States participation in world affairs is a *datum* of our time. We cannot now withdraw. The nature of our international task has changed, the magnitude of that task has changed, and many of the kinds of activities we have been pursuing on an *ad hoc*, emergency basis are likely to remain as relatively permanent features of our relationship with the rest of the world.

2. Unless large-scale nuclear war comes, the outcome of the competition between two ways of life hinges largely on the success with which we carry out the varying programs designed to further our political, military-diplomatic, economic, and psychological objectives. The specific character of these programs may be expected to change from time to time. Our preoccupation with the goals they serve will continue. And whatever modified forms the programs take will continue to entail extensive overseas operating functions—hence the problem of their effective execution and coordination. The general character of the problem is revealed by the operating activities in which we are already engaged.

   a. We have undertaken programs of economic and technical assistance, scattered widely around the globe, in which we enter into partnership with recipient countries to work toward basic improvements in their economic structure, functioning, and levels of life. These activities go far beyond the emergency relief, rehabilitation, and reconstruction programs which we undertook following both world wars, both in conception and in practical operating consequences.

b. We have come to the conclusion that it is of prime importance for the nations of the world (friends, potential enemies, and neutral or "uncommitted" peoples) to understand our aims and to relate our actions to those aims. We are convinced that this cannot be done solely through ordinary diplomatic exchanges or left to private cultural and communications media. We have concluded that we need to speak directly to the people in all these kinds of countries, to create a favorable understanding of United States goals and activities in those countries and in the world at large, insofar as that may be possible through publicity, information, and cultural communications.

c. Almost twenty years after the end of World War II, we have military troops stationed abroad in many countries and are a party to solemn engagements that will keep them there for many years to come. Moreover, we are engaged in supplying military matériel and technical advice and assistance, both through international organizations and as a result of bilateral understandings on a country-by-country basis. Hence, in addition to troops as such, we have military missions stationed abroad and concerned in daily operations as accredited representatives to the nations and organizations to which they have been sent.

d. We have become engaged more intimately and extensively than ever before in numerous international and multilateral organizations, in which we function not only as an active member but as a prime mover. We have added to our basic reliance on bilateral diplomacy a wide and expanding array of international arrangements. This is not simply an increased reliance on multilateral treaty commitments involving general obligations and duties. It includes participation in international specialized agencies which require day-to-day operations on a continuing and long-range basis by large numbers of technicians and persons with special skills.

3. Success in carrying out these tasks overseas depends on defin-

ing the job, decentralizing its execution, getting the right kind of people, and organizing their relationships at the post, in the region, and with Washington. This means increased emphasis on the specialized requirements of these programs in the matter of technical personnel and autonomy in operational detail, but also increased emphasis on the problems of coherence and coordination.

4. The contest may well be won or lost in the field, in the countries themselves. It is not likely to be won unless our field representation is able and effective and is given the necessary latitude to operate and the prestige required to do so successfully. The long-run hope lies in building an effective representative structure abroad, setting general policies, providing over-all guidance, and letting the field do the job. The airplane and rapid communications may have diminished the discretionary role of the ambassador and his top staff, but the accretion of operating responsibilities has revitalized it and placed it in a somewhat different perspective. The ambassador cannot do the job if his role approaches that of glorified messenger boy. He probably cannot do the job if he is, in effect, simply a representative of the State Department. He must in fact speak for the President, and must have the organization, the staff assistance, and the prestige to make this possible. To a degree not yet fully reflected in our organizational arrangements, our overseas missions have become operating agencies. A significantly more important, if not new, dimension has thereby been added to the missions' classic jobs of observing, reporting, negotiating, and "representing"—that of obtaining efficient performance of the various functional activities, and of seeing that they are integrated with each other and are in fact carrying out established policy. The first of these may involve a considerable autonomy within the mission for the functionally specialized elements, but the second involves a considerable degree of unified supervision, coordination, and control.

5. Although many of our objectives can and should be accomplished through international, regional, and multilateral organizations, there will continue to be a significant and per-

haps decisive role for bilateral relationships and hence for the United States missions to individual countries.

6. So far as people are concerned, it is immediately clear that the role of the expert in overseas representation is becoming more and more important. The Marshall Plan demonstrated that in order to carry out economic-aid programs involving partnership with recipient countries, it was essential that the United States have highly trained economists on its missions overseas. The foreign information program has surely demonstrated the importance of the skilled technician and the costs of amateurism in a field calling for specialized skills. In neither case, be it said, can the ultimate policies be left to the expert, but likewise in neither case can the policies be carried out without him. A recognition of the role of the expert and of his continuing indispensability has broad implications for the recruiting and personnel policies of agencies concerned with overseas operations, particularly the Department of State. The issue is more complex than the traditional "generalist" versus "specialist" controversy. The career man interchangeable as to country and function—the "generalist" of the standard discussions—remains as important as ever, and a major aim of the system must be to find and develop him. This may involve, among other things, recruitment from a broader base and improvement of in-service training programs. But careers capable of attracting and retaining capable technicians and professionally trained experts, and of advancing those with suitable qualities to posts of increasing responsibility, need also to be established as a regular part of the overseas service. This will broaden its base by systematic inclusion and advancement of persons whose initial training and experience may be in a wide variety of professional backgrounds. Hence, it will benefit the top group of career officers who are engaged in activities calling more than ever for acquaintance with such professional skills. It will also assure the recruitment and retention of more capable experts in the continuing operational jobs which United States representation overseas now involves.

1. The Growth of American Representation Overseas

LINCOLN GORDON

Expanded Responsibilities

The impact of war and cold war, and the emergence from old empires of many new nations, superimposed on a long-run trend toward increased involvement in world affairs, have vastly expanded the old dimensions, and introduced major new dimensions, into American foreign relations. International problems hold the attention and interest of the public, the Congress, and wide sectors of the Executive Branch of the Federal Government as never before in a so-called time of peace.

On the administrative side, the war and postwar years have witnessed the creation and transformation of new agencies, and of new arms for old agencies, in bewildering variety. Some efforts have focused on strengthening the structure and staffing of long-established departments. In other cases, new methods and new institutions have been improvised to handle critically urgent tasks, some of these subsequently disappearing when their job was done, others being consolidated into older departmental structures, and still others becoming, apparently, permanent. With the changed position of the United States in the world, moreover, many policy areas once considered of exclusively domestic concern now have international repercussions that must be taken into account.

Traditional Functions

The traditional functions of overseas representation were fourfold: *negotiation* with foreign governments; *intelligence*—gathering and reporting information on foreign events, conditions, trends, and prospects of interest to the home government; *representation* in the narrow sense of informing foreign governments as to official United States views and interests and acting for the United States in formal and informal contacts with foreign officials, fellow diplomats, and influential private citizens; and providing *consular* services with respect to foreign trade, passports and visas, and the protection of American nationals abroad.

With respect to top-level negotiation, the combination of rapid air travel and instantaneous communication has to some extent reduced the responsibilities of permanent overseas missions. It is now common practice for foreign ministers to negotiate through direct personal contact, either bilaterally or in conferences of three, four, fifteen, twenty, or more than one hundred nations at a time. In a few cases, even the foreign ministers have been displaced by direct contact between heads of government. As the power and influence of the United States have grown, moreover, there is a tendency for crucial negotiations to be conducted more frequently in Washington than in foreign capitals. Alternatively, emissaries with specialized knowledge of the matter in hand may be despatched from Washington. On questions of high policy, even where ambassadors participate, they are sometimes reduced to mere messenger boys whose every formal statement and almost every informal comment is controlled by cabled instructions. It is, indeed, a serious question whether this process of diluting the authority and reducing the discretion of the Ambassador has not been carried too far.

With the sole exception of top policy negotiation, however, the functions of overseas missions have shown an almost continuous and geometric expansion in both size and scope. Even on the top policy questions, the ease of travel and communications gives the overseas representatives the opportunity to advise on policy and to appraise and report foreign reactions with a degree of immediacy not previously possible. Below the highest level, there is a vast increase in the volume of negotiation handled by our overseas missions. As to intelligence and reporting on developments abroad, it no longer suffices for the home government to be informed of major political developments and the views of the foreign office on current international questions. Washington is necessarily concerned with *every* aspect of foreign happenings, whether they be domestic politics, military and strategic events, economic developments, or fluctuations in public opinion directly or indirectly affecting relations with the United States.

The reporting function has shown its most marked expansion in the economic, technical, and public-opinion fields. The American business community needs and expects prompt and accurate official reporting on economic developments abroad: production, trade, agriculture, employment and labor relations, finance, investment prospects and opportunities, and the maze of governmental controls that in even the most liberal countries affects foreign trade and investment. Similar information is needed on technical developments, whether military, commercial, or purely scientific.

Sound policy-making requires the best possible insight into trends in the internal political affairs and public opinion of other nations. Moreover, the shrinkage of the world through transportation and communications improvements, together with the pressures of the cold war and the emancipation of many formerly colonial areas, has meant that this sort of interest is world-wide in scope. There is no country about which we can afford to be officially ignorant.

It follows that the function of representation also has had to be expanded. It no longer suffices to have official contacts simply with foreign offices, diplomatic communities, and the small élite of social leaders in a foreign capital. Direct contact must be established with almost every department of a foreign government, including the treasury and central banks, the ministries of economics, commerce, labor, agriculture, transportation, fuel and power, and the military services. It must also extend to all types of organized and influential groups: labor unions; business and farm leaders; opposition as well as ruling political parties; journalists; editors and publishers; educators; religious leaders; and many others.

At the same time, the achievement of sovereignty in the former

European colonial areas has greatly increased the numbers of countries in which these overseas functions of the United States Government are performed. At the end of 1963, we had official missions in 112 countries, precisely double the number of sovereign areas on the eve of World War I. And in many of the regions where our official overseas representation is in its infancy, notably in Africa, the Middle East, and South and Southeast Asia, only few Americans have had previous acquaintance with the peoples and cultures, which are strikingly different from those of Europe or Latin America.

New Dimensions

All this is in essence an expansion of traditional diplomatic functions, but so radical in size and variety as to make for differences in kind as well as degree. Over and above these are the new dimensions that create especially difficult problems of coordination. They are foreign program operations of various types. In many countries, they include the establishment of American military bases, with large numbers of uniformed personnel and the inescapable resulting problems of public impact and relations with the local communities, of economic repercussions, and of formal status and privileges. In many more countries, there are military aid programs, with specialized missions engaged in providing equipment and training. In almost all the less developed countries of the free world, there are operating programs of economic aid and technical assistance, often requiring numbers of personnel that dwarf the regular diplomatic establishments, and there are programs of cultural and educational exchange virtually everywhere. In almost every country where diplomatic relations exist (and by shortwave radio to the rest), there are active information programs designed to improve public understanding of the nature, purposes, and attitudes of the United States and to win support for our policies.

Yet another new dimension has been added by the growth of international organizations in which the United States plays an active part. There are the United Nations, military alliances organized through the North Atlantic Treaty Organization, the Southeast Asia Treaty Organization, the Organization of American States, and the ANZUS Treaty (to which might be added the Middle East Treaty Organization, to which the United States is an observer although not a formal member); and on the economic side the Organization for Economic Cooperation and Development, the U.N.'s regional commissions in Europe, Latin America, Asia and the Far East, and Africa; the Organization of American States, the Inter-American Development Bank and the Alliance for Progress, the International Bank for Reconstruction and Development, the International Monetary Fund, the U.N. Specialized Agencies in labor, agriculture, health, child welfare, and refugee care, and the Colombo Plan—not to mention more technical agencies in atomic energy, telecommunications, meteorology, and aviation. Not only does our participation create difficult problems of representation in itself, which are the topic of a separate chapter of this volume; it also poses a problem of coordination between American viewpoints expressed to and through such bodies and our bilateral relations with the other member countries.

Overseas Representation Today

One index of the postwar problem of overseas representation is the sheer growth in size of civilian government employment abroad. Excluding the Department of Defense and the closely related American Battle Monuments Commission and Veterans Administration, the number of United States civilian employees, American and alien, in foreign countries expanded from 4,600 on the eve of World War II to almost 43,000 in mid-1963. Of this total, some 14,500 were American citizens.

There is no way of measuring the corresponding increase in the number of Washington officials concerned with foreign affairs, but it can safely be assumed to be at least in proportion. In mid-1963, the State Department (including the Agency for International Development) accounted for almost 10,000 employees in Washington, to which must be added large segments of the Departments of Defense, Commerce, Agriculture, Treasury, and of other agencies. The following tabulation of American civilians working abroad excludes those under technical assistance contracts and Peace

Corps volunteers, whose status is semi-official but whose work must be harmonized with that of the official missions.

It will be the purpose of this chapter to explore in some detail the record of American overseas representation, especially in the postwar period, the occasional points of conflict, and the various efforts made at coordination.

Today's problem is essentially an amalgam of two streams of development. The first has to do with the relationships abroad and at home of the permanent "old-line agencies" of the government, as departments other than State have expanded their interest in activities and representation overseas. The second arises from the addition of a series of operating programs, most of them considered "temporary" when initiated, and all of them involving special organizational arrangements that in turn required some meshing with the established forms of overseas representation.

FOREIGN ACTIVITIES OF THE OLD-LINE AGENCIES

The Unified Foreign Service

The central responsibility for handling our foreign relations rests with the Department of State. The statutory basis for this responsibility is still the Act of Congress of July 27, 1789, which provides simply:

> The Secretary of State shall perform such duties as shall from time to time be enjoined on or entrusted to him by the President relative to correspondences, commissions, or instructions to or with public ministers or consuls from the United States, or to negotiations with public ministers from foreign states or princes, or to memorials or other applications from foreign public ministers or other foreigners, or to such other matters respecting foreign affairs that the President of the United States shall assign to the Department and he shall conduct the business of the Department in such manner as the President shall direct.

For well over a century of our national existence, these responsibilities were performed by an extremely small Department in Washington, represented overseas by amateur diplomats and consuls in whose selection political patronage played an important

CIVILIAN EMPLOYEES OF GOVERNMENT AGENCIES ABROAD
(BY AGENCIES, AS OF JUNE 30, 1964*)

	U.S. Citizens	Non-citizens	Total
Department of State	7,210	10,276	17,486
Agency for International Development	3,746	8,954	12,700
U.S. Information Agency	1,355	7,141	8,496
Department of Commerce	386	143	529
Department of the Interior	431	12	443
Federal Aviation Agency	251	15	266
Department of Health, Education, and Welfare	201	79	280
Department of Agriculture	237	421	658
Peace Corps	234	126	360
Department of Justice	157	32	189
Department of the Treasury	183	52	235
General Accounting Office	79	—	79
Atomic Energy Commission	28	—	28
Department of Labor	8	19	27
National Aeronautics and Space Administration	15	—	15
Post Office Department	11	4	15
Library of Congress	7	—	7
National Science Foundation	4	—	4
Foreign Claims Settlement Commission	4	30	34
Other	8	—	8
Total Civilian Agencies	14,555	27,304	41,859
Department of Defense	119	—	119
Army	9,158	32,480	41,638
Air Force	4,354	16,274	20,628
Navy	2,301	15,502	17,803
American Battle Monuments Commission	41	391	432
Veterans Administration	32	297	329
Total Military and Related Agencies	16,005	64,944	80,949
GRAND TOTAL	30,560	92,248	122,808

* Data unavailable for the Central Intelligence Agency
(Source: Civil Service Commission)

part. In the generation before World War I, a start was made at building up a professional corps for both the consular and the diplomatic services. The concept of a united and systematically staffed professional foreign service, however, was officially adopted only in the Rogers Act of 1924. This measure consolidated the pre-existing diplomatic and consular corps, overriding the objections of many of the diplomats. It established a basic framework, which remains today, for a career service recruited at the bottom by competitive examination and carrying obligations akin to military service to work anywhere in the world at any time. Significantly, the Foreign Service, although governed by a Board of Foreign Service Personnel in the Department of State, was originally set up as a body distinct from the Department itself.

At this stage, it was taken for granted that the responsibilities of the Foreign Service should be simply the traditional diplomatic and consular duties. As the pressure for more specialized information and representation in the economic field developed, therefore, arrangements were made for each major domestic government department concerned with such matters to establish its own overseas service. Thus the Congress authorized in 1927 the creation of a Foreign Commerce Service, and in 1930 a Foreign Agricultural Service, and a few years later arrangements were made for the Interior Department to send mineral specialists overseas. The Treasury Department also had a number of customs specialists abroad, known after 1930 as Treasury attachés. These specialized officers were to be "through the Department of State regularly and officially attached to the diplomatic mission of the United States" in their countries of assignment. The State Department could also veto proposed nominations. No provision was made, however, for ambassadors to control their activities while abroad, and each service worked, in effect, as an overseas wing of its own department.

In 1939, President Roosevelt used his authority under the Reorganization Act to consolidate the Foreign Commerce and Agricultural Services into the general Foreign Service, and thus to initiate the concept of a unified Foreign Service handling all the overseas civilian representation needs of the government. While this unified service was to operate under the direction and supervision of the Secretary of State, the Board of Foreign Service Personnel was expanded to include representatives of the Departments of Agriculture and Commerce. The State Department was specifically directed to secure such commercial and agricultural information as the two sister departments might request. Arrangements were also made for special training for commercial and agricultural specialists destined to serve abroad.

This major step apparently resulted more from a general desire for organizational efficiency than from any heavy internal or external pressures. It was greeted with mixed feelings by the professional Foreign Service Officers, many of whom resented the transfer of these bodies of economic experts into their "elite corps" of political and diplomatic generalists. There was also one significant exception to the Foreign Service unification, the Treasury Department. Acting under its very broad authority to use proceeds from the Exchange Stabilization Fund "for any purpose in connection with carrying out the provisions of this Section," the Treasury, which at that time had its own pronounced views on foreign policy, began to place financial experts in a few foreign capitals. Now usually known as Treasury Representatives, this body has developed in effect into a small foreign service under the Treasury's Office of International Finance.

The Effects of World War II

How well the unified Foreign Service of 1939 would have worked was hardly put to a proper test, since it was soon submerged under the impact of World War II. No serious effort was made to expand the Foreign Service to meet war needs. This was not really desired by the Secretary of State himself. Many of the young officers were drawn off into military service, and recruiting was halted for the duration.

Apart from the direct military operations overseas, huge emergency civilian agencies were created in the foreign economic, information, and intelligence fields: the Office of Coordinator of Inter-American Affairs; the Board of Economic Warfare and the Lend-Lease Administration, later consolidated in the Foreign Economic Administration; the Office of War Information; and the Office of Strategic Services. In the latter stages of the war, as enemy-occupied territories became liberated and enemy areas were occupied by American forces, the Army developed its own vast organization for relief and rehabilitation and subsequently for government in occupied areas. While the State Department sought from time to time to assert its authority to coordinate at least civilian activities, and later the major policy aspects of occupied area government, during most of this period it was swamped by the emergency agencies and their specialized foreign missions. Conflict between such missions and the regular diplomatic establishments became common. Ambassadors were frequently simply disregarded. The authority of the State Department as leader in foreign affairs fell precipitously.

When hostilities ended, the emergency agencies were rapidly dismantled and their residual responsibilities transferred *en masse* to established departments. The State Department inherited the Office of Coordinator of Inter-American Affairs, the Office of War Information and part of the Office of Strategic Services (the rest going to the Central Intelligence Agency), while the Foreign Economic Administration was divided among State, Commerce, and Agriculture. It was evident that foreign representation would have to be maintained on a broader and larger basis than before the war, but it was the hope of the Foreign Service that this might be done essentially by rebuilding and modestly expanding the pre-war structure, with its central corps of professional "generalist" Foreign Service Officers. Under the Manpower Act of 1946, 166 officers were brought in at the middle and upper grades, in order to make up for the war-created deficiencies. These were mostly men with war-time military or civilian experience overseas who had developed a taste and aptitude for the Foreign Service career.

The Foreign Service Act of 1946

It was the Foreign Service Act of 1946, however, that was looked to both by the professional Foreign Service Officers and by the administrators of the old-line departments as a charter for the normal, long-run postwar needs of overseas representation. This elaborate piece of legislation was initiated by the Foreign Service Officer corps itself, adjusted to take account of the views and interests of the economic and information officers within the Department of State and the major outside departments concerned (Commerce, Agriculture, and Labor), and adopted by the Congress substantially without debate and without arousing any significant notice in the public at large.

While some Foreign Service Officers would have preferred to turn the nonpolitical work back to other departments, and simply to rebuild the Foreign Service as contemplated by the Rogers Act, with improved conditions and opportunities for officers to become chiefs of mission, this view did not prevail. Instead, the basic 1939 concept of a unified service was re-enacted, the Labor Department now being given a place on the Foreign Service Board alongside Agriculture and Commerce.

The possibility of consolidating the Foreign Service with the professional staff of the State Department in Washington, an arrangement common to the foreign services of most other countries, was considered briefly but rejected. The separate personnel and administrative system of the Foreign Service was maintained and its status enhanced by the creation of a statutory post of Director General of the Foreign Service, who had to be a member of the officer corps. (Following the recommendations of the first Hoover Commission in 1949, this position became purely advisory for some ten years, but it was revived and strengthened in 1960 as a part of the "Wriston reforms.") Provision was also made for temporarily supplementing the regular corps with Foreign Service reservists, who might be employees of the Department of State or of other federal agencies, or qualified private citizens. They could serve for periods of up to four years under the regular Foreign Service system of grades and pay, but without career rights or obligations. A Foreign Service Institute was created to provide advanced training during various stages of an officer's career. The basic emphasis was, as before the war, on lifetime service with entry by competitive examination at the bottom. The Navy principle of "promotion up or selection out" after a given number of years in any rank was introduced. The nonofficer employees of the service were consolidated into a Foreign Service Staff corps.

In short, the 1946 Act was intended to provide a system of overseas representation that, while administered under the State Department, would serve the interests of the United States abroad as a whole, provide adequate incentives for recruitment of able personnel, and make sufficient provision for economists and other appropriate professionals alongside the central body of "diplomatic generalists." Among the old-line agencies with substantial interest in representation abroad, only the Treasury Department continued to have a separate system.

Foreign Service Reform

For many reasons, the high hopes of this 1946 law proved illusory. The main reason was the addition of operating programs in the fields of military, economic, and technical assistance, foreign information, and intelligence, which are discussed below. Even among the old-line agencies, however, and between the Foreign Service and the Department of State itself, the experience of the subsequent decade was far from happy. The Department of State did not succeed in securing general acceptance, in either the Executive Branch, the Congress, or the public at large, of its claim for authority to direct and control, or at least to lead in coordinating, all governmental activities abroad. The Department's internal organization was beset with conflict between the geographical officers, largely led by Foreign Service Officers, and the civil-service–staffed functional offices concerned with economic, information, and intelligence matters. Foreign Service recruitment and promotion were frustrated by inadequate appropriations, lack of aggressive leadership, and discontinuity in administration. The Foreign Service Institute fell into very low estate. The morale of the service, already badly hit by financial limitations and administrative difficulties, was further undermined by a drastic internal security program.

Among other results, the agencies outside of State became increasingly dissatisfied with the performance of the State Department and the Foreign Service as their agents. This feeling was shared in varying degrees by the Departments of Agriculture, Commerce, and Labor. They complained that reporting of the specialized information they desired was inadequate and that, when personnel and funds were limited, they would always be given lower priority in competition with the needs and desires of the State Department itself. In some cases, they felt that the domination of embassies by Foreign Service political officers placed the more specialized officers at a disadvantage—in living and working conditions, in prestige, and generally in full acceptance as part of the government team abroad.

In 1954, the Department of Agriculture, with the help of friendly legislative committees in the Congress, broke away from the unified Foreign Service concept. The Agricultural Act of that year gave direct authority to the Secretary of Agriculture to encourage and promote the marketing of agricultural products abroad and to acquire information on such products in foreign countries, and for this purpose to appoint agricultural attachés on his own payroll, with the concurrence of the Secretary of State. These officers were to be attached to the diplomatic missions. The House committee, in reporting on this legislation, emphasized that this was not a new and separate Agricultural Foreign Service; nonetheless, the change was clearly a major breach in the unified Foreign Service concept. The new attachés were to take their instructions from the Department of Agriculture and to make their reports directly to that Department, a change that, in the eyes of the House committee, "should greatly improve the efficiency and value of our foreign agricultural representation." Voices were at once raised in the Departments of Commerce and Labor seeking similar arrangements for the same reasons. These efforts were not successful, but the question of the proper organization and range of responsibilities of the Foreign Service, and the extent to which it should be designed and staffed to serve all American civilian needs abroad, remained in a state of uneasy doubt.

In 1949, the internal organization of the State Department was drastically altered to place the major emphasis on geographical bureaus, each headed by an Assistant Secretary, together with a Bureau of International Organization Affairs to handle participation in the United Nations and other world-wide multilateral bodies. Parallel functional units were retained for economic, cultural, and intelligence affairs, as well as for public relations, Congressional relations, administration, and security and consular affairs. These were also headed by Assistant Secretaries, but their position was recognized as secondary to the regional bureaus. (This point was re-emphasized in 1961, when President Kennedy declared that the regional Assistant Secretaries of State were more important officers of the Government than most members of the Cabinet.) The top management structure was also reinforced by the creation of a second Under Secretary and two Deputy Under Secretaries, together with a policy planning staff.

There remained, however, the problem of overseas organization and its relations with the Department in Washington. Successive studies and recommendations on improved manning and structural changes went unattended until the report in mid-1954 of the Secretary of State's Public Committee on Personnel, under the chairmanship of Dr. Henry M. Wriston. The fundamental proposals of the Wriston Committee were: (1) integration of the personnel of the Foreign Service Officer Corps, the higher levels of the Foreign Service Staff Corps, and the Department of State into a single administrative system; (2) a broadened system of recruitment to provide a stable and adequate flow of officer material into the integrated Service; and (3) a major revitalization of the in-service training system.

With remarkable dispatch and vigor, perhaps reflecting a psychological overcompensation to the record of previous inactivity, the State Department proceeded with the implementation of these recommendations. By mid-1956, the process of "Wristonization" of the foreign and departmental services was substantially completed. The principle of integration was applied drastically and with a minimum of exceptions. It incurred the hostility of many old-line Foreign Service Officers, who thought that once again their élite corps of political generalists was being diluted beyond recognition. Integration also aroused the opposition of many specialized professionals in the Departmental service, who were reluctant to assume the obligation to serve overseas in any place and any capacity their superiors might determine. It subsequently became evident that in the latter respect, reforms were carried too far, depleting the economic and intelligence functions of the Department of specialized personnel they could ill afford to lose. In consequence, a number of positions of this character were returned to Civil Service status in the early 1960's.

On balance, however, the Wriston reforms marked a major step forward in the modernization of the Foreign Service framework, enlarging it, diversifying the backgrounds and specialized interests of its members, and providing for regular alternation between service in Washington and overseas. There remained major problems of securing and developing the best possible people to work within this framework. These were among the central concerns of the Committee on Foreign Affairs Personnel, under the chairmanship of former Secretary of State Christian A. Herter, Jr., which made its report in December, 1962. Its recommendations included methods of improving recruitment, wider use of lateral entry into the middle and upper grades, better planned career ladders, and a more systematic program of in-service training. There also remained the problem of overseas personnel apart from the State Department and other old-line civilian agencies, which had been explicitly excluded from the terms of reference of the Wriston Committee.

Overseas Military Representation

Alongside the overseas interests of major long-established civilian departments of government, there is a corresponding traditional interest of the military departments. The armed services obviously have a profound concern with foreign policy and foreign relations, which determine when they may be called upon for active intervention and which are the basic factors in fixing their needs for manpower, equipment, organization, and financing. In the nineteenth and early twentieth centuries, when there was little general public interest in the outside world, it was not uncommon for the armed services, especially the Navy, to carry out foreign policies of their own. For many decades, it has been accepted international practice to assign armed service attachés to the diplomatic missions in countries with substantial armed forces of their own—with the combined functions of securing technical intelligence and maintaining contact with their counterparts in the professional services.

This highly specialized form of overseas representation has seldom posed serious problems of coordination, however. Service attachés are now clearly subordinated to ambassadors. Much of their reporting is inherently technical and conveyed through military communications channels. More serious problems arise, as will be shown below, from the military operating programs abroad occasioned by the cold war and the resulting series of American alliances. To some extent, moreover, the broadening of our strategic interests to a global scale, which has made the coordination of national security policy a central concern of government in Washington, also has its reflection abroad in the need for closer working relations between overseas military and civilian personnel.

As the scope of foreign interests of the civilian and military departments other than State has expanded, there has developed increasing concern with assuring Washington direction to our overseas representatives. This problem has been attacked through a series of devices: lateral clearances of communications, Cabinet-level committees and interdepartmental committees of lower rank, statutory interdepartmental committees, and new machinery in the executive Office of the President. These developments will be reviewed in Chapter 6.

Adding the Operating Programs

It has been shown above how the Foreign Service Act of 1946 was designed to serve as a permanent framework for a unified Foreign Service meeting all the basic civilian needs of overseas representation. It provided an expanded corps of unspecialized officers to serve the main needs of the State Department, and it sought simultaneously to meet the technical needs of the Departments of Commerce, Agriculture, and Labor, and others as they might develop. Its reserve corps was to provide for additional short-term governmental and non-governmental personnel. The arrangements for lateral entry were to permit the strengthening of the Foreign Service in the upper and middle grades if this should prove necessary. The State Department was to serve as a focus of Washington direction for all overseas activities, but with due regard to the interests of the other agencies. Within the State Department, Foreign Service Officers were expected to man a wide range of positions, especially in the geographical offices, and thereby to provide cohesion with the missions in foreign countries.

This measure had hardly been signed into law when the pressures of new programs engendered by the cold war raised afresh, and repeatedly, the question of the proper role of the State Department at home and of the Foreign Service abroad. It was the character of these programs as major operating activities, requiring large and specialized staffs, which again posed this set of questions. New agencies, or new offices within the State Department, and specialized missions abroad, multiplied the opportunities for conflict and the problems of coordination. The European Recovery Program, and later the North Atlantic Treaty, added a regional dimension to these problems of conflict and coordination in both country missions and Washington.

At the start, most of these activities were considered temporary. With the passage of time, however, the cold war took form as an omnipresent feature of the postwar world. Multilateral diplomacy, relations with newly independent nations, and problems of economic and political underdevelopment became other major dimensions in our international relations. It slowly became evident that large-scale overseas operating programs of aid, information, and covert intelligence gathering would be essential instruments of American foreign policy for a long time to come.

Generally, the State Department had taken the initiative in formulating these programs and had the responsibility for operating them. In some cases, new agencies were created. Various experiments in organization were made. As certain of the programs were recognized to be of long duration, efforts were made to work out new relations. The ever recurring questions were: should the State Department operate all such programs? If not, could the State Department alone guide and coordinate them? If not, could this be done through interdepartmental committees under State or other chairmanship? Or did it require new machinery at the Presidential level?

One temporary set of programs—huge while it lasted—was government in the occupied areas. Here, the immediate postwar pattern was general policy guidance from the State Department with operating responsibility in the Army. This arrangement was marked by chronic friction and jurisdictional dispute, partly occasioned by fundamental disagreements of policy between Army commanders in the occupied areas and the State Department at home. As effective national governments were re-established in

Austria and Germany, a shift was made to civilian High Commissioners reporting to the State Department. Problems of coordination were greatly lessened, but they did not completely disappear until the restoration of sovereignty in these countries and in Japan put an end to the occupation status itself. The other new programs of continuing significance were economic aid and technical assistance, military assistance, the establishment of overseas bases, and the programs of foreign information, education, and cultural exchange.

Foreign Assistance

While the programs of economic aid and technical assistance have shown a high degree of stability over the postwar period, the idea that they would become long-run operating responsibilities of the United States in foreign countries was slow to develop and endured a highly checkered career. It is no surprise, therefore, that administrative and coordinating arrangements for such programs, both in Washington and overseas, were improvised rather than planned. Responsibility for them was tossed back and forth between established departments and new agencies. In the early official postwar reviews of foreign affairs operations, the problem of systematically manning these programs was given little attention, since it was generally assumed that they were a passing phase.

In fact, some of these programs were successfully completed and discontinued, but others arose to take their place. With the shift in cold war strategy away from the concept of moments of maximum danger at particular points of time, and its replacement by the expectation of an indefinite period of competitive coexistence —the competition extending over the whole range of political, military, economic, technological, psychological, and cultural activities—it became clear that these were long-run, and for all practical administrative purposes, permanent elements. This viewpoint was first expressly recognized by the Eisenhower Administration, and was reaffirmed with even greater vigor by Presidents Kennedy and Johnson.

There were many reasons, however, for regarding these programs in their incipiency as short-run responses to unusual crises, for which administrative improvisation was not only adequate but positively desirable so as to avoid interference with normal long-run activities. In the last months of the war, and the immediate postwar period, it had been hoped that the United Nations agencies established for relief and rehabilitation, for the governance of world trade, finance, and investment, and for collective security and disarmament would provide a stable framework of world order and reduce bilateral relationships to normal proportions.

This grand design unhappily did not come to fruition. The sheer destruction and economic dislocation occasioned by the war had been grossly underestimated. There had not been adequate appreciation of the urgency with which underdeveloped areas, especially those recently freed from colonial control, would seek acceleration of their economic development as a cardinal political objective. It was too lightly assumed that an adequate flow of private capital could be readily set in motion. Above all, the breaking of the wartime alliance into hostile Soviet and free-world camps, even if anticipated in a few quarters, was not generally foreseen, and it was certainly not translated into its economic, psychological, or long-run strategic implications.

Out of this divergence between bright hopes and grim reality there developed a series of bilateral supplementary aid programs. The first such programs were emergency measures to make good deficiencies in the postwar grand design. They included a bilateral post-UNRRA relief program and a special Philippine rehabilitation program. This was followed in early 1947, when Soviet pressure was brought to bear on Greece and Turkey and the British were no longer able to sustain their historic role in the eastern Mediterranean, by the announcement of the Truman Doctrine and the first large bilateral programs of economic and military assistance to those two countries. Meanwhile, it was becoming increasingly clear that neither the World Bank, the International Monetary Fund, nor the special $3.75 billion loan negotiated in late 1945 to underwrite sterling convertibility would suffice to remedy the general economic weakness of Western Europe or safeguard that critical region from the increasingly heavy political pressures of the Soviet Union.

Out of these conditions came the proposal for the Marshall Plan, the first foreign assistance program to be deliberately projected as more than an emergency remedy. Conceived on a scale sufficient to deal with underlying weaknesses, programmed over a four-year period, and instituted with the enthusiastic collaboration of the West European Governments, the Marshall Plan in fact achieved its goals of European economic reconstruction more fully, more rapidly, and at lower cost than had been hoped at its start. At the same time, the Soviet veto on the participation of Poland and Czechoslovakia, followed by the Berlin blockade and the Communist takeover of the Czech Government, made it crystal clear that political and military defense were necessary supplements to economic reconstruction—hence the Vandenberg Resolution of 1948 and the North Atlantic Treaty of 1949, backed by a new overseas operating program under the terms of the Mutual Defense Assistance Act providing for grants of military equipment and assistance in military training. With the fall of mainland China to Communist control, this program was extended not only to Europe but to Asian countries lying under the threat of Chinese military expansion. These efforts were greatly expanded with the outbreak of the Korean War in 1950.

Meanwhile, the possibility of developments adverse to our national security and welfare in the underdeveloped areas of the world, mostly as yet untouched by the threat of direct military aggression from the Communist bloc, did not go unnoticed. The major concern of these countries, especially in the areas recently freed from colonial rule, was acceleration of their economic development. Building on a decade of experience in Latin America as directed by the Office of the Coordinator for Inter-American Affairs, President Truman in "Point IV" of his inaugural address of January, 1949, called for "a bold new program for making the benefits of our scientific advances and industrial progress available for the improvement and growth of underdeveloped areas." He thus foreshadowed still another operating program overseas, world-wide in scope, focused on technical assistance and on the fostering of expanded private capital investment.

Under the original Point IV concept, this was to be primarily a multilateral enterprise organized through the United Nations, although substantial bilateral programs were also contemplated. After a year of debate, this program was given legislative backing in the Act for International Development of 1950. A few years later, Congress adopted the policy of selling surplus agricultural products for local currencies, with the proceeds to be used largely for economic development loans within the receiving countries. The Agricultural Trade Development and Assistance Act of 1954, commonly known as Public Law 480, has been repeatedly extended for varying periods of years. It also provides for grants of food to meet emergency needs arising from natural catastrophes and to assist school lunch programs and needy persons served by charitable agencies. Rechristened the "Food for Peace Program" a decade later, Public Law 480 has become a powerful auxiliary instrument of foreign assistance.

During the early 1950's, a more lasting pattern gradually began to emerge from the series of foreign-aid programs. In Europe, purely economic assistance gave way to direct military aid and indirect support for European defense budgets, imposing an evident need for coordination between the military and economic programs. In the Asian nations threatened by Communist Chinese expansion, this was even more evident, since they also required large-scale technical and economic aid to achieve a long-range increase in their standards of living. In other less developed countries, it became increasingly clear that the flow of private and public capital on conventional terms through the World Bank and Export-Import Bank, even when reinforced by technical assistance under Point IV, would not suffice to meet capital needs for a pace of development exceeding the rate of population growth and satisfying the deep desires for economic modernization.

In 1957, therefore, the Eisenhower Administration proposed the creation of a Development Loan Fund, offering capital assistance on longer terms and at lower interest rates than had been previously available. In Latin America, where the hostile reception of Vice President Nixon in Lima and Caracas was followed by the left-wing revolution of Fidel Castro in Cuba, it also became clear that a more affirmative use of public and private capital was indispensable in the effort to press on with economic and social progress. Under the impetus of the Brazilian initiative for "Operation Pan

America," it was agreed in 1959 to establish an Inter-American Development Bank, multilateral but financed mainly from United States Government resources. This was followed in 1960 by adoption of the Act of Bogotá, including an American commitment to finance an initial $500 million program of social development in Latin America, concentrated mainly on education, public health, housing, and improvement in rural living conditions.

Thus, from 1951 on, there was a steady trend toward recognition that economic, technical, and military assistance would be important elements of American foreign policy for many years to come. Legislative authorization for these programs was provided annually under the title "Mutual Security Program," and the successive versions of the legislation showed growing Congressional endorsement of the long-term character of these efforts. There were variations in the proportions of military and economic assistance, in the regional distribution, and in the relative emphasis on international institutions and bilateral programs, but in one form or another the programs continued, providing resources in the range of $4 to $7 billion per year.

The advent of the Kennedy Administration gave even further emphasis to foreign assistance as a long-range instrument of American foreign policy. New legislative form was given to the program in the Foreign Assistance Act of 1961, which marked a shift toward long-run development assistance as its major feature, while still conserving military and defense support programs inherited from the past. A Peace Corps was established, providing opportunity for thousands of young Americans to serve directly as volunteers in technical-assistance work in less developed countries. And within the Western Hemisphere, a ten-year Alliance for Progress to accelerate economic and social development was proposed by President Kennedy and subscribed to by twenty of the American Republics in the Charter of Punta del Este in August, 1961.

In its third year, the Kennedy Administration encountered increasingly strong public and Congressional criticism of foreign aid, and its requests for appropriations were drastically reduced. Nevertheless, while the amount, philosophy, and administrative organization of foreign aid were matters of intense controversy, the commitment of the United States to substantial foreign assistance programs, with a corresponding need for effective overseas administration, appeared to be a lasting one.

Foreign Information, Cultural, and Educational Exchange

As in the case of foreign assistance, the idea of large-scale systematic overseas information, cultural, and educational exchange programs is largely a product of the cold-war conditions since World War II. Until the late 1930's, nothing had been undertaken in this field beyond the traditional diplomatic functions of representation. Embassies were equipped to provide information on the United States to interested members of the public in their respective countries. Ambassadors sought to convey a degree of public, as well as official, understanding of American viewpoints through formal speeches and informal contacts. There was some cultivation of the foreign press as a normal diplomatic endeavor. Cultural and educational exchanges, however, were all private.

Beginning in the late 1930's, modest government provision was made for promoting scientific and cultural cooperation with the Latin American countries. These efforts were greatly expanded by the Office of Coordinator of Inter-American Affairs, established in 1940. To a considerable degree, these programs were a part of the cold war of that era, being designed to counteract the German Nazi penetration of the Western Hemisphere.

With our entry into the war, overseas information activities became a major official function. They were entrusted to an emergency wartime agency, the Office of War Information, which grew to huge dimensions. With the end of hostilities, both of these agencies were consolidated into the State Department, with the expectation in some quarters that they would soon be liquidated. The officials concerned with overseas information who foresaw the need for at least some continuing programs in this field had to fight a difficult and disheartening uphill battle during the immediate postwar years. Their efforts to secure legislative approval failed in both 1946 and 1947, and the program was maintained only by the skin of its teeth, appropriations almost being withheld because of the absence of explicit Congressional authority.

The difficulties of these years reflected a deep-seated and almost instinctive hostility in the American public at large and in the Congress toward the conduct of official "propaganda" programs in peacetime. It was widely felt that the best possible foundation for understanding of the United States in foreign countries lay in person-to-person relations and contacts among private groups. In keeping with this philosophy, Congress approved in 1946 American participation in UNESCO and the Fulbright program for teacher and student exchanges. But an official information program was considered not only inappropriate to our foreign relations in peacetime but also potentially dangerous as a possible instrument of governmental propaganda turned inward and abused for domestic political purposes. This hostility was overcome only as it became clear that the world was not genuinely at peace.

In 1947, as the pattern of Soviet designs against the free world became more and more evident and official Communist propaganda showed itself as a major weapon in the cold war, Congressional interest developed in an effective foreign information program. The lurking suspicion toward some of the personnel and practices of the wartime and early postwar information programs gave way to the conviction that the psychological aspects of the world struggle were too important to be disregarded. This viewpoint was strongly reinforced by firsthand observations in Europe during the late summer of 1947 by Congressional subcommittees from both Houses. As one Senate committee stated the problem:

> The present hostile propaganda campaigns directed against democracy, human welfare, freedom, truth, and the United States, spearheaded by the government of the Soviet Union and the Communist Parties throughout the world, call for urgent, forthright, and dynamic measures to disseminate truth. The truth can constitute a satisfactory counterdefense against actions which can only be described as psychological warfare against us as well as the purposes of the United Nations.

The resulting legislative charter, the United States Information and Educational Exchange Act of 1948 (the Smith-Mundt Act), contained broad grants of authority to meet these needs.

The Act's stated objectives were "to enable the Government of the United States to promote a better understanding of the United States in other countries, and to increase mutual understanding between the people of the United States and the people of other countries." To this end, it authorized establishment of "an information service to disseminate abroad information about the United States, its people, and policies . . . ; and an educational exchange service to cooperate with other nations in the interchange of persons, knowledge, and skills."

On the information side, a major "Campaign of Truth" was launched, and expenditures were built up from a $40 million level in 1950–51 to $100 million in the following year. While the program suffered many vicissitudes of organization, it soon became firmly established as an essential aspect of official overseas activities, involving the expenditure of some $155 million per year by 1963. One of its principal operations was the multilanguage radio programs of the Voice of America.

In the embassies overseas, substantial organizations were rapidly developed during the 1950's to carry on these information activities. Typically, responsibility for them under the ambassador was entrusted to a public affairs officer, who later came to double as the director of a United States Information Service (USIS) Mission. His functions, like those at home of the Assistant Secretary of State for Public Affairs, were of a dual character: serving as a staff adviser to the embassy on public relations matters and supervising the information program in the country.

The program would typically include the management of libraries designed to interest the public in the United States and to make available basic and current literature on all aspects of American life; work with the press, the radio and television industry, news film services, and other informational media of the country; arranging demonstrations and exhibits; organizing speaking programs for American residents and visitors; supporting a network of binational centers to promote the teaching of English and the stimulation of interest in American history and customs; and facilitating contacts with various types of organizations having an influence on general public opinion. In keeping with the heavy emphasis of the Smith-Mundt act on use of private American media, the program also involved assistance to their representatives operating in the country. Parallel with and leading into these activities was an important reporting task covering public opinion in the country, attitudes toward the United States and toward policies and issues of concern to us, and reactions to the information program, with the development of recommendations on both the content and the techniques best designed to serve its purposes.

With regard to cultural and educational exchange, the programs were developed in a somewhat more groping and gingerly fashion, partly because of the reluctance of many cultural and educational institutions in the United States to be involved at all with the federal bureaucracy, and partly because of doubts in these circles whether cultural and educational activities should be organized together with an overseas information program, which entailed some connotations of officialized propaganda. At the same time, however, it was evident that not only the Communist nations but also our European allies, working through semi-official bodies such as the British Council and the Alliance Française, had developed influence with artistic, literary, and intellectual circles, including teachers and students, which were of great importance in the shaping of broad national attitudes toward their countries. The United States could ill afford to leave such endeavors to private initiative, which could not in fact recoup the expenses of programs on the scale required.

The Fulbright program for educational exchange was one major advance on this front, and it came to be supplemented by gradually expanding programs of cultural and athletic presentations, expositions, and book translations and publications. These activities were substantially assisted by the availability in many countries of local currencies derived from the sale of agricultural surpluses under Public Law 480, as well as the so-called "local currency counterpart" of dollar grants under other aid programs.

In 1961, the educational and cultural exchange programs were given new support through Congressional passage of the Fulbright-Hayes Act, a far-reaching charter for all types of activities in this field. In 1963, some $37 million were available for these purposes, including both dollars and foreign currencies. Responsibility for the general direction of the program rests with the Assistant Secretary of State for Educational and Cultural Affairs, and the operating activities overseas are normally handled by cultural attachés working with the information missions.

A somewhat related development is the official sponsorship of scientific and technical interchange through the appointment of scientific attachés in a number of the larger embassies. Their responsibility includes the fostering of contacts between American and foreign scientific communities, and guidance to programs of technical assistance and educational exchange in these fields.

ORGANIZING AND STAFFING THE PROGRAMS

As the above record shows, the expansion of overseas operating programs has been an outstanding feature of our postwar international relations. Both aid and information activities are likely to be with us indefinitely. Although the substantive content of these programs has shown a remarkably continuous trend, their administrative history has been extraordinarily erratic. At two- or three-year intervals, changes have been made in the names and organizational responsibilities and relationships of the economic and technical-assistance agencies. Since 1953, there has been greater continuity in the administration of overseas information programs, but the record shows considerable confusion in the organization of cultural and educational exchanges.

Given these frequent changes, the problem of recruiting and retaining competent personnel, including those of a long-term professional staff, has been serious. While progress has been made, neither organization nor manning arrangements have achieved a stable or satisfactory pattern. Moreover, the relations between the operating programs and the organization at home and overseas for the more traditional international functions are continuing subjects of controversy and will doubtless undergo further evolution.

The Problem of Organization

The central question of organization of the operating programs has always been whether they should be administered directly under the Secretary of State as part of his department or should be organized independently, and, whether inside or outside the State Department, how they should be related to general foreign-policy guidance.

To trace in detail the administrative arrangements for foreign assistance would be a lengthy and unrewarding process. Suffice it to say that practically every conceivable type of organization has been tried at one phase or another. The post-UNRRA relief and Greek-Turkish aid programs of the mid-1940's were administered directly by the Department of State, although the overseas mission in Greece was independent of the embassy there. When the Marshall Plan was enacted in 1948, administrative arrangements were a major focus of attention by the Congress, which finally decided to establish a separate agency of Cabinet rank—the Economic Cooperation Administration. The ECA had separate missions in European countries, but it was subject to detailed statutory provisions for political guidance by the Secretary of State in Washington and ambassadors in the field and for the resolution of disputes should they arise. The administrative agency for Point IV, however, known as the Technical Cooperation Administration, was established within the Department of State. The technical aspects of military assistance obviously had to be handled by the armed services under the direction of the Department of Defense, but broad military-assistance policy was from the start made a responsibility of the Department of State.

In 1951, as coordination between military and economic assistance became increasingly important in both Europe and the Far East, the ECA gave way to a Mutual Security Administration (MSA); all aspects of economic, military, and technical assistance were coordinated by a Director for Mutual Security in the Executive Office of the President. In 1953, the Marshall Plan pattern was re-created with the establishment of a Foreign Operations Administration (FOA), again with independent Cabinet status but receiving policy guidance from the Secretary of State. After two years, it was felt that the Department of State should be given a stronger voice in foreign-aid administration, and the FOA was replaced by an International Cooperation Administration (ICA), whose director was placed within the State Department with the rank of Deputy Under Secretary. In practice, however, most ICA personnel continued to work in offices distant from the State Department, and the jurisdictional friction between aid officials and State Department desk officers was not significantly reduced. With its separate budget and personnel systems, the ICA could be said to be truly within the Department only at the top. Moreover, the Development Loan Fund was established independently of the ICA, and with less affirmative provision for policy guidance from the State Department. At the same time, the Export–Import Bank was coming to be an increasingly important source of capital development funds and balance-of-payments assistance, and it had no formal relationship to any of the other foreign-assistance agencies.

The most far-reaching effort to rationalize the organization of foreign assistance was made early in the Kennedy Administration with the passage of the Foreign Assistance Act of 1961. Through the fusion of the former responsibilities of the Development Loan Fund and the International Cooperation Administration, it was made clear that all economic and technical assistance, except for Export–Import Bank loans, would now be handled by a single agency, the Agency for International Development (AID). AID was also given responsibility for coordination of military assistance. At the same time, AID was placed within the Department of State—much more so than the old ICA had been. With its main internal structure based on lines parallel to those of the State Department's geographical bureaus, regional and country officers were placed "back to back" with their counterparts on the political desks, greatly facilitating day-to-day consultation and coordination. In Latin American affairs, this principle was carried even further by fusing the State and AID offices, thereby securing complete coordination at the country level. Staff services and functional offices, on the other hand, were separate from those of the State Department, and the overseas AID Missions retained their semiautonomous status under the guidance and policy direction of the ambassadors. The AID Administrator was given rank equivalent to that of the Under Secretary of State.

In late 1963 and early 1964, in view of the signs of the Congress' substantial dissatisfaction with various aspects of the foreign-aid programs, President Johnson called for a further review of these arrangements. The conclusion, in substance, was that foreign-aid administration had suffered from too frequent reorganization during the previous fifteen years, and that the real complaint had more to do with program content, direction, and execution than with organizational forms.

The administrative history of the informational and cultural programs is less complex. When they were first established in 1948, the Congress placed the operating responsibility directly with the Department of State at home and the embassies abroad. At the same time, the hope was expressed that administrative arrangements would pay due regard to the need for specialized personnel and businesslike management for such large-scale operations as the Voice of America. In practice, the information activities rapidly became the largest single unit of the State Department.

This operational program was not easily absorbed within the State Department hierarchy. It was placed under the general direction of an Assistant Secretary for Public Affairs, and much of its day-to-day operations was delegated to a working organization in New York City. Both at home and abroad, it required large numbers of technicians who did not readily fit into either Civil Service or Foreign Service patterns. Some thought was given to reorganizing the foreign information program under a special government corporation, but this proposal proved abortive.

In 1951, an effort was made to provide more affirmative direction to the information programs through creation of a Psychological Strategy Board that brought together the Departments of State and Defense, the Central Intelligence Agency, the ECA, and other interested agencies. This was a group on the sub-Cabinet level, with its own small staff; it was hoped that it would provide a more affirmative strategy for this aspect of cold-war activities than could be expected from an information service established as a junior handmaiden of the politically oriented State Department. The experiment was not strikingly successful, and it was abandoned two years later.

The philosophy of the Eisenhower Administration at its start was to reaffirm policy leadership of the State Department in foreign affairs but to divorce the Department from foreign operations. Pursuant to this philosophy, the information and library functions provided by the Smith-Mundt Act were transferred in June, 1953, to a new independent agency, the United States Information Agency (USIA), which also formally absorbed the information programs previously carried on by the aid agencies. Program policy and content were to be guided by the Secretary of State, who employed for this purpose an Assistant Secretary of State for Public Affairs. Overseas, USIA was to be represented by USIS Missions, with separate lines of administrative authority and personnel policy. Within the Executive Office of the President, an Operations Coordination Board was established, theoretically empowered to supervise the carrying out of all national security policies, but in practice devoting the lion's share of its attention to questions of psychological strategy and informational policy. This experiment was abandoned early in the Kennedy Administration, pursuant to its view that general foreign-policy guidance should be given by the State Department and that Presidential control should be exercised directly through the Cabinet rather than through formal inter-agency committees at the Presidential Office level.

The independent status of USIA, subordinate to the State Department on matters of policy and program content but autonomous in its operations, has been unchanged since 1953. Nor has its status been a matter of active controversy, although thorny problems have arisen in the relations between information activities on the one hand, and cultural representation and educational exchange on the other. The latter remain a direct State Department responsibility, even though their overseas administration is largely handled by USIS personnel.

Staffing the Operating Programs

As operating programs gradually took on permanent character, the problem of recruiting, training, and maintaining competent personnel to administer them came to the fore as the critical determinant of their success—far more important than the niceties of organizational relationships that occupied so much attention in the late 1940's and the 1950's. During the early postwar years, much use had been made of personnel carried over from the corresponding wartime activities. The Marshall Plan had the special attraction of an effort with fixed time limits concentrated in a geographical region well known to many Americans. The ECA, therefore, was able temporarily to draw high-quality personnel from business and professional life, as well as from other government agencies.

For operations of indefinite duration, however, many of them now concentrated in the relatively unfamiliar and often less attractive regions of Asia, Africa, and Latin America, these *ad hoc* staffing methods were inadequate. In the late 1950's and early 1960's, recruiting for professional needs was further hampered by the increasing lag of governmental salary levels behind those for corresponding work in private life.

The provisions in the Foreign Service Act of 1946 for a Foreign Service Reserve Corps might be thought to have offered a partial solution. Despite the implications of its title, however, the reserve corps was not a body of civilians specially enlisted and trained to be available for periodic overseas service, analogous to military reserve officers. It was simply a convenient label under which to classify civilians who were temporarily recruited for the operating programs, offering them during their tours of duty many, though not all, of the perquisites available to regular officers. Even had the reserve-corps concept been more fully developed, however, it would not have met the need for a core of full-time career professionals in AID and USIA, or for easy movement of personnel back and forth between these operating programs and the regular Foreign Service career. Since, in many countries, operating programs constituted a major part of the substance of relations with the United States, and since ambassadors and deputy chiefs of mission were being given constantly greater responsibility for general policy guidance and coordination of these programs, the logic of facilitating such interchange, and of including operating program experience in the Foreign Service career ladder, became constantly more compelling.

Nevertheless, most of the postwar official and semi-official studies of overseas representation focused only on the problem of manning the State Department and the Foreign Service. This was notably the case of the Wriston Committee, the most important of the series because its recommendations were implemented. In two major studies in 1951 and 1959, the Brookings Institution did propose a foreign-affairs personnel system including substantially all civilian foreign-affairs staffs at home and abroad, but these proposals were related to a radical plan for integrating the AID and USIA headquarters in Washington into a new superdepartment of foreign affairs.

Meanwhile, the operating agencies did the best they could, *faute de mieux* evolving toward *de facto* career services of their own. With its greater administrative continuity, USIA made comparatively good progress, establishing a "career reserve officer corps" generally patterned on the Foreign Service, with recruitment by examination at the junior level and arrangements for systematic career planning and promotion. In the absence of legislative authority, however, there were some limits to the development of this system into a full-fledged professional career service.

The aid agencies, on the other hand, were badly hampered in developing similar arrangements by the frequent changes of organizational form and top leadership, and by the chronic uncertainty as to the duration of the programs. Turnover was much more rapid, and the agencies depended far more on direct recruitment at the upper and middle levels for comparatively short tours of duty. While the infusion of fresh blood at upper and middle levels is a desirable element in any such program, not excluding the Foreign Service itself, the administration of aid suffered badly from a disproportion between short-term recruits and long-term career professionals. Many man-months were lost in the indoctrination of successive waves of newcomers and in accustoming them to governmental methods.

The diversity of personnel needs for the operating programs obviously complicates the development of career services. They require many technical specialists—radio and television experts, highway and electrical engineers, agricultural researchers, and the like, as well as top administrators of the missions, country program officers at home and abroad, and other management personnel. While some technical specialists may wish to make a lifetime career abroad, for many the most satisfactory career includes both overseas governmental work and private professional activity within the United States. The need for a permanent career service is especially great in the more generalized positions.

This problem was one of the main topics dealt with by the Committee on Foreign Affairs Personnel under the chairmanship of Former Secretary of State Christian A. Herter, Jr., which filed its report in December, 1962, under the title *Personnel for the New Diplomacy.* The Herter Committee considered the possibility of a further expansion of the Foreign Service itself to meet the professional core needs of the operating agencies, but it concluded that this major step should not be taken at the time. Instead, it recommended that statutory provision be made for both a career Foreign Information Service and a career Foreign Development Service, and proposed that, together with the Foreign Service itself, these two new services constitute "a family of compatible services governed by uniform statutory provisions regarding personnel management," with substantial uniformity in personnel policies, equality in conditions of service, joint conduct of personnel operations to some degree, systematic interchange of personnel, and "consideration of senior personnel of all three services in filling top executive posts in foreign affairs." At the same time, the Herter Committee made extensive recommendations for improving the recruitment, promotion, and career-planning arrangements for all foreign-affairs operations.

The Problem of Coordination

Through this kaleidoscopic flux of diverse policies, programs, agencies, and staffing arrangements, there runs one persistent question. *How can these many efforts be fitted together into a single pattern of effective and harmonious United States foreign policy?* This is the basic problem of coordination, which affects not only the actions, but also the posture and appearance of the United States abroad. In Chapter 6, this problem will be reviewed in some detail as it is currently posed at the country, the regional, and the Washington levels.

2. Economic Representation
of the United States Abroad

JOHN LINDEMAN

Nearly five hundred years ago, Machiavelli advised his Prince, "There is nothing more difficult to take into hand, more perilous to conduct, or more uncertain in its success, than to take the lead in a new order of things." This might be construed as a warning not to take the lead, but rather to sit back in relative safety and comfort and go wherever the current of events should lead. Such a warning would be of small value to the United States. Whether we like it or not, we have been forced into a position of leadership in an utterly new world order of things. And we have to face all the difficulties, perils, and uncertainties which go with that leadership.

This is true, of course, in all fields of the New Diplomacy—political, military, cultural, information, and intelligence—as well as in the economic field. It cannot be said that the task of securing adequate and creditable U.S. representation abroad is any more complex in the field of economics than it is in the others. However, the task is different because of a number of factors. Chief among these factors are the highly varied types of professionalism required; the number of people involved (second only to the military); and the many and often subtle channels through which economic representation takes place.

Moreover, economic affairs are intricately involved with political and military affairs. It used to be a popular interpretation of inter-

47

national relations that political and military decisions more often than not had their roots in economic conditions or objectives. In today's changing world, and especially with respect to year-to-year economic problems, the opposite is more nearly the case. For the United States, at least, purely political and military (security) problems have come to the fore. Paradoxically, however, this does not mean that economic matters have been relegated to a lower place in the scheme of things. Far from it: new political and military developments have spawned many major and hundreds of minor developments in U.S. economic policies and actions. For example, political and military considerations certainly account for most of the United States' interest in European and Atlantic economic institutions; the Alliance for Progress is a creature more of political than of economic strategy; our technical-assistance programs are largely a response to politically inspired independence movements in ex-colonial countries; and a major fraction of our annual foreign economic aid goes to governments whose military commitments are overly burdensome to them but important to us.

The upshot of this is that the people who represent us abroad in economic affairs must have more than a nodding acquaintance with the political and military realities that affect their work. Conversely, the representation officers in other fields, and especially the political officers, require more than the usual sophistication about technical economic matters.

How should we define the term "economic representation" abroad? We might use the traditional definition, which would encompass only those people and activities normally thought of as falling within the competence and responsibility of the regular diplomatic establishment—those involved in formal negotiations, the gathering and transmission to Washington of economic intelligence, and the recommendation as to how the intelligence should be used. This definition would focus almost exclusively on the overseas representation that flows through the old-line agencies in Washington, principally through the State Department.

Such a definition, however, would be too restrictive. It would leave out of account many of the very important representational functions of groups of people whose actions, in the economic field, significantly affect the conduct of American foreign policy, and who are to a greater or lesser degree responsive to American foreign-policy objectives. It is therefore convenient and useful to use the term "representation" here to mean something broader. Specifically, there will be a discussion of the representational functions of foreign-aid personnel (under whatever agency they happen to work currently), and the problems connected with them—including the Peace Corps. There will also be a discussion of the activities abroad of private American entities, such as large foundations and businesses.

The three categories for discussion are, then, traditional representation, foreign-aid representation, and representation through private entities. At first sight, the general lines and dimensions of the three seem clear and exclusive enough. But in fact they tend to merge. Traditional functions are often performed by the foreign-aid mission. Members of the diplomatic mission are usually deeply involved in foreign-aid and Peace Corps programs as a legitimate part of their jobs. In some countries, the technical-assistance activities of private American entities outweigh those of the U.S. Government.

It is precisely this merging of the categories that makes them significant. An important element in the development of the postwar activities of the United States in its dealings overseas has been the conscious effort to bring into a single focus all the instruments of foreign policy. A single focus is not possible when there are clear lines between categories. Some merging is necessary. One purpose of this discussion will be to describe and appraise the success of the merging efforts within the special field of economic representation, as well as between it and others.

Traditional Representation

The story has been told of a Texas tycoon who, at the tail end of a heavy evening, handed a few bills to an airline ticket clerk and said, "I want a ticket."

"A ticket to where?" asked the clerk.

"Never mind the details," said the Texan. "Just give me a ticket. I've got business everywhere."

This is the way it is with the United States in its economic involvement with other countries. We've got business everywhere. American embassies are established in more than 100 countries; there are nearly 200 consulates. There are also about eighty AID missions and numerous AID outposts.* All of these installations have traditional economic representational functions. The total number of people in them who are concerned with economic affairs can be numbered in the thousands.

In spite of the large number of installations, the geographic extent of our economic representation is no greater than it was before the last war. Indeed, the exclusion of mainland China and a few other places around the world from the orbit of our overseas representation makes it smaller than it was then. Before the war, however, we could manage an extensive geographic coverage by manning fewer posts: an embassy in the metropolitan capital could cover a vast colonial area, for example. Now, the proliferation of independent countries, especially in Africa and Asia, has greatly complicated even the relatively simple task of staffing the overseas installations.

More important than the increase in numbers of posts and the required numbers of people, however, is the drastic postwar change in the nature of the tasks that our economic representatives abroad are supposed to do.

Some Historical Perspective

Prior to World War II, the principal economic function of the American Government's overseas staff was to represent and promote specific domestic economic interests. Generally speaking, the purpose of the job was uncomplicated: to acquire and provide economic and commercial intelligence for the use of American businessmen who needed to know something about economic conditions abroad, and to negotiate favorable (or not unfavorable) arrangements for American exporters and investors. As a rule, the

* A small qualification must be made concerning these figures. They are not additive, because in most (but not all) cases the consulates general, the consulates, and the AID missions are offshoots of the embassies. Also, the embassies in a few countries are technically classified as legations.

job stopped there. The clientele was wholly American and easily identifiable.

The 1930 act that set up the Foreign Agricultural Service stated in its enacting clause that it was for "the purpose of encouraging and promoting the agriculture of the United States and assisting American farmers to adjust their operations and practice to meet world conditions."

This language not only was in the spirit of the times, it also reflected the whole of the spirit. Commercial attaché posts had been created to provide the same sort of service for our mining, manufacturing, and commercial interests. The regular staffs of the embassies, legations, and consulates did most of the reporting. They also did most of the routine work of extricating Americans abroad from the red tape or worse in which their business ventures may have landed them. The economic staffs—or, rather, the people on the staffs who did economic work, for there were few professional economists among them—rarely were called on to do anything that could not be related clearly to a particular economic interest within the United States.

In short, the emphasis was on the American economy and on what was good for it. This was entirely consistent with the pursuit of our foreign interests as we saw them then and, incidentally, one that closely corresponds to the emphasis that most other countries still place on their economic dealings with us. We were then not interested to any significant degree with the internal economic conditions in other countries and their effect on our international policies or posture.

The war, its immediate aftermath, and the recognition of the cold war changed all this. As the United States gradually changed from a relatively isolated and inward-looking nation to the peacemaker and economic arbiter of the non-Communist world—the role of economic arbiter being now somewhat eclipsed by the success of the Marshall Plan—the purpose of our economic representation abroad and the quality of the people engaged in it had to change. Our representatives abroad necessarily became concerned more and more with the internal affairs of the countries to which they were assigned.

This meant, in short, that in our own interests—however vaguely or explicitly they may have been expressed—we became directly involved in the internal economic affairs of other countries. This required that our economic intelligence and our ability to negotiate on economic matters with foreign countries had to take on an entirely new dimension.

Even though the transition period was gradual, the operational change was abrupt. With some minor qualifications that need not be given here, it came with the Marshall Plan, when we committed huge sums of money to the restoration of Western Europe because of the disruption caused by World War II. This commitment of funds was made on the condition that European countries would produce a program that held out reasonable prospects of success. The judgment as to whether or not a program would or would not do so had to be a joint one, arrived at by the U.S., the individual countries concerned, and the Organization of European Economic Cooperation. Under the circumstances, we had to know what we were talking about, and we had to talk (i.e., negotiate) with representatives of these countries on a basis of at least roughly equal appreciation of their economic problems.* This abrupt shift in emphasis required an entirely new breed of economic officers in our representation abroad. Through some miracle of recruitment, they were found, and, on the whole, our economic representatives in European countries were highly successful. (Attributable to their success is at least some part of the reduction in the cost of the Marshall Plan from an estimated $17.5 billion to roughly $12.5 billion, and its phasing out a year ahead of schedule.)

The Marshall Plan organization has long since gone by the board, but there has been another transition. To date, the transition has been in three basic areas: (1) helping the development of the aspiring new nations in Asia and Africa, and the new aspirations of the older nations in Latin America; (2) maintaining the economic viability of countries on the Communist periphery; and (3) agreeing with the economically viable industrial countries on economic policies that should be adopted to help maintain peace

---

* I was once chided by a high economic officer of a sophisticated European country because of this. The U.S., he said, actually seemed to know more about his economy than did the people in his own government.

and world security.* In all three cases, we must know a great deal about the internal economic conditions of the countries involved and must be able to negotiate with them not only on our own domestic economic interests, but also on their economic policies and prospects, in our common interest.

The Current Situation

It should be clear that there is a continuing need for a radical reorientation of all economic officers abroad in the field of economic representation. They no longer simply report "the number of camels crossing the desert" (as one foreign officer characterized the pre-war purpose of economic representation) or the likely market in some far-off country for American sewing machines. They must now be well versed—and in a position to brief their superiors—on such formerly esoteric matters as fiscal policy, exchange rates, development potential (and theory), terms of trade, commodity questions, etc. Also, and this is of considerable importance, they must be able to relate their economic analyses to the political and social realities of the country to which they are assigned.

For a number of years, the various groups that have studied the problem of staffing the Foreign Service have been aware of this new condition and have recommended that there should be a greater emphasis on the recruitment and training of foreign service officers with a good background in economics. The State Department has taken this advice seriously and has, at least on paper, upgraded the job of economic officer to the point that it is as prestigious as that of the "generalist" political officer.† One striking change is that the entrance examination for foreign service officers has been refined by the inclusion of additional options: the general examination, as in the past, is relatively unchanged; but the options now offered to candidates have been expanded to

* On this last point, much of the representational activity of the U.S. is in international agencies or in international *ad hoc* conferences. International and multilateral representation is the subject of another chapter and will be mentioned further here only in passing.

† A dozen or more of our present ambassadors are professionally trained economists.

meet the needs of the foreign service of more specialized skills. For the latest entrance examination the four options were the usual generalist one (political), and those in the fields of economics, commercial work, and administration. The Department states that: "The Economics, Commercial, and Administrative options represent manpower requirements of the Foreign Service which are currently in short supply. By providing specific options it is hoped that more applicants with these specialized skills and interests will take the examination."

In spite of its best efforts, the Department has not been notably successful in recruiting officers who choose economics as their field. The deficiency has been partly overcome by lateral entry into the Foreign Service of experienced people from AID (and its predecessor organizations) and, more importantly, by reliance in the field on AID personnel to carry out what normally should be embassy tasks.

To rely on AID personnel to provide some of the brains and manpower needed for intelligent economic representation is both good and bad. It is good in those countries where competent AID missions exist, for the comprehensive and highly professional analyses AID requires provide the basis for excellent economic representation. It is bad in that the country emphasis in AID changes from year to year—in relation to the requirements of the foreign-aid program, not in relation to the United States' needs for competent economic representation in the countries concerned. When the Marshall Plan was phased out in Europe, a tremendous gap was left in our economic representation. Now that AID is phasing out—or down—in many countries, the same kind of gap may again appear. It seems incongruous that our best economic representation throughout the world is connected to the foreign-aid program rather than to our need for good economic information and skillful negotiation on economic matters, but this appears to be the case.

The concept of the Country Team—which is discussed in another chapter—is, of course, a good and sensible one, but it makes the ambassador's life quite burdensome, especially in such specialized fields as economics. According to the Herter Report, the requirements for effective leadership in the field "cannot be made through experience only in the traditional mold of the diplomat: a striking illustration of the new dimensions in diplomacy is the extent to which economic problems have come to occupy the time of virtually all ambassadors abroad." If the ambassador is to handle these problems well, he must have high-caliber economic advice at hand, and he needs it whether or not there is an AID mission in his country.

Thus, one important problem with respect to traditional representation is that of manning through regular Foreign Service channels our embassies and other installations in which we do not have AID missions, and of being prepared to take over economic representation when AID missions are no longer there.

Another problem is that of adequate coordination. It has already been pointed out that in many of our major diplomatic missions abroad there are agricultural attachés and commercial attachés; there are also Treasury representatives and representatives of a number of other branches of the Executive. In all, twenty or more agencies of the federal government have their own representatives stationed abroad. Of course, there are not twenty or more in each embassy, but an ambassador is likely to find himself with representatives of at least five or ten.

In accordance with the Country Team concept, the Ambassador is supposed to coordinate the activities of these representatives. But the simple fact is that the people from agencies other than the State Department have their spiritual homes, as well as their career interests, in their own buildings in Washington. Too often this means that the ambassador finds it necessary to reconcile conflicts that actually originate in differing departmental or agency views about foreign policy. As a rule, this happens with departments or agencies that have relatively little interest in foreign affairs. It might be that this is a throwback to the pre-war days when our main concern in economic representation abroad was to take care of special and specific American interests. But this is small comfort to an ambassador who must now adapt to the present, principally outward-looking, posture of the U.S.

The ambassador's job in this respect is not that of policy coordination, but of operational and representational coordination. This type of coordination is much simpler when policy is consistent, and when the departments and agencies in Washington direct their people in the field along lines that have been properly coordinated at home. Basically, of course, this is a question of how the Executive Branch is organized to make decisions and determine objectives. If organization in Washington is poor, there is bound to be lack of coordination in the field. This is particularly true when field officers feel responsible to differing agencies in Washington. The basic responsibility here rests in Washington, not in the field.

The pulls and tugs in Washington on domestic versus foreign policy objectives have so far made it difficult to send consistent policy directives to the field. The result is that our field representatives are often confused among themselves and give a confused picture of American foreign economic policy to the government to which they are accredited. But it is not their fault.

Coordination of the activities of economic representatives at a single post abroad is relatively simple. But it is much more difficult to coordinate activities in several places and head them in the same direction. There are two circumstances that make this kind of coordination especially important in the economic field. The first is that economic arrangements we make with a given country (or countries) very often have economic consequences in other countries. If we negotiate a sale of surplus grain to India, we may throw the economies of the rice-producing countries such as Thailand and Burma out of kilter. If we persuade a nation to take measures to eliminate its balance-of-payments deficit, we create balance-of-payments problems in other nations. If we have anything at all to say about a government altering its nation's exchange rate—and very often we do—we have to consider the effects in many other lands. A major job of our economic representatives abroad is to evaluate properly what these inter-country consequences will be, so that Washington can make sound policy decisions. This requires more knowledge and objectivity than is necessary when only local problems are considered. It also requires good communications. These we have, daily with a fast cable service, and periodically in regional meetings of key economic personnel that permit our representatives to get an appreciation of our total economic program abroad.

The second circumstance is that we often deal with the same

question at different places. Representation is not only at the capital city of individual nations. It takes place also in numerous regional and international bodies, where a second group of American representatives negotiates on matters also being dealt with on a continuing basis with individual governments. For example, we deal with trade matters both bilaterally and at GATT negotiations; with fiscal matters both bilaterally and with the International Monetary Fund; with military-economic matters both bilaterally and in NATO, SEATO, or CENTO. Furthermore, we may deal with much the same problem in two or more international bodies. The essence of proper coordination is good communications and frequent conferences, which we appear to have. It takes a real effort to see to it that all economic representatives abroad who might conceivably be interested in a particular question are fully informed of what is going on, and the reasons for it.

Finally, there is the obvious need to coordinate what our economists do overseas with what is being done in other fields of representation—political, military, and information. The objective, of course, is to tie together all official American activities overseas so that they strengthen each other and do not cancel each other out. The concluding chapter of this volume deals with the problems of over-all coordination of this type and with the organization that has been developed in Washington and in the field to achieve it. But it should be pointed out here that our current requirements make it more important than ever before to coordinate economic activities properly. While in earlier days our economic representatives dealt mainly with routine reporting of a commercial intelligence nature, their activities seldom affected the principal formal business of our top diplomats. Consequently, it became customary in most of our embassies and legations to look upon the economic staff as essentially a service group and to keep it outside the mainstream of diplomatic business. This attitude no longer fits our requirements. Responsible officials in the State Department and most ambassadors recognize this fact.

Manpower

The need for special recruitment of economic personnel into the regular Foreign Service should not be minimized. Nor should the current failure of the Foreign Service to recruit adequate economic personnel be overlooked. This is not the place to propose new recruitment policies, but it should be made clear that present policies tend to repel rather than attract the better young people in the field of economics. It is usual that the applicant for a Foreign Service appointment has to wait twelve to eighteen months from the time of his application before he finds out whether he is accepted; by the time the decision is made, he is often comfortably settled in some other, and more lucrative, position.

Along with this general recruitment difficulty, the Foreign Service has the problem of manning a large number of specialized economic posts abroad. The Department of State lists nineteen specialties (plus a final category called "Other") in the economic field. They are: strategy, international trade, military relations, commercial, finance, international organizations, investment and economic development, industrial analysis, agriculture, commodity policy, fuel and power, minerals and metals, atomic energy, transportation and communications, civil air, shipping, telecommunications, fisheries, and reports evaluation. In addition to these, there are twenty-four different geographic areas of specialization, and a general category of Intelligence Research and Analysis.

From this it is clear that if the Foreign Service is to have adequate manpower, there must be some means of recruiting people on a firm basis with a minimum of delay in appointment. Other government agencies have found a way of making firm offers, mostly on a probationary or "internship" basis. It would be only sensible for the State Department to do the same.

At this time, there are less than 500 Foreign Service officers with economic functions stationed in the field, and a fair percentage of them are working with international or multilateral agencies rather than in regular diplomatic establishments. (The regular Foreign Service officers are augmented in the field by some 300 AID personnel whose functions are, by and large, representational in the traditional sense.) Many economic posts are vacant because of the difficulty of finding qualified officers to fill them.

The vacant posts, the uncertainty about AID personnel, and the growing importance of economic representation make the current and future manpower situations a matter of concern to State Department officials. Programs are under way to offer a new entrance option in economics, to increase lateral entry, and to provide mid-career training in economics. To quote the Herter Report again: "There are acute shortages of persons who combine specialized knowledge in the fields listed below with experience and broad understanding of foreign affairs. In all these fields, the needs can be expected to grow in the future." The first of the fields listed was that of "Economists with practical competence in planning economic and social development, including specialists in international trade and other fields."

Complexity and Diversity

Another view of the complexity and diversity of economic representation may be had by considering the kinds of tasks the economic specialists must perform:

—In the trade field: routine reporting on market conditions and trends, and straight intelligence; negotiation of trade agreements and reciprocal concessions; investigation of American allegations of unfair trade practices; analysis of inter-regional trade; negotiation of agreed restrictions on East-West trade, and reporting on East-West trade developments; and active promotion of U.S. interests with the host country—trade, licensing agreements, investments, investment opportunities, etc.

—In the commodity field: negotiation of international commodity agreements; arranging purchases of materials for U.S. stockpiles; routine reporting on demand, supply, and price trends; investigating requirements and end-use of commodities under international allocation or U.S. export control; active promotion of host country's production and export of specific commodities; and active promotion of the sale abroad of specific U.S. commodities, especially agricultural products.

—In the economic-development field: exhaustive analysis of investment and consumption needs, resource availability, internal financial conditions, foreign exchange potential, etc.; negotiations to put into effect policies leading to economic progress; occasionally, working out details of a national economic program with the government of the host country; occasionally, operational control of some aspects of an economic development program, as, for example, the use of counterpart funds for investments; and investigation of end-use of U.S. aid.

—In the military field: analysis of the economic potential of the host country to finance its military requirements; negotiation of the character and level of the host country's military budget; analysis of the economic effect in the host country of American expenditures for (and by) American forces, bases, lines of communication, etc.; analysis of the industrial capacity of the host country to produce military goods; and advice on placement of offshore procurement contracts.

Incomplete though it is, this list illustrates the wide range of subject matter. Furthermore, our economists deal with these things at varying levels of importance. A report, for example, is often the inconsequential and overburdening chore inspired by Washington agencies that (to quote the Brookings Institution) "apparently seek to obtain all possible information on every conceivable subject within their official jurisdiction without regard to its immediate or ultimate usefulness." Similarly, negotiations can be cut-and-dried affairs conducted in the field on the basis of precise instructions from Washington.

On the other hand, reporting can be penetrating, technically impeccable, and, above all, persuasive about important economic matters. When it is, it can contribute significantly to the articulation of our foreign economic policy and to the effectiveness of our negotiations. This negotiation is often at the highest level where it involves important matters of national policy for the host government, and where it requires of our negotiators not only great technical competence as economists, but also mature judgment and an appreciation of relevant noneconomic factors.

It hardly seems likely that the need for competent economists will diminish in the future. Not many years ago, there was a generally accepted assumption that once we were past the postwar economic crisis we could revert to more "normal" international economic relations. Events have proven this to be a false assumption. It is more likely that we shall continue to be involved in other people's economic affairs for many decades to come. The need for more and better economic officers in the field is not only a problem for today—it is also a problem for the future.

FOREIGN-AID REPRESENTATION

Apart from the people in the economic field who provide traditional representation for us abroad, there are thousands of Americans employed to administer and carry out foreign economic-aid programs. Very few of these people can be classified as economists. We find specialists in soil and water utilization, for example, and in ranch management, epidemiology, or school administration. But their function is primarily economic, in that their basic job is to help raise the standard of living in the countries to which they are assigned.

Our foreign economic aid did not begin, as many people suppose, with the Marshall Plan in 1948 or with the Greece–Turkey program the year before. On a massive scale, it began with Lend-Lease and the Middle East Civilian Supply Program, and carried over into UNRRA and the several improvisations between the termination of UNRRA and the beginning of the Marshall Plan. On the technical-assistance level, it began in 1940 with the *servicio* programs of the Institute of Inter-American Affairs; the *servicio* attitude still exists in Latin America, in spite of the new look that the Alliance for Progress was supposed to have provided. Thus foreign economic aid as a major American activity has had a fundamental continuity for a quarter of a century.

During these years, a remarkable and experienced cadre of officers has been created. Many mission chiefs, administrative officers, and program officers have twenty or more years of experience in the foreign-aid field. A number of them have been absorbed into the Foreign Service. Some have been appointed as ambassadors. This cadre has been built with a minimum of career security.

The foreign-aid legislation, and hence the existence of the agency administering it, is on a year-to-year basis. But many of the officers of the foreign-aid program apparently ignore the inherently tenuous nature of their jobs. And the AID agency itself has ignored—or overlooked—its temporary character. It has now set up a quasi-career service with some rules of tenure, selection-out and promotion panels, mid-career training, rotation between field jobs, and rotation between the field and Washington. This applies mainly to people at the executive level. For the foreign-aid agency, in spite of its many reorganizations and difficulties, anticipated one of the Herter Report's observations:

> Foreign development work is particularly demanding of executive talent. AID programs entail heavy operational responsibilities, and most of them operate exclusively in the areas of the world where the forces of change are moving most rapidly. There is almost no way to obtain experience in the United States in coordinating the special interests of a variety of technical fields and fitting them into the complex, changing needs of total societies. The need for sustained development programs for executives in foreign assistance work is critical.

The Field versus Washington

It is an axiom of bureaucratic organizations that field offices and headquarters frequently clash. Such clashes are the rule rather than the exception in the foreign-aid program.

In part, this results from the necessarily divergent perspectives. The field offices tend, to paraphrase a familiar quotation, to be "more Martian than Mars." And the Washington headquarters thinks that it looks austerely and objectively at the whole of the world with infinite wisdom, able to call the turn properly on any matter overseas, no matter how trivial it may be. To field officers, it appears that too many desk men in Washington, whose job description calls them "officer in charge of" a particular country and who think they actually are in charge, can hardly keep up with the name of the current prime minister. At the same time, the desk officer wonders how in the world the men in the field could have failed to heed Manual Order No. XXVI, or to send in an amended form G1, with amended E1 and AD attached.

The fact is that foreign-aid personnel in the field and their counterparts in Washington live in different worlds. At a recent conference, a man with many years of experience in the field explained that "in the field we look upon Washington as the enemy." The rejoinder, from a participant who was equally experienced, but at headquarters, was "And we think of the field as a cross we must bear up Capitol Hill several times a year."

The field representatives, although they may resent it and argue about it, must respond to orders from Washington. Thus, much of the substance of our foreign economic representation comes from an understandably timorous evaluation of Congressional opinion, rather than from a real evaluation of economic needs. The only cure for this is to put our economic aid program on a continuing, rather than year-to-year, basis. For representation abroad is bound to be less effective if it must be carried each year, as a cross, up Capitol Hill. The fault lies not entirely with Congress and its committees. There have been many hostile committees, but to place the blame on them alone is a specious argument. Most of the fault lies with the Executive Branch. Until very recently, the foreign-aid program has been presented to Congress annually with a degree of diffidence that invites suspicion. If and when it is presented with assurance and conviction, then, perhaps, the field-*versus*-Washington problem will be in better proportion to the over-all dimensions of the issue.

The Technicians

Numerically, technical-assistance experts (apart from the Peace Corps) make up our most important body of economic representatives abroad. On direct hire and on contract, there are some 6,000 of them—nearly ten times as many as the people who engage in traditional economic representation. But their representational role is crucial, for they deal daily not just with government ministers, but with middle-level civil servants and community leaders. Their representational impact perhaps strikes harder than that of the embassy staff. This large number of technicians overseas is a logical result of the shift in emphasis in our foreign-aid programs: we started by advising the West European governments in the use of Marshall Plan aid; now we are trying to transmit knowledge and technology to remote parts of the world. It is a different job.

The change in the character of our foreign-aid programs in recent years has intensified an already serious problem of economic representation overseas—namely, the problem of recruiting, training, and holding large numbers of good people. The great diversity of skills required makes this problem difficult enough. But the mission system, which emphasizes the emergency nature of the job, and thus the probability that employment is temporary, adds to the difficulties.

In their study on training specialized mission personnel, Wallace Sayre and Clarence Thurber have described the average person recruited for mission work:

> The typical staff member of a specialized mission may be assumed to have certain general characteristics, although it would perhaps be difficult to find among them a single individual who did not differ in some important way from the following description. This somewhat hypothetical typical staff member is a specialist of mature years; he has been trained in a special field and has earned through experience as a specialist the status of an expert in some degree; his training and experience have been mainly if not solely within the United States; he knows no language other than English; his acquaintance with United States foreign policy is that of the average citizen in his professional group; his knowledge of overseas environments (their culture and their economic and political systems) is very slight. He is, in short, what he was selected by the government to be: a competent specialist possessing skills and knowledge needed to carry out some aspect of our program overseas.*

The authors might have added that the recruit must be psychologically well-balanced and able to adjust to unusual living conditions in a way that will reflect credit on the United States. If he is to be abroad for long, his wife and children must also be able to make a good adjustment. Finding such adjustable people with essentially American specialties is not easy today, when many of our missions are located in so-called hardship posts. The hardship post carries a salary differential that helps in persuading people to go to it, but the differential does not eliminate the basic problem. A few years ago, most of the personnel of our economic missions were in Europe, where adjustment is relatively simple. Today, the missions that employ most of the American personnel of the AID agency overseas are in Asia, Africa, and Latin America. More than

* Wallace S. Sayre and Clarence E. Thurber, *Training for Specialized Mission Personnel* (Chicago, Ill.: Public Administration Clearing House, 1952).

forty headquarters posts are classified as hardship posts. But this only begins to tell the story. With operational missions there is a great deal of activity outside capital cities, in remote areas where the problem of adjustment is particularly acute. In Nigeria, for example, there are thirty posts outside the capital city.

The recruiting problem therefore is to find people who possess professional qualifications in combination with a stable and well-balanced personality to take a temporary job in an entirely strange environment. Training must be brief, and there is little time for apprenticeship in the field. This is one of the most challenging personnel problems in the government today. Is it, however, a necessary one? Could we not face the fact that the mission system no longer adequately responds to a nonrecurrent emergency—that, for example, some of our Latin American missions have been in existence for twenty-odd years, that the list of active missions grows every year, and that our national interest will probably require an indefinite continuation of technical-assistance programs? Having faced this situation, should we not try to build up a permanent personnel system to go along with a regular operation?

The answer is not clear-cut. In the first place, the year-to-year authorization for foreign-aid programs works against building a career service, no matter how permanent the Administration may consider the programs to be. In addition, even though the mission system continues and even though the life of some missions may appear to be indefinite, there is a constant change in the kinds of skills required in technical-assistance programs. The specialized jobs that must be done can usually be completed in a relatively short time (and should be, if they are done correctly by developing local technicians to take over), and there is no assurance that similar jobs must be done elsewhere. Thus many of the technical experts on mission staffs are bound to be temporary employees. And finally, there is this to say in favor of the temporary employee: if he is well selected, he is apt to do his job better than the permanent man; his zeal and flexibility often combine to let him turn in a superior performance.

Sayre and Thurber did not describe another type of mission employee. This is the man who has already proved his ability to adjust to his environment, usually with long experience in government service before going abroad, who does a generalized job in the mission structure or one with a counterpart in most other missions. There are many such men, and the AID agency guards them jealously. These men are, in effect, the permanent cadre around which the agency fits the technicians needed for temporary assignments. Many of them are now mission chiefs, deputy chiefs, administrative officers, and program officers. They provide the missions with the hard core of professionalism that offsets many of the obvious disadvantages of the truly emergency mission staffed at all levels with temporary personnel. Also, since most of the employees with long experience are in supervisory positions or in positions that require the most contact with officials of the host government, they set the general tone of representation by which the temporary personnel are guided.

For a variety of reasons, the AID agency and its predecessors found it convenient to make contracts with outside agencies for many technical-assistance projects. One-quarter of our technicians now abroad work under contract, rather than directly for the United States Government. It is likely that their number will increase, if for no other reason than that there is a growing sense in the Congress that contractors can often do a better job than direct-hire employees, and that they do not tend to become permanently affixed to the government agency.

There is no hard and fast rule as to what kinds of projects will be undertaken directly and what kinds on contract. Considerations include the relative ease of recruitment of personnel; the likely duration of a project (it is easier and often more economical to contract with an organization to provide a cadre of its own permanent staff for a one-year job than it is to set up an organization by direct hire); the degree of "team" expertise required (for example, a road-design project requires several different kinds of engineering skills from people accustomed to working together; a contractor can provide these better than direct hire).

Another important consideration is the degree to which the project is likely to impinge on a sensitive area of national policy. Many projects, particularly those which have to do with economic planning and programming and with public administration training, do so impinge, and in such cases, both the United States and the host country are likely to be wary of too close a connection with technical-assistance experts who are directly employed by the United States Government. A contractor is at least one step removed from this onus. Many of AID's more than 100 contracts with universities (which usually also call for training in the United States of planning and public administration officials from the host country) are in this category.

Despite the fact that contractor personnel are somewhat removed from direct identification with the United States Government, people in the host country, nevertheless, consider them to be representatives of the United States. Their actions, their dedication (or lack of it), and their on-the-job efficiency all create a representational picture of the United States. Very few people in the host country take the trouble to distinguish between contract and direct-hire personnel when they evaluate what the Americans are up to.

The Peace Corps

This is not foreign representation in any usual sense. Nevertheless, to many people in other countries, as well as to their governments, the Peace Corps represents the United States more dramatically than any other overseas activity of our government. The Peace Corps carries with it an idealism and sense of dedication to the furtherance of the welfare of mankind such as no other U.S. Government program can profess to provide.

President Kennedy said about the Director of the Peace Corps: "I handed him a lemon, and he made lemonade." The Director made lemonade only because he had the enthusiastic backing of many thousands of Americans who wanted to export their particular knowledge and expertise to the less developed areas of the world. Their motives, though most likely very diverse, are not important for this discussion. The important thing is that more than 10,000 Americans* are now in the Peace Corps overseas; additional numbers are in training to take their places.

Is this economic representation? If not, under what category

* Mostly young, but not entirely. Some Peace Corps volunteers beyond retirement age have been accepted.

does it fall? One of our difficulties is to define what we mean when we use the word "economic." The best definition seems to be all encompassing: that which relates to the welfare of people. In this sense, the participants in the Peace Corps program are doing a job related to both economic representation and economic development.

In the area of formal representation, these people have no status. It is regrettable, but true, that in several foreign countries the embassies and foreign-aid missions (which ought to provide logistical support for the Peace Corps volunteers) think that the whole Peace Corps effort is a nuisance. They would prefer not to be bothered with it. Very probably this is because of a too constricted view of the purposes of American economic representation abroad.

The percentage distribution of Peace Corps volunteers, including those in training, as of the end of 1963, was as follows (the percentages are about the same today):

Secondary Education	32
Rural Community Action	21
Elementary Education	10
Health	9
Agricultural Extension	7
Urban Community Action	6
University Education	6
Physical Education	3
Public Works	3
Vocational Education	2
Multi-Purpose	1
	100

As of the same date, the Peace Corps was operating in forty-six countries, all of them in the so-called underdeveloped part of the world—Africa, South Asia, Southeast Asia, and Latin America. By geographical areas, the largest number of volunteers were in seventeen countries of Latin America, the next largest in seventeen countries of Africa, and there is representation in four countries of the Far East, with heavy concentration in Malaysia. The Peace Corps is just beginning its programs in the Near East and South Asia, with volunteers in eight countries.

Unlike the majority of AID technicians, Peace Corps volunteers usually work in remote areas where the purpose of their "representation" is to project an image of the United States to people who have little political involvement or aspiration. Incidents involving friction or any other kind of unpleasantness from the people in the host country have been extremely rare, with the result that the Peace Corps has been enormously successful among government officials and other influential people on the local scene. Many of the countries that have received volunteers have formally requested that more be sent. (In this connection, it should be noted that we seldom receive a formal request to augment our embassy personnel or AID missions).

The Peace Corps policy is to withdraw any volunteer who for any reason is unsuitable to his mission; yet, out of the many thousands of volunteers in the field, only 4 per cent have been recalled for this reason. Perhaps this is due to the high degree of enthusiasm and dedication that most Peace Corps volunteers bring to their jobs—qualities that might, in some cases, outweigh the quality of technical expertise. (Why send Peace Corps people to a country like Chile, for example, to teach road-building in villages? Santiago is full of sophisticated Chilenos with technical capacities far superior to the average Peace Corps volunteer.)

However, the comparative success of the Peace Corps is also largely due to the care with which the volunteers are selected and to their orientation and training before they leave the United States. The Peace Corps is unique among government agencies in that it does not have to do much active recruitment. Typically, nine out of ten applications are turned down after a preliminary and almost cursory examination; the remaining 10 per cent represent the cream of the crop and are selected as candidates, but not yet as employees. Candidates are given an intensive orientation course on the country to which they will be assigned, which includes language instruction, courses on political and social factors, and a rigorous physical-fitness program. There is an axiom among the universities that offer Peace Corps training that the instructors are exhausted long before the trainees have even begun to slow down.

Of the candidates chosen for orientation, however, usually 30 per cent drop out during the training period. Thus only seven out of ten candidates finally make the grade, and these people go into the field well prepared to do their assigned jobs and represent the United States in a most satisfactory way.

Another unique feature of the Peace Corps is the relatively short term of service. Volunteers sign up for two years, which includes the training period; they may not renew. The short-term policy also applies to headquarters and field staff officers, but here the limitation is partly informal because of Civil Service regulations. Stated broadly, the policy is that nobody shall make a career of the Peace Corps, the objective being to limit staff employment to five years or less.

It is somewhat incongruous that the three months' orientation program of the Peace Corps is in sharp contrast to that of AID. As a rule, a new AID technician receives not more than two or three weeks of orientation; during that period, he must get his shots, alert his wife to the climatic and dietary problems that she and her children will find, buy a new wardrobe, and take care of the other dozens of details that surround a major family move. Partly, this is because AID has so much difficulty in recruiting: when the Agency finds a satisfactory man, it is usually anxious to get him on the job as quickly as possible. Nevertheless, AID might well learn a lesson from the success of the intensive and relatively long orientation that has contributed so much to the success of the Peace Corps.

ECONOMIC REPRESENTATION BY PRIVATE AMERICAN ENTITIES

It may be unusual to include the representational activities of American private entities abroad in a discussion such as this one. But it would be misleading to omit all references to them. For good or ill, they and their personnel present to people in foreign countries certain facets of America that cannot be seen elsewhere. And in recent years, there seems to be in their presentation more good than ill for the achievement of United States economic objectives abroad.

Voluntary Organizations and Foundations

The Technical Assistance Clearing House lists ninety-eight voluntary organizations and foundations that, to greater or lesser degrees, cooperate with AID in economic or quasi-economic activities in the less-developed countries. Some of them are very small, with all field operations being conducted by perhaps one man and a part-time secretary from a one-room office. Some are highly specialized. One of them, for example, does nothing but send baby chicks to Latin America on a farmer-to-farmer basis; another has enlisted a corps of home-based experts who, without fees, will answer unusual technical questions that come in from the field.

The foundations, of course, operate on a much larger scale. For example, in the economic field, the Ford Foundation (which usually maintains only a small field staff of its own, and makes operational contracts for its projects with universities and other non-profit institutions) has financed an economic advisory group for India and one for Pakistan; has helped to organize an Administrative Staff College in Pakistan which heavily emphasizes economic planning; and in Burma has supported an agricultural college, a team of accountants to try to straighten out the books of the government-owned commercial and industrial corporation, and a team of American professors in the School of Commerce at the University of Rangoon.

Most of the voluntary agencies and foundations have this in common: they present a sincerely altruistic and nearly nonpolitical face abroad. We must say "nearly" nonpolitical for, while all these agencies would undoubtedly deny that they are an arm of U.S. foreign economic policy, there can be no doubt that they are allies. By and large, their activities are designed to implement and to supplement those of the United States Government.

This is especially true of the large foundations. It was mentioned above that AID contract employees (especially university advisory teams) can deal much better with foreign government officials on such delicate matters as national economic planning and policy because they are at least one step removed from the onus of being directly on the United States payroll. The foundations are even further removed; their personnel, especially in the economic policy and planning fields, enjoy the confidence both of foreign country officials and of United States agents and economic representatives abroad.

As a result, foundation people can often act as a bridge between the American officials and those of a foreign country. In view of the sometimes almost incomprehensible language of formal diplomatic interchanges, and in view of the protocol that very often inhibits knowledgeable people in two different countries from even talking business to one another, this kind of bridge is invaluable to our more traditional type of representation abroad.

American Business Entities

It is a far cry from the pre-war stereotype of the American embassy (and its offshoots) as primarily a representative of American business interests to the hopeful trend today that American business interests abroad are more and more consciously representing the broader objectives of United States economic policy. Yet this trend exists.

Most observers agree that, with a few eccentric exceptions, the management of any American (or other) business will be motivated to do what it considers best for the welfare of its own company. But this generalization covers a broad spectrum of possible lines of action, which can be based on policies that are short-run and opportunistic, on policies that are long-run and "socially responsible," or on policies that fall anywhere in between. The place of each company in the spectrum will depend on a number of factors or conditions: the corporation philosophy, the personal convictions of senior officers, the degree of the corporation's financial and other commitments in the country, the nature of the company's business, the importance of overseas operations in the company's total business, etc. Thus, as far as advancing American economic policy abroad is concerned, a highly variable quality of performance should be expected among the different companies that make up the American community. There is no such homogeneous entity as "American Business Abroad"—any more than at home.

Very few companies are unconcerned about the "image" they project in the communities in which they operate, whether at home or abroad, and in many countries the appearance of a genuine interest in the local economy is an important aspect of image-making. At the very least, most American companies operating abroad try to surround their actions with an aura of civic consciousness. But pure image-making—in the sense of getting the most public-relations value out of ordinary operations—is apparently being met with growing cynicism in the less developed countries and the company that is concerned with its image is finding it more and more necessary to become genuinely involved in the community life in order to create credibility. Of course, such involvement does not always imply actions that meet local aspirations, but when it does, and when the involvement is genuine, the motivation toward image-making is just as useful as any other.

More and more American business men have discovered that the more closely their activities become identified in the public mind with the economic aspirations of the whole country, the more likely they are to be successful and to help create and maintain a favorable business in the future. It is in this area of identification and accord with the country's economic aspirations that the foreign economic policies of the United States and the interests of many American businesses abroad coincide.

In part, this emerging attitude in American business is a reflection not simply of a feeling of responsibility of top executives for the welfare of their own companies. It also reveals an uneasiness about their role in society now that management and ownership have been increasingly divorced. On the domestic scene, we seldom hear the flat statement by a high executive that "my duty is to my stockholders." He is more likely to say "my duty is to my stockholders, my customers, my labor force, and the public." It makes no difference that there is little consensus as to how these many responsibilities can be put into operational terms: they do not show up on the balance sheet, or in profit-and-loss data. The important thing is that the uneasiness is there. And there is clear evidence that more and more businessmen are asking the State Department or the ambassador what they can do abroad, rather than asking for the State Department or the ambassador to do something for them.

SUMMARY

From the foregoing, it is obvious that the United States today has many sources of economic representation abroad, and that each is important with respect to its impact in other countries—

especially in the less developed ones—and in its feedback to Washington.

There has been a change from an emphasis on our own domestic economic problems as they are affected by economic events abroad to an emphasis on trying to influence economic events abroad in the interest of our *total* foreign policy, often on a very long-range basis.

"Change" is perhaps too mild a word. In some cases there has had to be a complete turn-about; and in view of the deeply entrenched ideas which have in the past characterized the State Department and the large American corporations with interests abroad, there has been little time in which to make the change. On the whole, because of a number of perceptive people in the State Department, the various foreign-aid agencies, the Peace Corps, and private business, we have accomplished the turn-about in economic representation abroad pretty well.

However, it is fair to forecast that "pretty well" will not be good enough for the future. From the experience of the past two decades, we should have learned a number of lessons about how to adapt our methods of getting good economic representation abroad to our total foreign policy objectives. As the United States gradually becomes less dominant in the economic affairs of the world, the need for further adaptation will increase.

3. *American Information and Cultural Representation Overseas*

HOWLAND H. SARGEANT

For a nation that issued its Declaration of Independence "out of a decent respect to the opinions of mankind," we Americans have shown a strange and perplexing indecisiveness about how we wish to make our way of life, our values, our aspirations, known and understood by the rest of the world. We have a reputation for the slickest use of the mass media in selling soap, automobiles, refrigerators, and other products of our technological civilization. We have a profound desire to be "liked" by other peoples in this world —and we are wounded and hurt when some foreign action or statement reveals that a position of great strength in world leadership is not necessarily compatible with being universally liked. We see so clearly our own ideals, buttressed by some of the most unselfish acts that any nation has embarked upon, that many of us feel instinctively that other peoples of the world will see us and our actions and our motives much as we like to see ourselves.

Unhappily, this is not true, but we still persist in acting as though it were. Clearly these are not *new* problems. From the beginning of our history, we Americans have been forced to find ways to make ourselves understood abroad. In times past, especially under the compulsions of war, we have made concerted and extraordinary efforts to do so. But it is only since the end of World War II that we have come to grapple with some of the problems below the surface and to probe more deeply our real motives and intentions. We have been spurred into this kind of self-examination largely because of our experience in two world wars, where it became increasingly clear to all Americans that victory—survival of our free and open society as we know and cherish it—depended in some mysterious but indisputable way on persuading other peoples that our cause was just and our victory ultimately assured.

This paper will discuss where we stood on this vexing problem of international persuasion at the end of World War II and how we have moved haltingly and in a kind of blindman's buff to our present position. More than 8,000 people in more than 100 foreign countries are now trying to represent the United States on various firing lines of the cold war, so as (1) to show foreign peoples that American interests and goals have much in common with their own, (2) to build mutual understanding between the American people and the peoples of these countries, and (3) to counter hostile attempts to distort and frustrate American objectives and policies.

This paper deals with only a few of the many activities by which we Americans affect the attitudes and actions of other nations. Harold Lasswell defined the major ways in which a nation seeks to achieve its objectives as "deals," "goods," "force," and "ideas." This is shorthand for saying that a nation may try to win its goals and secure acceptance for them by foreigners through the negotiations of traditional diplomacy; through use of its economic resources; through use or the threat of use of its military strength; and through the symbols with which it clothes its policies and actions. American cultural and informational representation overseas works mainly in this fourth area. By itself, it can accomplish little. In concert with diplomatic, economic, and military programs, it has enormous potential. For a democracy, words without deeds achieve little—and may even boomerang. On the other hand, even the right actions need explanations so that other peoples will give the meaning to these acts we intend them to have.

Much of this paper will necessarily deal with "problems." American information and cultural representation—as for any democracy—must be based on "truth." We Americans have been highly successful in solving many of the problems of sheer survival, in providing an increasingly high standard of living for all of us. Because we have solved certain basic economic problems we now have time to indulge in a great deal of healthy self-criticism at every level, and to reflect the deep inner ferment of American life today in a running debate on our values and aspirations. American public opinion takes part in shaping our foreign policy through wide public discussion.

The result of this self-criticism and "government by public debate" is to leave a highly confusing series of images of us Americans in the minds of foreigners. American cultural and information representatives overseas work against a backdrop resembling the Tower of Babel. Further, our objectives are *constructive*. We want to build. The Soviet objectives are *disruptive*. They want to tear down. So sometimes Communist propaganda looks skillful and effective in comparison with what we are doing. Remember: we could look successful in propaganda too if we wanted to tear things apart.

In the long run, however, we have some great advantages in this struggle for the expectations of men. Truth serves us well in that we are compelled not to promise more than we can perform—and the gap between Communist promises and performance remains one of their major vulnerabilities. Our objectives help us too. We are not just trying to explain America, or gain acceptance by foreign public opinion of "the American point of view." We are stressing the objectives the great majority of foreign peoples have in common with us—a peaceful world, a materially prosperous world, and one in which the spread of freedom holds the promise that every individual may have the greatest opportunity to develop to the fullest his or her potential for growth.

How U.S. Information and Cultural Representation Overseas Began

Although opinions will differ as to the exact points in time when the United States Government began to embark seriously upon programs of international persuasion through information and cultural representation overseas, most will agree that World

Wars I and II forced us into a war for the minds of men, for the "conquest of their convictions." The Creel Committee on Public Information was created; and, in 1917 and 1918, in the words of George Creel, it "not only reached deep into every American community, but . . . carried to every corner of the civilized globe the full message of America's idealism, unselfishness, and indomitable purpose."

The Creel Committee was liquidated on June 30, 1919. Until almost the time of the Japanese attack on Pearl Harbor, the United States officially did little or nothing to cultivate the opinions of mankind. It was true that a few feeble beginnings in the cultural field were undertaken.

The interchange of persons, which has existed for scores of years on a private and individual basis, became a small part of the conduct of American foreign relations in 1936, when the United States signed the Buenos Aires Convention for the promotion of inter-American cultural relations. Congressional action followed in 1938 to enable the United States to adhere to the provisions of the eighth International Conference of American States. In 1938, the State Department set up a Division of Cultural Relations, directed to confine its activities to the Western Hemisphere, and President Roosevelt established under the Secretary of State the Interdepartmental Committee on Cooperation with the American Republics to plan and execute the program of scientific and cultural interchange. By 1939—largely as a result of the needle of Nazi penetration among our good neighbors to the south—we were carrying out a cooperative program there including exchange of persons and books; maintenance of libraries; distribution of documentary films; aid to binational cultural centers and American-sponsored schools; and the beginnings of technical-assistance–type cooperative projects like developing agricultural experiment stations.

In 1940, Nelson Rockefeller, appointed to a post later known as Coordinator of Inter-American Affairs, undertook a massive program of persuasion through both information and cultural representation. Although Mr. Rockefeller had broad programs in economic and political fields, he set in motion some important information and cultural representation overseas; through his programs he presented convincing evidence of United States power and laid the basis for producing much of the era of inter-American good neighborliness in the 1940's.

However, Americans were not doing very much in the rest of the world. In the spring of 1941, Robert E. Sherwood and William J. Donovan developed a "Foreign Information Service"—without any Congressional authorization—but it was not until June, 1942, that the Office of War Information was set up under Elmer Davis, charged with coordinating the Government's domestic information activities. Robert Sherwood and his international propaganda team were thrown in under OWI, which also conducted cultural operations, ran United States overseas libraries, and distributed cultural materials.

During the remaining war years, America learned a great deal about the arts of international persuasion. We welded together the eleven private short-wave stations then broadcasting to overseas audiences and made them the first official Voice of America. We set up information offices in nearly every country abroad. We sent out Americans to friendly, to neutral, and to military areas. "Psychological warfare" became a common term as civilians using leaflets, loudspeakers, and radio broadcasts worked in newly created psychological-warfare units in military theaters.

By the end of World War II, Americans were deep in the business of international persuasion. We were using most of the techniques in use today, including documentary films, translations of American books, radio broadcasts, photo displays, American libraries, exchange-of-persons programs, news releases, press photographs, magazine articles, posters, film strips, pamphlets. These techniques were applied by Americans abroad, operating with much assistance from local citizens. They were learning how to represent the United States in ways which were new to us. "Psychological warfare," as an integral part of military operations, achieved some spectacular results—including the mass surrender of complete enemy units, enormous supporting service to the D–Day invasion of Normandy, and the broadcasts in the Pacific by Captain Ellis Zacharias, which were held by some to have precipitated the final Japanese surrender.

America Plays Postwar Blindman's Buff with
International Persuasion

On August 31, 1945, President Truman's Executive Order 9608 began the disbanding of our overseas persuasion program at a pace even quicker than our military demobilization. The overseas information functions and personnel of the OWI and of Nelson Rockefeller's OIAA were transferred to an Interim International Information Service in the State Department. The Secretary of State was required to study the problem of whether we needed any kind of permanent activities of this sort although the Executive Order itself said: "The nature of present-day foreign relations makes it essential for the United States to maintain information activities abroad as an integral part of the conduct of our foreign affairs."

But Americans were not as sure as the drafters of the Executive Order that this in fact was called for. Assistant Secretary of State William Benton led the fight during the next two and a half years to win executive, legislative, and public support for the necessity in peacetime of permanent overseas information and cultural representation of the United States. When this finally came with the signing on January 27, 1948, of Public Law 402 (the Smith-Mundt Act), American indecisiveness and perplexity over the significance of these new and strange functions had been amply demonstrated. Out of the long and violent debate, a few of the perplexities emerged in sharp focus:

1. Is it right for the American government to be engaged in "propaganda"—which is somehow a dirty business—and is there the danger that a government that propagandizes foreigners may some day attempt to propagandize the American people?

2. Now that the shooting war is behind us, is all of this vast bureaucracy, put together like our military forces in wartime to achieve victory, any longer necessary?

3. Can't we do all that is needed simply by making it possible for peoples to speak to peoples?

Postwar American public support seemed firmest for exchange of persons: if you want to convey an idea, do your best to wrap that idea in a person and send the person to the place where persuasion is needed. We Americans did not formulate the proposition quite so precisely. We did show that out of our tradition we had acquired and retained a great faith in the ability of individuals to communicate with each other across the barriers of race, language, religion, and national boundaries. Even before it was willing to authorize the rebuilding of an international information program, Congress had acted in response to a groundswell of American public opinion. In 1946, Congress authorized United States participation in the United Nations Educational, Scientific, and Cultural Organization, dedicated to the use of education, culture, and science to permit peoples-to-peoples communication in an all-out attack based on the assumption that "wars begin in the minds of men." In 1946, Congress, under the leadership of Senator J. William Fulbright, authorized the use of millions of dollars of foreign currencies to finance the international exchange of students and teachers.

This faith in the concept of peoples speaking to peoples runs like a connective tissue throughout the whole postwar period. So strong was this faith that many believe the Congress would have authorized nothing more than cultural relations and educational exchange programs, excluding any information service, had it not been for the fact that nearly half the members of Congress had travelled abroad in 1946 and 1947. Most of them came back alarmed and angry over the Soviet Big-Lie technique of misrepresenting and maliciously distorting America and American motives. The United States Information and Educational Exchange Act of 1948 was the result.

The concept of peoples speaking to peoples provided a firm basis for American overseas representation, especially in the cultural field. We sought to provide means by which private American citizens, representing cross-sections of these United States, might talk to peoples of other countries. We said that we hoped other peoples might have a chance of coming to know us as we really are. We set up programs of communications supported and facilitated by the government itself. We were trying to wash out age-old jealousies, animosities, prejudices, and misunderstandings. We were acting on the premise that we must have an understanding among peoples if we are to have a peaceful world. We were expressing our prophetic faith that in a hydrogen-bomb era, "truth is no longer merely the first casualty in war; today it must be assassinated before war can be started," as *The Economist* put it.

We were also saying that for a democracy, no governmental program could by itself do the job. We were saying that we are not like the Soviet Union, which speaks with but one voice, the voice of dictatorship; but that we, like any other democracy, make ourselves known abroad through the student, the tourist, the visiting professor, the soldier, the free press, radio, television, and motion pictures, as well as through our government spokesmen. Where the Soviet Union speaks with but one opinion, we speak with many. If we were to try to do otherwise, we would be imposing on ourselves the very totalitarianism we are struggling to avoid. Deeper down, and without ever making this specific point, perhaps we were saying that our ability to persuade other peoples can never rise above the level of the behavior and actions of the American government and of the American people themselves.

Certainly these were among the bases for our programs of international persuasion as authorized in January, 1948.

From the "Full and Fair Picture" to the "Campaign of Truth"

At the same time as these debates were rumbling through the halls of Congress, officers directing the surviving postwar programs were re-examining their basic assumptions. Our assumption at the end of World War II was that we should present "a full and fair picture of America, to make clear our aims and policies." It is probably true to say that from 1946 to 1950, our international information and educational exchange programs were essentially dedicated to meeting the conditions of a peaceful world. But events were moving fast and tended to outrun the policies set for these programs. By the spring of 1947, the United States gave ample evidence of recognizing that we had merely passed from a hot war to a cold war: Greek-Turkish aid was instituted; the Truman Doctrine was proclaimed; the Marshall Plan began; NATO was established.

As early as the spring of 1946, State Department officers in charge of information and cultural relations were beginning to study the ways that emphasis should be shifted. By May, 1947, one officer wrote: "As long as the objective of an information and cultural program is to present to the world a full and fair picture of the U.S., we'll be planting flowers in soil chemically unprepared to sustain them, and which has the further disadvantage of being continuously trampled by wild bulls." During 1947 and 1948, policies gradually evolved that made the information programs more and more a part of the free world's recognition that the cold war was a reality. We set about exposing Communist distortions and placing United States policies in perspective.

The next step was to be a giant stride, not simply gradual evolution. Under the leadership of Assistant Secretary of State Edward W. Barrett, the Campaign of Truth was planned and initiated in April, 1950. (Up to this point the peacetime program, still under fairly constant attack in Congress, had reached about $30 million annually for its operations in more than eighty countries overseas.) The Campaign of Truth sought about $90 million, plus a $41 million expenditure for enormous new transmitters for the Voice of America. The invasion of South Korea on June 25, 1950, provided the impetus for Congressional approval of what came to be known as a psychological offensive, aimed at four objectives: (1) to establish a healthy international community by creating a climate of confidence in the free world; (2) to present America fairly and to counter misconceptions, so that other people would want to cooperate with us; (3) to deter the Soviet Union from further encroachments; and (4) to help roll back Soviet influence.

We Tell Our Neighbors: We Share Many Goals and Interests

The Eisenhower Administration brought another important phase in national policy toward international persuasion. President Eisenhower's Committee on International Information Activities, a group of distinguished private citizens under the chairmanship of William H. Jackson, made a fundamental study in the early months of 1953. About the time of the Jackson Report, the Senate's Special Subcommittee on Overseas Information Programs, chaired by Senator Bourke Hickenlooper, proposed, after months of review, certain changes designed to strengthen the foreign information program.

Following and to some extent taking into account the recommendations of both these groups, on August 1, 1953, all foreign information programs and operations were removed from the State Department and consolidated in a new United States Information Agency, independent of the Department of State. The new USIA embraced the Voice of America, United States libraries overseas, the motion-picture service, and the press and publications service. The Department of State retained the educational exchange program, however.

The President's definition of the new USIA's mission was "to submit evidence to peoples of other nations by means of communication techniques that the objectives and policies of the United States are in harmony with and will advance their legitimate aspirations for freedom, progress and peace." In carrying out its responsibilities, the USIA was to: (1) explain and interpret "to foreign peoples the objectives and policies of the United States Government"; (2) depict "imaginatively the correlation between United States policies and the legitimate aspirations of other peoples of the world"; (3) unmask and counter "hostile attempts to distort or to frustrate the objectives and policies of the United States"; and (4) delineate "those important aspects of the life and culture of the people of the United States which facilitate understanding of the policies and objectives of the Government of the United States."

The first Director of the independent Information Agency, Theodore C. Streibert, stressed the fact that the new mission given this agency "embodies the concept . . . that psychological activities and psychological strategy do not exist apart from official policies and actions"—the bedrock of the Jackson Committee philosophy. As interpreted by Mr. Streibert, American information and cultural affairs officers would now "emphasize the community of interests that exists among freedom-loving peoples and show how American objectives and policies advance the legitimate interests of such peoples. . . . We must make every effort to show the mutuality of our interests and goals with the legitimate goals of other peoples. We must explain those goals in ways that will cause other peoples to join with us in achieving them."

By the time USIA was established, President Eisenhower had taken three other important steps, designed to serve broader needs but important to American information and cultural programs: he had appointed a special assistant to advise and represent him in all matters of this kind; he had set up the sub-Cabinet level Operations Coordinating Board to coordinate the plans and oversee the execution of projects in which several government departments shared responsibility for carrying out a national security policy; and he placed authority for foreign policy squarely in the Secretary of State and, through him, in the chief of the U.S. diplomatic mission in each foreign country. Such actions added support to the President's declaration in his State of the Union message of February 2, 1953, that we "must make more effective all activities related to international information" and that "a unified and dynamic effort in this whole field is essential to the security of the United States and other peoples in the community of free nations."

President Kennedy's statement of the mission of USIA, a decade later, made more explicit still USIA's responsibility not only for influencing public attitudes in other nations, but for "advising the President, his representatives abroad, and the various departments and agencies on the implications of foreign opinion for present and contemplated United States policies, programs and official statements."

USIA activities were to—

> encourage constructive public support abroad for the goal of a peaceful world community of free and independent states, free to choose their own future and their own system so long as it does not threaten the freedom of others; identify the United States as a strong, democratic, dynamic nation qualified for its leadership of world efforts toward this goal; and unmask and counter hostile attempts to distort or frustrate the objectives and policies of the United States.

How United States objectives and policies harmonized with those of other peoples and governments for freedom, progress, and peace was to be emphasized, as well as those aspects of American life and culture awareness of which would facilitate sympathetic understanding of United States policies.

Characteristics of Our Information and Cultural Activities

The United States Information Agency's overseas staff serve in more than two hundred posts, which are integral parts of the regular Foreign Service establishments of the United States; they are called the USIS (United States Information Service); they are served and supported by the headquarters offices in Washington.

USIA has more than 100 "one-man" posts—where one American must cover the whole range of program activity with several helpers. At the opposite end of the spectrum, there is the Public Affairs Officer in the American embassy in the capital of a large country, who must build a smooth-working team of Americans and local employees not only in the capital city but in several provincial sub-posts as well. Since he is the top representative of the Information Agency and responsible for USIS performance in the country to which he is assigned, we might do well to take a look at the world through his eyes.

His job is to know at first hand and to evaluate and interpret the attitudes, beliefs, and opinions of the people. Armed with this knowledge, he must use his resources—which include not only the tools of information but also the programs of educational exchange and other cultural activities—so as to build support for the "peaceful world community of free and independent states" and recognition of the vital contributions of American leadership to this goal. He must try to show how American policies and objectives are in harmony with their own aspirations, and increase mutual understanding.

He is not just trying to influence group attitudes. He is also trying to contribute his knowledge of public opinion and of how his resources can be used to the pool of facts available to the ambassador, so that any action taken, or statement issued, or policy announced will be most likely to meet with a favorable response from the people of the country—and carry the meaning we want accepted. This function, relatively new when USIA was set up as an independent agency fighting hard for recognition and acceptance, has strengthened and is more universally accepted. This is an important advance, since much of the Public Affairs Officer's effectiveness will depend upon his ability to make his chief (and colleagues) recognize the value of this contribution.

Whatever he does will be under the direct control of the American chief of diplomatic mission, in keeping with the President's determination when the U.S. Information Agency was established that:

> Not only must the Department of State be given clear authority to provide guidance on our foreign policies to all other agencies of the Federal Government, it is equally important that each chief of diplomatic mission in each foreign country provide effective coordination of, and foreign policy direction with respect to, all United States Government activities in the country.

Let us assume that our Public Affairs Officer is located in a large country capital, and that his chief of diplomatic mission is a wise and experienced officer seeking to make the best use of the specialized talents of those around him. In such a case, our Public Affairs Officer is probably a member in good standing of what is often called the "Country Team," in which he participates with the officers of the diplomatic mission responsible for the political, economic, and military programs. He has a small staff. For every American working with him, there are four to seven employees hired locally, usually natives of the country.

What are the Public Service Officer's chief means of communication to reach individuals and groups in his country?

1. He operates information centers—with libraries, extension services, motion pictures, lectures and discussion groups, musical performances, English-language instruction, special exhibits, and displays of various kinds.

2. He supplies news and feature materials and related services to the press and local groups to assist them in providing their audiences with a better understanding of United States foreign policy, motives, purposes, and mutual interests.

3. He arranges to show motion pictures (often produced locally) to key officials, opinion leaders, and other important cross-sections of the public.

4. He may distribute specially prepared magazines to select groups, or to particular audiences, through mailing lists or through commercial channels.

5. He arranges for press, photo, radio, and motion-picture (sometimes television) coverage of special events of mutual interest to the United States and the peoples of the country.

6. He plans projects and selects local talent for local production of radio programs, using technical facilities of local stations or facilities operated by USIA.

7. He arranges presentations of books or of magazine subscriptions to key groups and individuals.

8. He helps local publishers to obtain book translations.

9. He tries to provide low-priced books by American publishers working through their foreign counterparts.

10. He provides support to binational centers and other local institutions through cash grants, grants to Americans needed in the operations of the centers, and the supply of needed materials.

11. He sees that contacts are maintained with local cultural groups; he promotes and takes part in cultural events in which the achievements of American scholarship, music, drama, and other creative arts are brought to the people of the country.

12. He carries on the administration of the exchange-of-persons program for the Department of State.

This list constitutes the bare bones of what a Public Affairs Officer and his team do. In many countries, they carry on, to a greater extent than any other members of the United States Mission, a host of individual contacts with government officials, editors, writers, educators, executives, labor leaders, intellectuals, and other influential leaders and opinion-makers.

A Public Affairs Officer may have on his staff an Information Officer, a Press Officer, a Cultural Affairs Officer, a librarian, a motion-picture officer, a radio officer, and others to whom he looks for effective performance in different areas. In most cases, the Public Affairs Officer and his key assistants will be career Foreign Service Officers, appointed by the President and with Senate confirmation, holding commissioned diplomatic and consular titles and rank on the same basis as Foreign Service Officers of the Department of State.

What Supports USIS?

The top USIS officer looks to the headquarters of the U.S. Information Agency in Washington for a variety of supporting services. More than 3,000 Americans are at work there. About 1,200 of these are concerned with radio broadcasting. The Voice of America broadcasts to a world-wide audience over a network of about 100 transmitters and operates thirty-six language services. Radio is still the primary means of communication with the peoples under Soviet and Chinese Communist domination.

More than 400 Americans are in the USIA Press and Publications Service. Some are sending our Public Affairs Officers 10,000 words of news and background material by wireless seven days a week, separately tailored to each major geographic area, often carrying overseas *in full* the only available texts of such important official papers as the President's State of the Union message. Feature articles and photos, picture stories, plastic printing plates, cartoon strips, pilot model pamphlets for local adaptation, magazines in English and other languages, and other special materials reach him from this same source.

From a group of more than 160 Americans at home constituting the Motion Picture Service, the Public Affairs Officers will receive documentary films, newsreels, and monthly news magazines. Much of USIA's motion-picture production takes place in more than fifty foreign countries where authentic locale and native persons are used. Adapted in more than fifty major foreign languages, the films are exhibited in commercial theaters, on television, and in non-theatrical showings.

From the efforts of more than 200 Americans in the Information Center Service, our Public Affairs Officers will receive books, magazines, newspapers, exhibits, English-teaching materials, musical scores, and recordings for use in his information centers, libraries, and binational centers. There will be translations of books of particular local usefulness; paperback overseas print runs of useful books from American book publishers, which can compete with heavily subsidized Communist publications on sale; books in serial form for use in local publications. He will receive occasional exhibits, such as "U.S. Progress in Space Sciences," "Medicine USA," or color panels showing John Glenn's orbital flight.

From the Voice of America, he may receive programs for rebroadcast over local radio networks. From more than 100 Americans in the Television Service, he may receive complete television programs on videotape or film for placement on local TV stations, both original productions and special acquisitions of programs first produced for American domestic audiences.

In addition to such tangible products for use in the media of communication, the Public Affairs Officer may have the good fortune to entertain in his country several cultural presentations by top American performing artists—arranged by the Department of State through its Office of Cultural Presentations. Perhaps the New York City Ballet, the Robert Shaw Chorale, the Baird Marionettes, or a jazz revue. He will be working with a number of Americans as well as nationals of the country under various types of exchange programs which offer a great opportunity for carrying out his objectives.

To supply these services and to give top direction, USIA has reached a headquarters strength of over 3,000 people. Nearly three times as many employees are overseas—over 8,000. Somewhat less than half of USIA's funds are allocated to the overseas missions. Well over half of all USIS personnel overseas are assigned to the Far East, Near East, and South Asia. The trend has been to cut down on personnel assigned to Western Europe, and to increase in other areas, with staffs in Latin America and Africa in recent years rising sharply.

Appropriations authorized for USIA have stabilized somewhat, avoiding the pattern of earlier years in which sharp rises were followed often by steep and disconcerting drops. Recent operating budgets have ranged from $125 million to $150 million annually.

Less Washington Master-Minding; More Field Autonomy

This highly oversimplified sketch makes our Public Affairs Officers look as though they were well-equipped to handle their job—perhaps a misleading impression. "You can't generalize!" is a safe rule to follow about the USIS operations in any particular country. One of the greatest advances made in recent years has been the recognition of the fact that each country program has its own individual needs and character. Accompanying this recognition has been a willingness to reduce the abundance of Washington master-minding and to offer increasing autonomy in determining the objectives of the USIS program in any given country and the ways in which the program will try to reach these objectives. Most Public Affairs Officers seem to agree that there is indeed a refreshing atmosphere in Washington—a greater disposition at headquarters to tackle a problem with the idea: "Let's start by finding out what the officer in the field thinks about this."

Further, when in 1953 the U.S. Information Agency was separated from the Department of State—leaving behind the educational-exchange programs—there were many who believed that if there was to be greater independence in Washington, there would have to be greater cohesion and integration in the field between those responsible for providing coordination and foreign-policy direction and those responsible for our persuasion programs. Edward R. Murrow, Director of USIA at the end of its first decade as an independent agency, concluded that this was exactly how it had been working. Chiefs of mission knew that the Public Affairs Officer and his staff had a dual responsibility: (1) to advise the mission on the psychological implications in the country of U.S. policies, plans and actions; and (2) to serve as the information, cultural and psychological link between the mission and the people of the host country. USIS was functioning as an integral part of the overseas country teams—in effect, a small cabinet at each post.

The Public Affairs Officer can thank for his greater degree of local independence the development of some important means of delineating policy and keeping it current. To simplify it somewhat, the State Department establishes United States foreign policy and reviews the policies programmed by USIA. The USIA has a plan for USIS operations in each country, consisting of four parts: a statement of global objectives, of area objectives, and of country objectives (including short term objectives), and an operating plan. The global objectives are translations of USIA's statement of mission into specific objectives to guide worldwide program operations. Area objectives show courses of action applicable to all or almost all the countries of a given area, to be interpreted in relation to local conditions. The country objectives are actually initiated by the individual posts; they are approved or modified by USIA in Washington and established only after mutual agreement between the Public Affairs Officer and his headquarters.

The operating plan likewise is prepared by the Public Affairs Officer in the field and submitted to Washington. In the operating plan, the Public Affairs Officer discusses audience groups, including their categories, priorities, geographic locations, estimated total number of individuals, and special problems involved in contact. It deals with the themes devised to reach each audience group and projects planned to present each of these themes.

Using this basic tool of the Country Plan—despite some criticism that occasionally the process is too cumbersome and slow—and relying on a good policy-guidance mechanism set up by the Deputy Director for Policy and Plans at USIA headquarters responsible for the formulation of basic information policies, themes, and program emphases, a Public Affairs Officer can usually be sure that he knows his objectives, that he is working under an approved operating plan which he and his supporters in Washington understand, and that he is being kept up to date on policy decisions and the evolution of policy. In cases where the guidance is too slow, or where the United States behaves like a man with two left feet, the Public Affairs Officer can only do his best to convey to the people of the country the meaning that the United States wants accepted for the particular act—or failure to act. Occasionally, no amount of guidance can help the Public Affairs Officer out.

Delineation of policy and keeping it current for USIS officers then depends essentially on the Country Plan, the provision by the chief of mission to the Public Affairs Officer of full guidance concerning the foreign policy of the United States, and up-to-date and prompt guidance from USIA headquarters in Washington on the policy to be followed on important developments.

What has been helping the Public Affairs Officer most of all in recent years has been the strengthened role of the USIA Director and his senior officers in the formulation of foreign policy. No longer is USIA handed a policy and told to make the best of it. There is impressive evidence that USIA's counsel is sought when most national policies with foreign implications are formulated. The Director himself takes part in all meetings of the National Security Council. There has been a growth of "awareness throughout the entire Government of the impact of day-to-day governmental actions" and a more and more successful attempt "to coordinate and time such actions so as to derive from them the maximum advantages," in the words of the Jackson Report.

Much remains to be done, however, and honest differences of opinion still persist on whether it was wise in 1961 to abolish the Operations Coordinating Board, characterized by the Sprague Committee on Information Activities Abroad on the basis of seven years of OCB performance as a "major step forward in improving the effectiveness of U.S. psychological and informational activities."

Cultural Relations

The last half of the 1950's and the early years of the 1960's were marked by an intense preoccupation with the role of cultural relations as an essential and integral part of international relations, in the same way as the searching scrutiny given to America's international information programs characterized the years immediately after World War II. A spate of surveys and reports examined cultural relations as a whole and such important aspects as exchange of persons, the part played by the arts and humanities, American studies abroad, international scientific activities, or the university and world affairs. Passage of the Fulbright-Hays Act (Public Law 87–256) on September 21, 1961, consolidated a complex network of legislation and a hatful of Executive Orders, considerably broadened the exchange program, and emphasized the concept of reciprocity and the two-way street in cultural relations, as the formal title "Mutual Educational and Cultural Exchange Act" implies.

The Public Affairs Officer and his chief aide in the field of cultural relations—the Cultural Affairs Officer—must still occasionally scratch their heads in bewilderment when they look back to the United States to see how best to carry out the legislative intent and comply with the injunctions of advisors and experts. The Cultural Affairs Officer sees that the hard core of any cultural-relations program he can carry out must center on programs of interchange of persons. He probably agrees that through exchange of persons more influential people in his country will become valiant supporters of America and American policies than through any other single activity with which he may be concerned. But his handicaps are in proportion to the enormous potential rewards. Even less than the relatively clear-cut field of the dissemination of information can cultural relations be precisely described.

When he looks to the basic authorization and the mechanics for carrying out these interchange-of-persons programs, he sees that progress is being made. Since June 25, 1962, the Secretary of State, by Executive Order, has had "primary responsibility for Government-wide leadership and policy guidance with regard to international educational and cultural affairs." An Assistant Secretary of State for Educational and Cultural Affairs, whose post was created early in 1961, was charged specifically with assisting the Secretary of State in this responsibility, as well as with conducting a major program of his own that the Cultural Affairs Officers execute in the field and, in some (but by no means all) cases, help to plan and shape. In spite of clear and encouraging progress, however, foreign currencies and United States dollars still have to be blended with a magician's skill. A host of private subcontractors, both in the United States and in his country of assignment, share the responsibilities. The Public Affairs Officer is likely to deal with a binational commission or committee that will be extremely helpful to him but that further dilutes his control over the programs. In the case of Fulbright grants, the U.S. Government does not have responsibility for the final selection of persons receiving them.

This sounds complicated—and it is. There are historical reasons for this labyrinth of perplexities. Although exchange of persons and cultural relations had feeble official beginnings before World War II, the only permanent authorized program for cultural activities and educational exchange when the war was over was the cooperative program with the other American republics. No government grants were made in other areas of the world until 1948, when the first exchanges under the Fulbright Act were effected. The Fulbright Act authorized use of foreign currencies derived from the sale of surplus war materials abroad for these exchanges, and operated therefore only in countries where such funds existed and could be made available. Its programs did not depend on any official judgment on the priority or order of importance of countries with which exchanges might be needed. The Board of Foreign Scholarships, made up of Presidentially appointed private citizens, had final authority in the selection of grantees. Overseas, binational commissions composed of private American citizens plus top intellectual leaders in the country, drew up the proposed annual program of grants.

The reasons for some of the complexity seen by our Cultural Affairs Officer emerge more clearly in the debates leading up to the first permanent authorization of international information and educational exchange activities—the Smith-Mundt Act of January, 1948. These Congressional debates are filled with key words and phrases like "reciprocity," "mutuality of interests," "cooperation," "sharing," and "partnership." There was to be no "cultural imperialism"—no imposition of one people's culture on another. Just as it is the American tradition to divorce education and similar activities from federal government control, so our legislators, strongly aided and abetted by organized groups of private citizens, viewed these programs as involving "direct face-to-face communication and contact between the people and institutions of the United States and those of other countries." They felt that these activities were traditionally accomplished through private individuals and groups, speaking as such. "The authentic educational, scientific, and cultural institutions of the country . . . with minor exceptions, are not to be found in the national government." An even stronger emphasis was that these activities were *not* to be "used as instruments of power relations by individual nations." Senator H. Alexander Smith said, "Educational exchange service . . . to be truly effective, must be objective, nonpolitical, and above all, have no possible propaganda implications."

Many viewed these programs as long-range and lasting. They differentiated sharply their purpose in promoting the foreign relations of the United States from those of any information activities. These were not designed to project a prearranged message but to offer experiences from which conclusions might be freely drawn by those who participated. The legislators viewed the information programs, on the other hand, as "an instrument of national public relations abroad" seeking "to implement the diplomatic policies of the Department of State," and they sometimes referred to them as "the psychological warfare approach." They felt in general that the information programs, primarily the radio, press, and motion-picture services, were unilateral rather than reciprocal and cooperative; they felt that their goals were to be achieved through mass-communication techniques to primarily mass audiences; they felt that the information-program operators would think of immediate impact more often than the long-term objectives of building mutual understanding by the slow process of international exchange of ideas and knowledge.

What was to be the business of the government in the cultural-relations programs? Principally, "to stimulate, facilitate and coordinate activities arising in all areas of the nation"—in other words, to offer necessary official support, help solve problems at the governmental level, negotiate intergovernmental agreements; facilitate desirable exchanges of any kind under any reputable sponsorship, match private funds with public funds where necessary and desirable, and execute only those projects which private groups were unable or unwilling to undertake.

As the years have gone by, we have learned, of course, that many of these positions are indeed extreme. The United States Information Agency is involved in a complex of activities, many of them cultural in every sense of the word. USIA executes overseas on behalf of the Department of State's Bureau of Educational and Cultural Affairs the governmental sector of the educational-exchange programs that form the matrix of our cultural relations with other countries. We seem now to be more in agreement that educational exchanges and cultural relations cannot be planned in the same way that information activities are planned to reach national objectives. Most agree that disseminating truthful information in order to influence attitudes and actions abroad must be linked with what former Assistant Secretary of State Edward W. Barrett calls "specific actions, clear policies, and grand strategy." Is there an emerging national consensus about the role of educational and cultural programs?

It seems clear that there is. Our educational-exchange programs, which form the hard core of the government's officially sponsored cultural activities, have real elements of purposeful direction to them, although they are firmly rooted in the conviction that political values come as by-products of free cultural exchanges. Most people agree that these programs are not designed to serve narrowly political ends, and to try and make them so would undermine their effectiveness and be self-defeating. However, in the words of Philip H. Coombs, the first Assistant Secretary of State for Educational and Cultural Affairs, "for their greatest effectiveness, these educational and cultural activities must be planned and conducted in close conjunction with all other international programs, both at home and overseas; . . . must also be directed consciously at specific objectives, country by country and within the United States, not treated as ends in themselves."

Further, there is greater agreement today that in a broad sense these programs *can* support foreign policy without having to pass the short-range political test of immediate and visible results. The U.S. Advisory Commission on International Educational and Cultural Affairs, under the chairmanship of John W. Gardner, President of the Carnegie Corporation, summed this up eloquently:

> In increasing mutual understanding, in demonstrating American character and achievements, in furthering the grantee's own development and career and the strengthening of his country, the exchange program has effectively supported one of the nation's most basic international objectives—of helping support strong free societies able to work together, in mutual trust and understanding, on the grave issues of our time.

There is perhaps less general understanding and agreement on the importance of respecting the mutual and reciprocal nature of these programs not only in lip service but in deed as well. Robert Blum, former President of the Asia Foundation, puts it well when he reminds us that "cultural activities . . . are also a way for us to understand others better, and, in seeing ourselves as others see us, we may understand ourselves better and clarify our own role in the world." Walter Lares and Charles Thomson, in their comprehensive survey "Cultural Relations and U.S. Foreign Policy," conclude: "Shared goals and responsibilities make for stronger commitments and mutual respect."

Exchange Programs

The Cultural Affairs Officer, when he plans a program for exchange of persons, is in a different position from the USIS officer primarily concerned with spreading information. He wants to develop programs around the interchange of actual or potential leaders who by virtue of their positions at home and their activities and contacts while abroad, can be of mutual benefit to the peoples of both countries. Such people include:

1. Americans who spread knowledge of American literature, language, history, and political and social institutions (and of characteristically American organizations like public libraries or agricultural extension services). They may have special skills, as in teaching the peaceful uses of atomic energy, or they may demonstrate American educational, artistic, and cultural achievements (as in performances of *Oklahoma!*, the New York City Ballet, Duke Ellington and his orchestra, the New York Philharmonic, Martha Graham and her dance company).

2. Those who help us to develop and broaden our knowledge of foreign areas—foreign professors teaching at American institutions, or staff members of American universities studying abroad.

3. Those who play special roles in the lives of their own countries—members of national legislatures, key government officials, trade-union leaders, journalists, and—these have been emphasized in recent years—university students, youth leaders, and academic opinion-makers.

4. Those who establish and strengthen contacts in significant institutions like universities, libraries, and national professional organizations.

5. Those who complement the work of United States Government agencies, private organizations, or international bodies of which the United States is a member, like social scientists working on projects essential to the technical-assistance programs.

In the fifteen-year period, 1949–63, some 81,500 grants were made under the international educational and cultural exchange program of the Department of State. For the first seven years, the cost of the programs amounted to $17–22 million in annual Congressional appropriations. In the early 1960's, the budget gradually increased to more than $50 million a year and provided for sending cultural attractions overseas as well as grants to individuals. These grants enabled foreigners from more than 130 countries and territories to visit the United States. The emphasis from the beginning has been placed on bringing foreign nationals to this country—in fact, more than two foreign nationals came here for every American sent abroad. In a recent year, 5,200 foreign nationals came here and about 2,100 Americans went overseas.

The most broadly based survey ever made of the State Department educational and cultural exchange program was prepared by the U.S. Advisory Commission on International Educational and Cultural Affairs and submitted as a report to Congress (which not only created the Commission but specifically required it to make this study of the program's effectiveness). The report, entitled "A Beacon of Hope," was published in April, 1963. It focused on the foreign grantee—the chief matter of interest to the Congress. Only American professors and lecturers, among American recipients of grants, were studied. Pointing out that the State Department's programs are but a small part—less than 5 per cent—of the great flow of exchange taking place today between the United States and the rest of the world, the Commission concluded: "Testimony is overwhelming from all sources that the program as a whole is effective. . . . The evidence is also conclusive that the program has proved itself an essential and valuable part of America's total international effort."

Sixty per cent of these exchanges have been with Europe; about 12 per cent with Latin America; 14 per cent with the Far East; 11 per cent with the Near East and South Asia; 3 per cent for the rapidly expanding exchanges with Africa.

Some regional differences other than size stand out:

Latin America. The programs with Latin America were considerably expanded when foreign currencies became available for purposes of educational and cultural exchange. Agreements were signed with eight Latin American countries. The exchange programs themselves became essential to the accomplishment of the goals of the Alliance for Progress.

Near East and South Asia. For every American sent there, three grantees were brought to the United States.

Far East. The number of Far Easterners brought to this country was four times greater than the number of Americans going there.

Africa. Although the program remains small, the increase in number of grants has been phenomenal. Emphasis has been placed on bringing African students to American institutions of higher learning.

Europe. The largest exchange programs have been conducted with European countries—Germany, the United Kingdom, and France. There have been half as many American grantees as European. During the fifteen years surveyed, of all American grantees throughout the world, 90 per cent of the students, more than half of the lecturers and research scholars, two-thirds of the teachers, and nearly half of the specialists went to Europe. For all foreign grantees, about half of the students, two-thirds of the lecturers and research scholars, more than half of the teachers, nearly two-thirds of the leaders, and one-third of the specialists came to this country from Europe.

In recent years, however, the exchange-of-persons program in Europe has been reduced in size and dollar grants cut back. (There has also been a gradual reduction of USIA programs in Western Europe, moving toward more direct personal contacts with European intellectuals and opinion-makers, reducing mass distribution of American books, movies, and periodicals, closing regional cultural centers, and curtailing direct English teaching.) Proposals to cut back on the exchange-of-persons programs in Europe have caused a good deal of concern. The Advisory Commission seriously questioned the wisdom of such a policy. And the participants in the twenty-second American Assembly on Cultural Affairs and Foreign Relations in their final report said: "We should maintain and strengthen our cultural exchanges with those countries of the West with which we share a common heritage and whose present and future are intimately bound up with ours."

W. McNeil Lowry, Director of the Ford Foundation Program in Humanities and the Arts, and his associate, Gertrude S. Hooker, in their background paper for this American Assembly, concluded that "our international cultural activities should be expanded, and primarily in Western Europe."

Unusual and contributing features of the international educational and cultural exchange program have been the financing in part with foreign currencies generated by the sale overseas of surplus war equipment and agricultural products. These funds gave the program its start and continued to expand its activities. The other element of assistance is the generous contribution made each year by several hundred non-government organizations and groups of individuals. Some idea of the participation of private American citizens in these programs is suggested by these statistics:

The Institute of International Education census conducted recently showed nearly 65,000 foreign students, 7,300 medical interns and residents, and 5,800 foreign scholars and faculty members in the United States. (For the past decade, the number of foreign students here has been growing at the rate of about 7 per cent each year. If this continues, we will have almost 132,000 foreign students here in 1970.)

There are about 3,400 private programs officially designated as "exchange visitor programs" under which foreign nationals are admitted to the United States for educational purposes. In addition there are 180 government programs so designated.

In summary, the U.S. Advisory Commission concluded that educational and cultural-exchange programs: (a) increase mutual understanding; (b) help to dispel many misconceptions about the American people among foreign visitors; (c) provide in an "outstandingly successful" way a valuable educational experience to foreign grantees; (d) benefit the home country of the foreign grantee (for this, the "evidence is significant, though somewhat less conclusive"); and (e) establish effective channels of communication between people in other countries and the United States. (More than two-thirds of all returned grantees are in positions in which "they can readily communicate their broadened perspectives—whether as teachers, journalists or top-level administrators.")

As a USIS officer overseas, then, I would know a good deal about the images of America that people held in the country in which I served. In the exchange of persons, I would see my greatest opportunities to change some of the false and distorted images. (A study made in Germany, for example, indicated that half of all the German people recognize a German visitor to the United States as the most important and credible source of information about us.) I would be pleased, but not surprised, at some of the Commission's findings of how attitudes of foreign visitors changed: such visitors found Americans to have warm personal qualities and discovered that the American character was refreshingly unlike the prevailing stereotype. American thought had vitality—"its capacity to stimulate, its curiosity, its open-mindedness." Of course, there was not a uniformly favorable reaction on all aspects of the American scene. America's race relations were found by all grantees from all areas to be the least admirable of American attitudes and customs—but even here it is significant that proportionately more grantees from Africa than from any other area felt it important to tell their countrymen about the improving racial situation in the United States.

As seen by the U.S. Advisory Commission, "better coordination among the various government agencies involved in exchange of persons continues to be the highest priority objective for improvement of the program." The Commission commended the Assistant Secretary of State for Educational and Cultural Affairs for the important steps already taken to coordinate diverse programs, but stressed that much remains to be done—not just in Washington but at embassies abroad as well. It pointed out that country-by-country planning is essential, so that coordination of all exchange programs with the country's needs as a whole are well thought out, but that in the majority of countries "there is little to no planning of exchange programs in relation to a total country plan."

The Commission found a number of areas in which other improvements might usefully be made. Noting that "fiscal starvation" was often cited as a recurrent weakness of the program—including not only failure to finance the program adequately, but also late appropriations and short-term financing—the members felt a special study was needed of the "problems created for the program and limitations placed upon it by the heavy reliance on foreign currencies." They called attention to the "ridiculous inadequacy" of official hospitality funds for use at home and abroad for foreign grantees sponsored by the Department of State—about 20 cents each per year!

The Commission hoped more young potential leaders, and more young adults generally, would be selected to receive grants, especially from developing countries. Foreign grantees in the past had been drawn too often from favored economic and social groups, too seldom from the "have-nots" on the way up. Far too few had been under 35 years of age. The orientation and information received by such foreign grantees before they came to the United States could be improved, too, perhaps through a global network of field selection centers. The Commission supported continued use of private agencies in programming and placement of foreign grantees but recommended a "fresh appraisal be made of the most important" to weigh their effectiveness. More contacts with Americans and more visits to their homes were urged. Weakness in following up foreign grantees who have returned to their home countries needed correction.

Although the Commission concentrated its study on the foreign grantees and limited its consideration of American grantees to professors and lecturers—about a fourth of the total—they concluded that "the quality of American professors and lecturers is not consistently as high as it should be." They also felt that the program should send more American teachers abroad to strengthen institutions in the developing countries.

The Commission also noted, as had Dr. Coombs, the need for upgrading the quality, competence, and status of Cultural Affairs Officers who carry out the educational-exchange program abroad. But neither of these authorities (nor the Herter Committee on Foreign Affairs Personnel, in its detailed recommendations on tripartite management in foreign service) actually grappled with the basic and prickly issue: is the split that keeps the base for the educational and cultural program in Washington in the State Department but delegates its management in the field to USIA in the best long-term interests of the program? The Commission contented itself with the observation that "this whole question . . . needs considerable study." Dr. Coombs was not willing to say that "the present pattern of governmental organization . . . is satisfactory" but observed that "the foremost requirement . . . is not better organization but stronger conviction and stronger support." He went on to observe: "A good case can no doubt be made, at least on paper, for one or another such reorganization, but as a practical matter right now it might well have the negative effect of creating confusion and dissension which would slow down the whole effort for a considerable time."

Participants in The American Assembly at Arden House in October, 1962, who considered Dr. Coombs' paper took a somewhat different view. In the Final Report, Recommendation 16 was: "In view of weaknesses in the present organization of governmental administrative machinery in the field of cultural relations, immediate action is urged to bring an early correction of continuing hindrances to effective governmental cultural activity."

Fortunately, good men can make even bad organizations work, and this in effect has been what has happened. Important steps have been taken to make the split-personality program workable. The Fulbright-Hays Act and the President's Executive Order were important initial steps to make clear the primary responsibility of the State Department for leadership and policy guidance. The USIA Director was made a participant in the planning. The Assistant Secretary of State for Educational and Cultural Affairs set the pattern of picking as his First Deputy a senior USIA officer; established his Bureau of Educational and Cultural Affairs on a regional basis to make coordination easier with other government agencies operating under geographic forms of organization; created interagency or other advisory committees to untangle knotty problems of English-language teaching abroad, government efforts in book publication and distribution overseas, more effective programs for reaching young leaders; and even grappled with the "complex frictions and tensions between private and public agencies dealing with Africa."

Coordination remains a mammoth problem, however. The official educational and cultural exchange programs administered by the State Department are only about one-third the size of the Defense Department's training programs in the United States for foreign military personnel. Nor are they as large as the technical-assistance programs of the Agency for International Development, which brings more foreigners to the United States and sends more Americans overseas for training activities. Further, private activities in the 1950's grew even more than the federal program, and in total far exceeded the governmental effort (if we exclude technical assistance). Federal activities helped to stimulate them, but they grew fragmented, confused, uncoordinated—and remain so to this day. Even coordination with the educational institutions that are the heart of the exchange program needs improvement. Our colleges and universities meet most of the costs of most foreign-student grantees, and of research scholars and lecturers who are frequently provided only with travel grants from official funds. Perhaps universities which receive these foreign grantees should receive "cost-of-education" grants to meet the additional expenses —a proposal endorsed by the U.S. Advisory Commission on International Educational and Cultural Affairs. They should clearly be drawn far more closely into both policy and planning if they are to make their most effective contributions.

The United States Government is closer today than it has ever been to deciding what role should be assigned to educational and cultural activities within the broad framework of American foreign policy. Stimulated somewhat by the Soviet cultural offensive which began as early as 1950, and by increasing appreciation of the extraordinary effort made by Kremlin propagandists to depict us as a nation of barbarians and materialists interested solely in the mass product of a technological civilization, official and private Americans have worked together to reach a more precise understanding of the value and place in our international relations of these flexible and valuable instruments, serving a wide variety of objectives. The Congress has enacted consolidated basic legislative authority to support a much wider variety of programs—although lagging in providing funds to carry out some of the reciprocal programs that are authorized and that would give even greater meaning to the concept of *mutual* educational and cultural exchange. The importance of these activities to the conduct of American foreign relations has been recognized in the creation of the position of Assistant Secretary of State for Educational and Cultural Affairs. New and important dimensions have been added in the cultural presentations abroad, and in opening up broader cultural contacts with the Soviet Union and the Communist nations of Eastern Europe.

Coordination, however, is still unsatisfactory. The Executive Order of June 25, 1962, did not give the Secretary of State a clear Presidential mandate to lead and guide all governmental international educational and cultural activities, since he was enjoined to take "into account the statutory functions of the departments and other executive agencies concerned." What appears to be happening is that there is greater awareness and willingness to cooperate than in the past. Attitudes and good will within the Executive

Branch are bringing about more coordination, but much of this simply adds up to whatever it is that people are willing to do. Other agencies frequently interpret the policy guidance that the Secretary of State is required to give as being narrowly limited to *foreign policy guidance*. This is far less than what is required to fulfill the enormously important responsibility of the Secretary of State as implied in the language of Section 6 of the Executive Order: "in order to assure appropriate coordination of programs. . . ."

On a less spectacular scale, thousands of Americans are receiving foreign visitors in their homes and giving them a first-hand view of American life and aspirations. Hundreds of private organizations are helping with parts of the huge problem of America's cultural relations. Unfortunately these efforts do not provide:

1) A clear, understandable United States Government policy as to the importance of and strength of support to be given to our international cultural relations activities.

2) A sustained attack by the great American foundations on these deficiencies—although encouraging steps have been taken by their recent establishment of the new organization, Education and World Affairs, by major Ford Foundation grants to the performing arts, by current studies on the present and future of the performing arts in America, and by the encouraging trend in the early 60's for major foundations to rank support for international activities as second only to education in priority.

3) Proof that government can succeed in making sense out of the separate fragments of programs directly affecting American cultural representation overseas carried out in a vast variety of different executive departments and sub-divisions of these departments.

Private American Information and Cultural Representation

The Smith-Mundt Act of 1948, providing basic authority for governmental information and educational exchange programs, incorporated a principle which stressed Congressional intent that private resources should play an important part. Section 1005 directed the Secretary of State "to utilize, to the maximum extent practicable, the services and facilities of private agencies." The reasons for this section being incorporated in Public Law 402 were complex. In part, it was a recognition that, in a democracy, the government will never produce more than a fraction—perhaps no more than 5 or 10 per cent—of the impact made by the nation abroad on other peoples. In part, it was simply that American legislators did not believe the United States Government should go much beyond a hard core of activities in these fields where government must do something. In part, it was a testimonial of faith in the concept of peoples speaking directly to peoples. In part, it was implicit recognition that our ability to persuade other peoples can never rise above the behavior and actions of the American Government and the American people themselves.

Consider for a moment the impact of the private American on foreign public opinion. If we genuinely believe that persuasion is most effective in changing attitudes when done on a man-to-man basis, by far the greatest part of this most effective persuasion is done by private American citizens. Whether they persuade wisely or foolishly, create confidence or mistrust, it is nevertheless in these private channels that the broad tides of persuasion really flow. The Soviets have learned in their Agitprop apparatus the necessity and effectiveness of this man-to-man contact. Professional agitators, disseminated throughout every level and every area of the U.S.S.R., carry on an internal indoctrination program beyond the wildest fantasies of free-world propagandists.

How greatly do American unofficial grass-roots ambassadors of persuasion outnumber our official ones? There are overseas or afloat more than 1 million American military personnel and nearly 300,000 civilian employees of the military services—*and* their dependents. Another 640,000 Americans are residents abroad, including employees of American business and of civilian government departments. In a recent year, well over 2 million Americans travelled abroad (excluding Canada and Mexico), and in that same year, about 700,000 foreign travellers entered the United States.

Each one of these Americans overseas, whether he or she knows it, helps every day to create the authentic voice of America.

In addition to these individual Americans abroad, there are other private contacts of enormous importance in influencing public opinion and in changing attitudes of foreign people. The American commercial motion picture plays to about 75 million admissions *each week* outside the United States. American newspapers and magazines reach millions of foreign readers. American television production is seen more and more on the screens abroad. American books—which many believe ought to be far more widely distributed, at much lower cost, and in many more foreign languages—also contribute to this private image of America.

For the most part, little has been successfully done to reduce the Tower of Babel impression of these many clamoring voices of America on our foreign audiences. In a different category are private groups purposefully carrying on important tasks of information and cultural representation. In the years immediately following the end of World War II, the government of necessity carried the major burden in penetrating the Iron Curtain and reaching peoples in the Soviet orbit to counteract the Orwellian 1984 thought-control and brainwashing of the totalitarian secret police state. For more than a decade, however, private American organizations—like the Free Europe Committee, supporting Radio Free Europe and its broadcasts to the Eastern European nations, or the Radio Liberty Committee, supporting Radio Liberty in its broadcasts by former Soviet citizens in Russian and sixteen other languages to the peoples of the Soviet Union—have shown that even in the area behind the Iron Curtain, private enterprise has a vital and increasingly important role to play in communication. By the mid-1950's, somewhat greater opportunities began to open for private initiative in contacts with the Soviet orbit. The signing of the first cultural-exchange agreement between the United States and the Soviet Union in 1958 opened much greater opportunities for private American cultural activities during those periods of "peaceful coexistence" when the Kremlin was emphasizing smiles and promises.

In the free, open-society areas of the world, the role of purposeful private American activities is even greater. In the early 1960's, American philanthropic foundations increased their support for international activities to over $100 million a year. Only education now receives a greater share of foundation grants. (In 1960, their grants for international activities were less than $33 million—and ranked sixth among the categories of major beneficiaries.) People-to-People, Inc., of Kansas City and its constituent national committees have been responsible for a number of projects aimed at creating good will overseas. The U.S. National Commission for UNESCO is finding ways for American education, science, and culture to contribute through an international organization to building a more peaceful world. The Institute of International Education has for nearly fifty years been at the center of programs of interchange of persons.

Government and Private Cooperation in Overseas Information

We have many lessons still to learn about cooperation between the government and private Americans in the task of persuasion abroad. Problems of private cooperation with government in the cultural field were accentuated by the split between educational exchange programs and information programs. But one cannot accurately describe the programs of educational exchange carried out under the sponsorship of the government without identifying this extensive private American participation. The programs of USIA, despite their extensive use of private resources, can be described in their essentials with only a passing reference to such private efforts. This is a significant difference.

Let us take as an example of private and government cooperation in overseas information the USIA Office of Private Cooperation: staff—about 30; funds in a recent year—around $500,000 (less than one-half of 1 per cent of USIA's total budget). In the 1950's, the Office encouraged a very wide range of efforts to engage Americans in all kinds of international contacts. The Office's philosophy in the 1960's is to use private agencies and the private sector to the maximum extent *to accomplish USIA objectives*.

Under the much sharper focus dictated by this change in philosophy, the Office has become first of all a service arm for USIS field posts and, to some extent, for USIA media divisions. This is a service arm without money, "USIA's official scrounger." It gets for the posts and the media the things they need but have not the money to buy—or which just could not or should not be bought with appropriated funds. Examples of some recent activities:

1. Shipment in a recent year of about 1 million books abroad, obtained free of charge. Almost all are new, mostly from publishers' returns, superseded editions, etc. (USIA has the right to reject any titles offered it.) All the books that wind up in the Post Office Dead Letter Centers—some 200,000 a year, again almost all new—come to USIA. USIA wives, on a volunteer basis, sort them under a Field Librarian's supervision and prepare them for shipment. About half are useful for USIA purposes and are sent abroad—always in response to specific field requests, with about half the transportation free, also. (The other half goes to the District of Columbia for use in libraries, penal institutions, etc.) These books are not used in USIS libraries but are now the mainstay of the USIA book presentation program, carried out as a joint program with the Peace Corps.

2. To help further in filling the reading gap, the Office recently helped organize Books USA, Inc., a private, nonprofit corporation that gives Americans an opportunity to send useful paperbacks abroad. It sells for four dollars packets of ten books especially selected for overseas impact, distributed by USIS and the Peace Corps abroad to universities, libraries, schools, or other recipients whose needs are great. Each packet is put in a category, such as "Understanding America," "Learning English," "Science for Children," or "American Literature." A number of American paperback publishers are participating. Requests from USIS field posts for 70,000 packets to be distributed in the first year were received within weeks after the announcement.

3. For over four years, in cooperation with the People to People Magazine Committee, the Office has seen to it that annually about 1.5 million copies of magazine newsstand returns are sent to field posts, with another 500,000 being given to them directly by overseas distributors.

4. There are 250 American cities affiliated with cities in forty-seven countries of the free world under the Sister City program, promoted by the People to People Civic Committee and the American Municipal Association, but aided and guided by the Office, especially in making known to the American affiliates projects that USIS posts feel would be of greatest usefulness.

5. In cooperation with the People to People Sports Committee,

the Office has a joint program selling kits of sports equipment for presentation by USIS and the Peace Corps abroad. Sports Kits available include baseball, basketball, boxing, soccer, softball, and volleyball.

6. Several tons of recreational equipment were collected at the request of USIS, Algiers, for use in Algerian youth centers.

7. As a joint project with the publisher of *Scientific American,* almost 24,000 copies of an issue devoted to "Technology and Economic Development" were made available free for distribution to interested foreign leaders and institutions. Similar distribution was made of 5,000 copies of the *General Electric Forum* on "The Developing Nations," and of CBS President Frank Stanton's 1962 speech on "Mass Media and Mass Culture" made at the opening of Dartmouth's Hopkins Cultural Center.

8. American business firms provided specially inscribed ballpoint pens for gifts in Laos; cameras for contest prizes in Latin America; American flags for USIS posts to present to schools and other requesting institutions.

The Office of Private Cooperation is very much aware of the importance of the 35,000 American businessmen overseas. To help keep them better informed on important matters of foreign policy, such as President Johnson's views on foreign policy, Berlin, Soviet-American economic comparisons, the Alliance for Progress, the partial test ban treaty, or U.S. views on disarmament, the Office sends them through their own home offices current information materials. Some 450 American corporations and about 7,000 American business representatives overseas cooperate in this project, which is designed to make the conversations of Americans overseas with foreign nationals based on more accurate knowledge.

Finally, the Office of Private Cooperation performs an important function by counseling a wide variety of groups that wish to play some part in USIA's area of responsibility. The Office can help by describing accurately those things which will be most useful to the USIS field posts and by providing advice and guidance on planning and execution. The Office assists and guides voluntary international programs in all fields of social, cultural, and economic interest that supplement USIA's own overseas program. It helps American organizations to create new international contacts and broaden existing overseas relationships, and it encourages them to use their own communications channels to build confidence abroad in the principles and practices of American democracy. For example, USIA works with business firms in stimulating programs under which individual firms or American business communities abroad undertake to tell the true story of the American economy overseas, explain the value of American business investment, and attack foreign misconceptions of the real nature of modern American capitalism.

There are more than 35,000 representatives of American business working overseas. In a recent year, 2,500 American companies were operating 7,000 branches abroad. Conscious of the fact that American capitalism has long been a prime object of Communist attack, leaders of American business have organized important programs to tell the true story of the American economy overseas. One important pioneer in helping American business to attack and correct foreign misconceptions of the real nature of American capitalism and of the private enterprise system is the Business Council on International Understanding. Its broad goal: to get U.S. corporations to work together to help improve economic and social development in foreign countries, wherever possible promoting more democratic social institutions. Among a number of specific services the Council conducts is a training program at the American University in Washington for administrative, technical, and advisory personnel of middle and upper management assigned abroad. The program consists of lectures and discussions on U.S. foreign policy and overseas operations, adjustment to foreign viewpoints and language study. In a recent project, the Council arranged for fifteen American businessmen to go to the Dominican Republic and work with key companies in the revival of that country's industry. Vocational programs were started in Chile, the Dominican Republic, and Tunisia, designed to accelerate the development of middle-manpower skills.

A number of other private organizations are active in promoting cooperation, and better understanding and relations, between the United States and foreign countries through business ties. Latin America has been the focus of many recent efforts, such as the U.S. Inter-American Council, which is the American section of the

Inter-American Council of Commerce and Production, and the Inter-American Relations Division of the National Association of Manufacturers. The Committee for Economic Development and the National Industrial Conference Board have also arranged conferences between American and Latin American business representatives for an exchange of views.

Lessons to be Learned

This account has somewhat presumptuously tried to give briefly a feeling of the flavor and texture of this enormously complex relationship of government and its citizens, and to indicate the potential and actual extent and impact of private participation in American information and cultural representation overseas. To do this, I have focused on the programs that are the responsibilities of the Department of State and the U.S. Information Agency. Nothing has been said about other important areas of government cooperation, such as the overseas programs of economic aid and technical assistance carried out by the Agency for International Development, involving extensive participation by American universities and colleges and hundreds of American specialists. Nor have I spoken of the broad programs carried out by the Department of Defense to help make American military personnel, their dependents and Defense Department civilian employees and their families better spokesmen for American aims and better representatives of American culture. Even from this relatively narrow examination, however, we may feel free to draw several conclusions:

1) Private efforts of these kinds have enormous potential effectiveness.

2) A generation of experience since the end of World War II demonstrates the willingness and eagerness of private American citizens to take part in projects for building good will abroad and developing greater mutual understanding. Many projects, however, lacked focus and provided at most the opportunity for foreigners to be brought into contact with Americans, without any particular concern for how much or what kind of effect these efforts would have abroad.

3) It is easier to state United States objectives with some pre-

cision in the field of information than it is in the field of cultural relations. Current projects in which the USIA Office of Private Cooperation is involved show clearly the important and highly useful nature of the support private American citizens can give to United States foreign policy objectives.

4) An American information or cultural representative overseas thus far has *less* opportunity for participating in the planning of such projects carried out with private cooperation and influencing the level and degree of activity for the country to which he is assigned than for programs the government is undertaking directly.

A Career Service for Information and Cultural Representatives?

A generation after the end of World War II, more than 1,000 Americans and about 7,000 locally employed foreigners were manning the firing lines at about 200 posts in more than 100 countries for the United States Information Agency. By late 1964, it appeared that at last the necessary steps were being taken to complete a genuine career system for these people.

At the end of World War II, the exodus of top-flight talent from the wartime information agencies was a rushing torrent. Only the demands of war seemed to command the talent of the ablest executives—wartime alumni include the publishers of *Time, Look, Fortune*; editors of magazines like *Holiday, Parade, The Saturday Review*; editors of several major dailies; heads of major publishing houses; key network executives; partners in large advertising agencies; social scientists of note. Those who stayed or could be induced to join the beginnings of the peacetime program found they were working in an activity not even authorized by Congress and therefore not legitimate until January, 1948. The principal overseas employment vehicles were a temporary appointment in the Foreign Service Reserve or appointment in the stepchild Foreign Service Staff (not the career Foreign Service) of the State Department.

With the adoption of Reorganization Plan No. 8 on August 1, 1953, and the creation of an independent United States Information Agency, new hopes—and new problems—appeared. USIA was born toward the end of a period of violent and disturbing attack, of continuing and chronic investigation of all of our overseas information activities and some of our chief cultural ones, such as the use of books in our overseas libraries. When the new agency was born, it looked back on eight years of almost continuous public debate, Congressional investigation, and a great deal of irresponsible criticism including occasional use of smear tactics directed against top executives and lesser employees both at home and abroad. It was a program for which the appropriation level had fluctuated violently and unpredictably. Drastic reductions in staff were made, only to be succeeded by equally massive recruiting efforts to build back to meet needs which had existed all along —but unrecognized, like so much debris swept under the carpet.

American information and cultural representatives overseas today are still being appointed under the temporary authority granted by the President's Executive Order. The President explained in transmitting Reorganization Plan No. 8 to Congress that the Director of USIA would need to exercise some administrative authorities of the Secretary of State: "This is necessary because the legislation dealing with the information programs does not contain administrative provisions. For example, the Director of the new United States Information Agency will need personnel authority. I, therefore, plan to authorize an independent personnel system for this agency's foreign operations under authority of . . . Plan No. 8."

This authority was intended basically to permit the Director to appoint personnel and manage a personnel system based on the provisions of the Foreign Service Act of 1946, with the personnel receiving the same compensation, allowances, and other benefits as State Department Foreign Service Reserve, staff, and alien personnel received. The new agency was specifically prohibited from exercising any authority with respect to the appointment of career Foreign Service Officers.

The President added that although he thought these arrangements would "enable the new Agency to function with reasonable effectiveness from the outset, I do not consider them permanently suitable. There is need for a critical analysis of the various systems of employment and compensation for United States Government overseas civilian personnel. I am directing that this entire matter be studied with a view toward recommending appropriate legislation."

For the next decade, studies were made and legislation was actually introduced in Congress but no genuine career service for USIA employees resulted until on October 6, 1964, USIA announced in Circular No. 222 D and 222 F an agreement with the State Department under which a large percentage of USIA officers holding Career Reserve appointments would be "appointed as Foreign Service Officers," thus bringing "to a successful conclusion eleven years of Agency effort to provide statutory career status for its Foreign Service career officers." The basis for the agreement was laid by the skill and ingenuity with which USIA had used the temporary arrangements and authorities. Operating two different personnel systems—under Civil Service for jobs in the United States, with 90 per cent of these positions filled by Civil Service employees, and under the Foreign Service Act of 1946 authorities granted to USIA for positions overseas held by American citizens—USIA established in 1960 by administrative action the Foreign Service Career Reserve Officer Corps. More than 800 Career Reserve Officers had successfully passed a qualifying in-service or entry examination. The Career Reserve Officer Corps was modeled on the State Department's Foreign Service Officer Corps. USIA gave examinations like those for the Foreign Service (and on the same days) to junior officer candidates. Its promotion system and many other personnel practices were similar, and senior State Department officers served jointly with USIA officers on personnel boards and panels.

But USIA had moved as far as it could by administrative action. The Agency still lacked authority to eliminate low-performance officers. Reserve Officers could not be employed beyond a ten-year maximum without special Congressional authorization. Its Foreign Service employees were under the Civil Service rather than the Foreign Service retirement system. Senior officers were not eligible for promotion above Class I.

The October, 1964, decision that the Foreign Service Officer authorities of the Foreign Service Act could be used to give Foreign Service Officer appointments to USIA Career Reserve Officers cured these defects and enabled USIA to complete its Foreign Service personnel system.

The main points of the Agreement with the State Department were:

1. The authorities of the Foreign Service Act will be used to appoint a large percentage of Agency officers who hold Career Reserve appointments as Foreign Service Officers. In the future, Junior Officers and lateral entry candidates for the Career Officer service of USIA will be examined and appointed as Foreign Service Officers.

2. A career specialization field for USIA Foreign Service Officers will be established within the Foreign Service of the United States. These officers will be administratively designated as Foreign Information Officers.

3. The Director of USIA will retain control and operational autonomy over Foreign Information Officers. Foreign Service Officers administratively designated as Foreign Information Officers will be USIA employees and will be under the administrative control of the Agency.

4. Uniform and compatible policies and procedures and common standards will be applied to all Foreign Service Officers, including Foreign Information Officers, consistent with the flexibility needed by the Department and the Agency in performing their particular missions.

Initial recommendations for Foreign Service Officer appointments would be made after review of records of USIA Career Reserve Officers by joint USIA–State Department Selection Panels to assure that only those demonstrating sustained performance at a high level of excellence would be included.

The fact that educational-exchange programs are kept in the Department of State but are carried out overseas by the U.S. Information Agency has resulted in some anomalies that are not yet cured. The man or woman working in the State Department on educational-exchange programs who accepted integration within the policies recommended by the Wriston Committee presumably also accepted an obligation to serve overseas. But the State Department has no overseas positions for specialists in educational exchange and cultural relations. USIA conducts overseas exchange-of-persons activities for the State Department's Bureau of Educational and Cultural Affairs.

The situation for a USIA Cultural Affairs Officer, although not as difficult, is still not completely satisfactory. When the Cultural Affairs Officer returns to the United States for a headquarters assignment, the increasing emphasis within the U.S. Information Agency on cultural programs affords him a widening variety of opportunities for service. Nevertheless, if he undertakes direct work in the educational-exchange field, he will have to be detailed to the State Department to do it.

The common denominator—if there is one—for both the good Cultural Affairs Officer and the good Public Affairs Officer is a fund of knowledge of the peoples with whom he is trying to communicate and a deep understanding of American life and culture. Knowledge of a foreign language on a really fluent and idiomatic basis is a great asset. But nothing can replace the intimate acquaintance with the attitudes, beliefs, values, aspirations, misconceptions, and questions in the hearts and minds of the people themselves. For many newly developing areas of the world, especially in Asia and Africa, we still have too few Americans who can qualify on these counts as experts, and competition for their skills is exceedingly keen.

Special technical skills are required for certain jobs, as in radio engineering or motion-picture production, and here technicians are also indispensable. Labor Information Officers, Space Science Lecturers, Information Officers for the Agency for International Development programs, and Television Officers are also required to have special skills. Basic knowledge of communications techniques is important for overseas officers—but much less so than some other qualities. It does *not* follow that a man highly skilled in American radio broadcasting, journalism, advertising, or public relations will be effective as a Public Affairs Officer or Information Officer overseas—nor that a man who comes from a successful academic experience will necessarily be a good Cultural Affairs Officer. (Although no analysis exists of backgrounds of present Public Affairs Officers, many do have newspaper experience, and many Cultural Affairs Officers come from universities or colleges.)

The top officers overseas—Public Affairs Officers, Information Officers and Cultural Officers particularly—must have broad general understanding of the planning and conduct of the whole mission. They often are not experts in a particular medium but possess instead a combination of talents. Oren Stephens sums up the good Information Officer well: a good propagandist, he says, has a sense of mission; knows the United States; understands people and has an inherent quality of leadership; understands politics; understands the theory and technique of communicating information and ideas. (He also operates effectively in foreign environments.)

Contrary to popular folklore, the Cultural Affairs Officer is not set apart from the struggles of the cold war. He inhabits no ivory tower. In some countries, it would be more correct to think of the Cultural Affairs Officer as a hard-hitting political in-fighter. He is sometimes successful in this because he does not seek in his activities immediate political advantages. On the other hand, he is dealing with a host of personal contacts and with those elements in the life of a nation that vibrate warmly and most genuinely— a people's music, art, books, theatre. Creation of a genuine climate of mutual understanding about these elements of national culture affords a long-term influence difficult to evaluate and dangerous to underestimate. The Cultural Affairs Officer is dealing with schools and education (including adult education), with the entire spectrum of the flow of intellectual life in the country to which he is accredited; in the broadest sense he is reflecting the American people's way of life.

There are special problems of cultural officers. A hardy perennial, not yet resolved, is whether the cultural officer should be a career government person or someone brought in from private life for periods of temporary duty. There are arguments and good ones on both sides and as usual in such cases, the answer is probably neither one nor the other exclusively, but some combination of career cultural officers and people temporarily recruited from private life. Howard Nostrand summed this up fairly well:

A career officer can do the administrative job more neatly and with less strain. . . . The [Cultural Affairs Officer] loaned from another position can give more on the creative side. He represents some part of his nation's culture far more authentically and interestingly than anyone can who makes a profession of it. . . . He has more in common with unofficial people, and with creative intellectuals, than the career official.

Ideally, these officers must be willing to accept assignment to any foreign post. They must have a knack for working with "local employees." Whether he be a cultural affairs officer, an information officer, a press officer, a librarian, radio officer, or motion picture officer, he will be happiest and do best where the top position of Public Affairs Officer is filled by a man who can create a working team, both *for* his subordinates, and *with* his chief of diplomatic mission and his colleagues in political, economic, and military affairs.

More and more attention is being paid to the locally hired foreigners who work for USIS abroad. As many an American representative has come to know, they are the unsung heroes and heroines of the cold war. We are learning to take advantage of the partnership which can be built with such people who share our American beliefs and are genuinely dedicated to the building of a greater understanding between their fellow countrymen and us Americans. These are the people who know the folkways and deep emotional responses of their own countrymen. They know how to edit material effectively for their audience. They speak the language. In countries where there may be a racial or color problem, they know instinctively the right and the wrong ways of approaching communication. Remember that in the more than 100 foreign countries in which the United States Information Service is operating today, we have more than 1,000 Americans as compared with over 7,000 locals, including those working in VOA overseas installations. Training programs began about 1949 to permit the local employees who were doing outstanding jobs and had real potential for growth to pay visits to the United States so that they could supplement their intimate knowledge of their own countries with a first-hand experience in America. This experiment has paid off handsomely—in fact, USIA in 1963 began bringing a few outstanding previous visitors back to Washington for a second tour to reinforce their impressions and to share their observations with headquarters officers.

Perhaps one way of measuring how far we have come in laying

the foundations of a permanent career service is to compare the findings and recommendations of the Herter Committee on Foreign Affairs Personnel with what is now provided for information and cultural programs. In its December, 1962, report, *Personnel for the New Diplomacy*, which focused on the needs of the Department of State, including the Agency for International Development and USIA, the Committee enumerated major previous personnel studies beginning with some made before the end of World War II. The Committee remarked that it "was impressed by the fact that many of the basic conclusions and recommendations of these earlier reports, though formulated by different groups, and at different times, are essentially similar, and further, coincide with many of the Committee's own proposals."

To what degree do our information and cultural representatives today have what the Herter Committee considered essential and desirable?

1. USIA does *not* have membership in a distinctively indentified service, one of a family of compatible systems reflecting substantial conformity in personnel policies and coordinated personnel operations, with domestic as well as overseas personnel administered outside the Civil Service System and paid on the basis of a single salary schedule. USIA uses the Civil Service at home, but by bringing its Foreign Service career officers within the authorities of the Foreign Service Act, the Agency is moving much closer to meeting the Herter Report goals of more compatible personnel systems and greater uniformity in the management of foreign service personnel. Headquarters educational exchange officers now serve in the State Department under the same general Civil Service System as USIA domestic personnel. USIA overseas officers who must carry out these programs abroad are in a different career system.

2. The Herter Committee felt that the recruiting machinery of the three foreign-affairs agencies should be merged and examination processes consolidated. (There is no lack of talent skilled in the various communications media to draw on. USIA employs its own separate recruiting machinery. While bringing in relatively more appointees at intermediate and higher levels than the State Department, it also has a junior professional recruitment program

seeking junior officer candidates principally from college seniors. This program is similar to but separate from the State Department program. A common written examination is given on the same day, with the sections on general ability, English expression, and foreign languages similar for all candidates—but the general background portion differs for USIA and State Department candidates. In a recent year, three and one-half times as many persons took the State Department written examination as USIA's. On the average, three classes made up of twenty junior officer trainees enter USIA each year—60 per cent with masters' degrees.)

3. Even more important than recruitment is the kind of special training given. The Herter Committee felt so strongly that the quantity of training and education available to foreign affairs personnel should be increased, and its quality improved, that they recommended replacement of the Foreign Service Institute by a new National Foreign Affairs College to provide in-service training at an advanced level for professional people. Noting that in the absence of such an institution USIA had developed its own training programs, the Committee characterized them as "parochial," not "well equipped to consider United States policy as a unity." (USIA Director Edward R. Murrow strongly supported establishment of such a National Academy of Foreign Affairs in Congressional testimony in 1963. He regarded existing USIA training programs as supplementary to what the Academy might offer.)

USIA has been building expanding training programs for employees at various levels. Junior officer trainees get six months of intensive indoctrination, including the eight week basic officers course at the State Department Foreign Service Institute. They thus receive essentially the same basic preparation as do junior diplomats. Heavy stress is put on language training, and they are then dispersed to overseas posts, where they are given on-the-job training for ten months. Next they are transferred to a different post and given a work assignment. They are on probation until promoted.

USIA now has twenty to twenty-five officers a year in mid-career training courses. About half (nearly 400) of its Foreign Service Career Reserve Officers are in mid-career grades R–5 and R–4.

USIA normally enrolls twelve senior officers in each of the six sessions held during a year in the Country Team Seminar on Problems of Development and Internal Security—now supplemented by training for many more officers in USIA's own course, which is taken by all USIA officers above Foreign Service Grade 6.

USIA has the privilege of sending a select few of its most promising people to the National War College, where they spend a year in intensive studies with their counterparts from the military services and the political and economic officers of the State Department.

A training deficit still exists, however, for USIA—as for all the foreign-affairs agencies. The Herter Committee compared the proportion of officer-time dedicated to training, exclusive of language study, to total officer-time: "Among the USIA Reserve Officers, this proportion is slightly over 2 per cent; in AID, including its participating agency personnel, it is about the same; among Foreign Service Officers and Reserve Officers in the Department of State, it is about 5 per cent. The comparable figure in military departments is roughly 12 per cent."

4. Language training deserves a special note. The Herter Committee noted "the present high level of the Foreign Service Institute language program" as "a striking example of the success that high quality research can bring to a training program," and observed that USIA—though to a lesser extent then the State Department—had made "significant progress in raising the level and extending the scope of the language competence of its Foreign Service Officers." (USIA has encouraged language training for junior officer trainees, 50 per cent of whom study languages other than French, German, and Spanish, by assigning the officer after completion of his training period to his training post or area for at least one tour of duty. More senior officers work harder at language training under USIA policies of lengthening overseas tours, except in critical hardship posts, from two to three years, and making regional specialization the rule, so to the extent possible they now spend most of their overseas careers in a single cultural or ethnic region.)

5. Career development and manpower planning were important areas in which the Herter Committee found all the foreign affairs agencies deficient. Its Report urges USIA and AID to give "con-

siderably more attention to program planning" and concludes: "Neither agency, however, has yet developed effective means for translating program plans into long-term projections of personnel needs."

USIA career development was described as "a modest program restricted largely to junior officers," and both USIA and AID were advised to reorganize and model their programs on the conceptual approach developed by the State Department, despite the admittedly disappointing impact of this approach on actual operational decisions.

To sum up, the basis for a genuine career service has now been provided for American information and cultural representatives overseas. Because USIA developed a sound personnel system, parallel so far as possible in most important respects with the State Department Foreign Service, required its career reserve officers to satisfy standards comparable to those required of State Department Foreign Service Officers, and because the State Department was an active and cooperative partner in establishing and developing the Career Reserve System, it was a relatively simple step to convert the career reserve to full career status and so recognize the fact that "the information and cultural programs are an enduring and organic tool of American foreign policy."

Much is still left to do. USIA still has to develop that kind of manpower planning system which would permit the projection of training requirements further into the future, and find out how to operate a genuinely effective career planning system for individual officers "within which training assignments could be firmly predicted and scheduled." Much can still be done to emphasize area specialization even more, and to develop new kinds of communications officers for newly-developing countries. More can be done to assure the more frequent refreshing of the USIA officer, who must have a deep understanding of life and culture at home, by "systematic re-exposure to the domestic scene."

Finally, plans should be made to enable USIA's best people to acquire experience outside USIA—in the State Department, in AID, or other agencies concerned with international relations—so that more of them will qualify for posts of top leadership and responsibility in the conduct of our foreign affairs.

The Future of American Information and Cultural Representation

America is now spending around $200 million a year to maintain these worldwide programs of information and cultural relations. This is a good deal less than the three companies that make most of our soap and synthetic detergents spend in a year for advertising.

Propaganda by itself, for a democracy at least, cannot accomplish much. We best persuade abroad when we take the right action as part of a grand strategy—and do everything we can to explain the action and to gain acceptance for the meaning we intended to give to our action, since the psychological response to any action is *not* automatic.

We must be clear on our objectives. We must not think we can proclaim to the world one set of objectives—and actually have different ones at the heart of our policy. We must have the right grand strategy. Much of this paper deals with the orchestration of action. No conductor, whatever his talent, can command great music from his orchestra unless there is a score and all of his musicians are reading from the same score.

We are learning some hard lessons. We are learning that words without deeds are ineffective in a democracy's programs of persuasion. We are learning that we must not be preoccupied with day-to-day events to the exclusion of ultimate purposes, since this is the role of a press agent and not of a persuader. We are learning that persuasion must be based upon the true and tried instruments of national policy: a military undertaking such as the Berlin airlift, the commitment of American troops to Europe or to the United Nations forces in Korea, or military aid in South Vietnam; a program like the Marshall Plan or the Alliance for Progress in the economic field; a statement of policy like the Truman Doctrine, or President Eisenhower's appeal for "a true and total peace," or President Kennedy's American University speech calling for a re-examination of our attitudes toward the Soviet Union and the cold war; the development by diplomacy of NATO or SEATO—using these and other instruments, a nation can secure support for its national objectives and for the different things it does day by day. These are what give American information and cultural representatives overseas an opportunity to perform effectively.

We have learned painfully and to our sorrow that there are many occasions when Madison Avenue huckster techniques of selling the sizzle and not the steak will boomerang if applied to attaining American objectives overseas. We seem to be slowly groping our way to a firmer and more genuine conviction that we really want the rest of the world to have a much greater understanding of us and of our objectives—and that as Americans we really want to seek a comparably full and fair picture of other nations and peoples. We are learning how to compete with the Communists whose messages come primarily through one's friends and neighbors and are often disguised under the slogans of patriotism and nationalism. We are not able to create fifth columns of the Communist kind. Our information representatives overseas, however, are learning how to cooperate in the countries to which they are assigned with like-minded groups which share our views and find that the aspirations and values of their own peoples have much in common with those of Americans.

These front-line representatives of America in a major area of the cold war have found that in recent years it has become more generally true that the policy of the United States Government is to analyze each action that we propose to take in the light of what world opinion will probably think of it. Our representatives overseas report that we are more often requiring that some measures or plan be adopted at that time which will attempt to influence world opinion in its favor and which will form part of the action we finally adopt. They see that we are gradually coming to understand that taking the right action is only part of the task. We must also strive to see that the meaning we want attached to that action shall in fact be accepted by those people who are not Americans.

There has been clear and impressive progress in these directions. Our overseas representatives can honestly begin to say that we as Americans are presenting some clear hope for a better future. We are not simply presenting a program that will leave room for no one except bigger and better Americans. We seem less occupied with the immediate present and less in the position of advocates of the *status quo*. We are beginning to show foreign peoples that the great dynamic qualities of American leadership are in fact leading us somewhere and therefore leading them somewhere that they want to go. It is far less easy to say today, as an important paper discussing this topic concluded a decade ago, that "the absence of a defined faith in the future deprives us of our best of all possible guides in planning for the future."

We seem also to have largely abandoned the occasional excesses of the skywriting school of international persuasion. There is greater genuine belief in, and less lip service paid to, the concept that if we are to have peace and understanding in the world, we have to know about each other's cultures. Our overseas representatives today are doing less to "sell America" and more to create mutual understanding and secure participation by our audiences themselves in the work to be done.

We may even in time move to the position where in each country in which we carry on a persuasion program of our own, we may invite some qualified person to assist the nationals of that country in a flow of information *toward* the United States. Where might this concept of mutual understanding lead us? As we go on in a genuine belief that we are sincerely trying to understand the ways of life, problems and purposes of other peoples, perhaps our work will become less that of Americans conducting persuasion on a foreign soil and more a partnership arrangement between us Americans and others for the mutual welfare of both of us. We might ask whether this would not lead to a more effective contest with the Communists for what has been called "an indispensable basis for credibility"—namely, that the persuasion in each country is carried on primarily by its own nationals. Perhaps at some future time the spokesmen of the free world will in fact appear to be speaking not in the name of some foreign power but in the name of the nationals of their own countries and of their fellow workers and their own neighbors. Perhaps brown, black, and yellow skins can speak to people of similar pigmentation—and not in the role of the White Man, feared and hated because of his history of colonial subjugation and exploitation of "inferior races."

The American people themselves appear to be more and more

sure that we are in this not just for the short run but for keeps, however long that may be. It is too much to say that Americans are yet willing to make those same kinds of sacrifices of inclination and personal choice for the purposes of persuasion in the cold war that all of us have been cheerfully and valiantly ready to accept in a hot war. But understanding is deeper and broader of the importance of American information and cultural representation overseas than it ever has been before in this country. Encouraging evidence that this is finally becoming recognized is the grant to our information and cultural representatives of the full career status warranted by the importance of their contribution to United States national objectives, but so long denied them.

4. American Military Representation Abroad

PAUL C. DAVIS and WILLIAM T. R. FOX

Today, the United States has deployed abroad more than 500,000 military personnel. Most are stationed overseas as members of combat and supporting troop units, but at least 20,000 are performing advisory and training functions in more than 65 nations. Both troops and advisors often work and live in unprecedentedly close association with foreign peoples. Their presence, therefore, not only bears importantly on America's global military posture; it can have great social and political consequences for both American policy and the internal dynamics of these countries. This post–World War II phenomenon implies a range of new purposes and it demands a range of new military skills.

It is the aim of this essay to explain the purposes of American military representation abroad, to describe its main forms, to indicate the new kinds of skill that military representation abroad demands, and to examine how the American military services are seeking to supply these skills. We shall also, in passing, touch upon some of the problems of military representation that remain unresolved.

Changed American Military Responsibilities

That the United States should have a large number of military officers representing it abroad, including many of its ablest career officers, is but one consequence of the changed military responsibilities of the United States today. Just to deal with the myriad problems connected with the stationing of forces on non-American territories calls for much diplomatic skill on the part of the commanding officers, and greatly increases the work load of the diplomatic missions. The need, however, for our very large military representation arises from three other circumstances. The first is that our armed services have to operate in many areas of the world as part of coalitions, and this calls for coalition military planning. The second is that the United States is providing economic and military aid on a multibillion-dollar scale to make our allies more effective members of these coalitions. The military aid, furthermore, takes the form not only of supplying weapons but also of carrying on a huge training program through missions overseas and here in the United States. The third circumstance is that military security in most of the underdeveloped countries depends in great part on channeling the forces of political and economic modernization and forestalling their subversion, tasks to which American military specialists have much to contribute.

What is the nature of the threat to American security that has led the American people to accept the necessity for maintaining and developing our military power at the high present levels and in a period of peace?

Essentially, the threat to American security arises from two fundamental changes in the structure of international politics that have taken place in recent times. First, the European balance-of-power system, with the relative decline in the strength of the West European nations, has been replaced by a world system drawing America permanently into it. Secondly, the Soviet Union, with basic aims inimical to ours, has risen to a position of strength that the West, in the absence of the United States, could not effectively oppose. These two changes have compelled the United States, step by step, to assume the leading role in a world-wide system of collective and bilateral defense arrangements and to accept the responsibility for stabilizing the governments of threatened countries in many areas of the world.

Military Representation in the Age of Total Diplomacy

In the era of total diplomacy, the character and scope of military representation abroad have changed drastically, with far-reaching implications for the kinds of skills that must serve it. The nature of representation has changed because the influence of deployed military force in peacetime has broadened and become more dynamic. And it has changed because in today's highly tense and unstable international climate, limited wars are quite likely and the possibility of all-out nuclear war ever present. These possibilities have required a basically new approach to war preparation, emphasizing deterrence of war.

Deterrence is not an entirely new idea. The great powers of Europe have for centuries sought to deter war by changes in the level, deployment, and composition of their forces. But deterrence has acquired today a far greater urgency in the councils of states. In a world where both the United States and the Soviet Union possess far more destructive weapons than needed to gain national political ends, the immense difficulties in limiting the proportions and destructiveness of war once it starts have elevated deterrence of general war to the number-one place among the goals of military and foreign policy. Because general war has been relegated to the "last resort" in a sense far more final than ever before, it has become vital to be thoroughly prepared for war in peacetime. Thorough preparation is necessary not only to convince adversaries of the folly of attack, but because preparations once general war begins are next to impossible. There are many who believe that even limited wars can easily get out of control and "escalate" to general war because the U.S. and the Communist powers are so sensitive to the dangers of small shifts in the balance of power as to find them intolerable. So it is that the U.S. places an almost equally high premium on the deterrence of limited war. Our military planning and representation abroad are consequently about as active in areas where local war threatens (e.g., in Vietnam) as in areas where war would probably be general (e.g., Western Europe).

If we are to deter war, we must convey to our adversaries with unambiguous clarity our intent and our ability to defend our interests. It is this purpose that has led the United States to take great care in war planning as token of that will and capacity. It is this purpose that has called forth the presence abroad of American military forces and representatives on a scale without precedent in history.

The scope of war preparation has not been the only basic

change. The influence of military forces and representatives abroad has ramified and taken on a dynamism that is also new.

When American political purposes abroad were accomplished almost solely through government-to-government contacts, the scope of significant representation was narrowly circumscribed and readily definable. With the emergence of public opinion as a major force in the more advanced states during the past seventy-five years or so, the character of representation has gradually broadened, at a continually accelerating pace. At the same time, we have learned in recent times a great deal about how to influence even under-developed nations through pressures and persuasion directed at the groups and élites in and out of government who have access to the reins of power. Today, armed with awareness of these forms of political power, our military representatives frequently can serve American political purposes not only by performing top-level advisory functions, but through contacts at lower staff levels and with nonofficial foreign groups whose attitudes help to shape the policies of their governments. The scope of these activities has inevitably broadened the staffing and coordinating responsibilities of those who represent the United States in its dealings with other governments. This is as true of military representation as it is, for example, of our informational and economic activities abroad. Though even more significant for our civilian representation, this fact, since World War II, has called forth a proliferation of new military activities and has led to the augmentation of military staffs abroad. Today's military representation is not, then, limited to attaché duties and staff exchanges as it once was. It includes the influence of more than half a million troops abroad, our representatives in a vast web of coalition military staffs, our personnel providing advice and training in the use of military equipment through military assistance groups and military missions, and most recently those who provide advice and training abroad in such new activities as counterinsurgency and civic action. At the same time, the basic and dual nature of representation has not changed. It includes both the representation of United States interests to others (influence), and the presentation of what is learned about others to superiors in Washington (reporting and intelligence collection).

At a time when it is not only America's potential power but her actual immediately available power that counts, peacetime preparedness imposes important new tasks on military planners. Our foreign military intelligence has to be especially reliable and it has to be available much sooner than in the past. It also must be far more extensive, since the United States can expect to play an active role in a variety of lesser conflicts in many parts of the world. Our foreign military intelligence has to be more comprehensive for another reason. In the era of total diplomacy and protracted high-level mobilization, strategic-economic and political intelligence has to be integrated with the more strictly military intelligence if American military policy is to be based on accurate estimates of our opponent's capabilities and intentions. Moreover, since the United States counts upon the strength of the many countries to whom it renders assistance and advice, it needs to know fully as much about its friends as it does about its potential enemies. Our military plans must be worked out in exhaustive detail and fully tested on maneuvers, since there may be no possibility of correcting deficiencies once war starts. This requires the existence abroad of complete staffs. Communications must be installed and operating. Supplies must be appropriately distributed and stocked on the probability that their flow will be interrupted if not permanently arrested when war starts. Where we belong to coalitions, complete air defense systems must be in place tying together the matériel of many nations with their array of complicated technical equipment. These are but a few of the necessities of modern war that require the presence abroad of large staffs for active military headquarters and of numerous mission representatives engaged in an almost bewildering variety of activities. Almost all require negotiation with foreign countries and, where we belong to collective defense organizations, with other coalition partners. Finally, as one of the two countries (Great Britain being the other) with recent experience in large-scale command and planning operations in which military power had to be applied from distant bases, the United States has necessarily assumed an especially large role in coalition military planning. In the performance of this task, the United States is not simply one among equals cooperating for defense. Our leadership has bestowed upon us the representational task of providing the "glue" for the coalitions of which we are members.

"*The Buck Stops Here*"

The motto that President Truman had on his desk now applies as much to the role of the President of the United States in the free-world coalition as it does to his position in the American constitutional system. The United States can hardly help those countries that do not choose to help themselves, but, given determination on their part and on ours to develop military power on a combined basis, the United States can hardly pass the buck to its allies for making sure that the total effort is not dangerously inadequate. In the mid-1950's, the hard choice could be measured in dollars: the United States contributed about 15 per cent of the defense costs of the European members of NATO through military assistance (besides the contribution of American forces to NATO). With the phenomenal recovery in Europe's economic strength, the American contribution via military assistance to the defense of Western Europe by 1962 declined to less than 3½ per cent of what the European NATO countries were spending on defense. Their defense expenditures in that year exceeded $17 billion. This was a level of expenditure more than 50 per cent above the European defense expenditures in 1955. In the same period, West European economic strength had grown more rapidly than that of the European part of the Communist Bloc. Whether Europe was to carry its share of the military burden was no longer an economic but a political question, centered chiefly on basic problems of strategy: the role and size of the shield force (mainly ground troops) based in Europe, the control of the nuclear deterrent, and the mechanics for restraining a premature, and insuring a prompt, retaliatory strike. The buck has continued to stop at the President's desk, for Europe has looked to the United States to redefine the tasks of the shield force, and to propose means for constructing a NATO nuclear force.

Meanwhile, American military assistance outside Europe since 1957 has exceeded American assistance to NATO, and the margin has steadily increased. This reflects a new dimension in the challenge of Communism, which has compelled the United States to determine with respect to *all* its global alliances how much is enough. More than that, these needs, as we shall see, have had to be measured in terms that go beyond the traditional military task of planning defense against external aggression. They have had to be measured in terms of the capacity of non-Communist nations positively to deter war, and to repress internal war stimulated or inflamed by external pressures.

Before examining specific forms of United States military representation abroad, let us review the broad tasks of American military policy in the 1960's.

Military Planning and Political Consensus

Two facts peculiar to the postwar environment have made it easier for the United States to fulfill its new military responsibilities. In the first place, Great Britain and the countries of Western Europe have ceased to consider war between each other as a real possibility. One can be fairly confident that their relations with each other and with the United States will no longer oscillate between war and peace but only between cooperation and non-cooperation. Secondly, while the heavy American burden is not lightened, the task of planning is simplified by lack of ambiguity when there are one or at most two possible major opponents in view. We may well deplore the decline in power of our leading European allies relative to that of the Soviet Union; but as long as the cold war threat persists, the American Government at least knows who is the target of its military-planning arrangements.

The detailed General Staff conversations that the British and French military staffs carried on in the years before 1914 were made possible by a similar lack of ambiguity about the target of Franco-British security arrangements. There was a tendency in that earlier period, when the Triple Entente faced the Triple Alliance, for coalition military planning to outrun coalition diplomacy. Perhaps it only reflects the soldier's natural desire to make definite arrangements and the diplomat's natural desire to keep the future open by avoiding unnecessary commitments, but in the first critical days of August, 1914, the military on both sides of the Channel had done their homework, while the politicians and diplomats were debating just how far England had committed herself to France and Belgium. A military consensus had again developed within NATO in the 1950's, this time regarding the crucial question of whether and how atomic weapons should be used. Meanwhile, the political consensus of the 1950's as to what provocation would justify invocation of the atomic sanction has dissolved in this decade, as the United States has quietly sought to increase the number of situations *not* requiring atomic retaliation by pressure to strengthen the conventional shield forces in Europe. This change in United States strategic thinking, influenced by the advent of the ICBM, has contributed to the European powers' insistence on a NATO nuclear force, lest the United States less promptly honor its commitment to strike than they would prefer. If the political consensus cannot be reclarified and shored up by some such means, the situation could parallel that of 1914.

Threats to NATO Solidarity

Coalition military planning and the continued development of the military-aid aspects of our mutual security program depend on maintaining our ability to meet a range of threats to the coalition policy consensus. In the European theater, there are several problems that must be solved if the combined military effort is to rest on a firm foundation.

Even where relations among NATO allies seem highly harmonious, Soviet diplomacy is sufficiently imaginative to impose strains on relations among them by peace offensives that appeal more to one part of the alliance than to another. It is difficult for the NATO allies to tax themselves heavily to support a common defense effort; every twittering in the dovecotes of Soviet diplomacy compounds the difficulty.

Even without the divisive efforts of Soviet diplomacy, maintaining a coalition policy consensus is difficult. France's decision to withdraw troops from the NATO command to restore order in Algeria; the American determination to broaden the base of Western opposition to Soviet expansion by encouraging West German rearmament, acquiring bases in Spain, and by aid to Tito;

the Anglo-French invasion of the Suez in 1956, and De Gaulle's decision to withdraw the French fleet from NATO command and to create an independent H-bomb force, are examples of national policies that have subjected NATO to significant strains over the years. More recently, the most urgent strain on the coalition has been President de Gaulle's insistence on a larger share in NATO planning, one that in effect would replace American leadership with Continental leadership, with France playing the major role. Beyond this role in NATO itself, De Gaulle evidently wants an influence equal to Britain's in shaping the American political decision on when to employ nuclear force. His position is based not on military considerations alone, but on his desire for an independent "Third Force" position in foreign policy, which indeed extends far beyond Europe. As long as there is divergence of opinion on the two sides of the Atlantic as to the appropriate circumstances for using atomic weapons, a threat to NATO solidarity will continue to exist. The legal prohibition to the release of American nuclear weapons to European countries no doubt suggests to some of their leaders that we have less confidence in their restraint than in that of the Russians. It is possible, of course, that modifications in the law governing disclosure of information on atomic weapons would enable the United States and its allies to develop a surer consensus in this area. If, for example, one could demonstrate that the use of tactical atomic weapons did not open the Pandora's box of unlimited thermonuclear warfare, the task of coalition military planning might be simplified. But this is a question that our military leaders cannot solve by themselves.

Even for our political leaders, these problems are not easy. The United States must deal with its European allies as sovereign equals. If the United States were providing economic, technical, and military aid out of charity, it might be free to withhold that aid if the object of charity proved too recalcitrant, but it provides this help for reasons of enlightened selfishness. Because the United States Government has decided that it gets the most for a defense dollar by direct grants to its partners, it cannot treat them as pensioners but only as real equals. This is true of both its diplomatic and its military relations with its allies.

Threats to Solidarity in Asia

Difficult as they are, these obstacles to political agreement with our European allies are still not so numerous or so serious as those to political collaboration with countries in Asia. In Europe, collaborative diplomacy and military cooperation have stabilized the situation to the point where the partners feel it safe to debate whether the threat has receded. In Asia, on the other hand, the United States has seen the whole military balance of power seriously threatened by the expansionist pressures of Communist China and by guerrilla warfare and subversion throughout Southeast Asia.

Since 1945, eastern Asia has not been stabilized against either war or revolution. The forces opposed to Communist expansion have not had the time for long-range or integrated military planning such as was possible in Europe. Our diplomacy in Asia has tended to be a fire-brigade diplomacy, and our military activities have also had a fire-brigade rather than a deterrent aspect. Even had there been time to form an effective NATO-like organization in Asia, the states in the area show no inclination to join such an organization on an all-inclusive basis. The Southeast Asian Treaty Organization (SEATO) includes in its membership only three of the Asian states directly threatened by Communist aggression, and it lacks machinery for coalition military activity as extensive as NATO's. In some parts of Asia, the rivalries among those countries still outside the Communist orbit are so intense that it is difficult to provide military help for one without alarming an immediate neighbor. India and Pakistan are cases in point.

Implications for Military Representation

In terms of the tasks of American military representation, what does this picture of the problems of American military power in the 1960's mean? We have long had military and naval attachés as part of our foreign missions. We continue to do so, and they are of particular importance in unfriendly capitals and in the capitals of uncommitted countries. Military training missions to

Latin America are not new either, but the step-up of Soviet and Chinese Communist activities following the establishment of an influence base in Cuba has given these missions new importance. If for no other reason than a preclusive interest in keeping non-American powers from maintaining missions in Latin America, United States missions are likely to continue there.

Some other forms of military representation abroad are by no means new, but they are new for the United States, particularly in Europe. There is a long history, for example, of General Staff conversations among European allies and of military missions sent and military assistance rendered by European powers to Asian countries. But it is new for the United States to participate in these General Staff conversations and new for the participation to take the form, as it does in NATO and in its various military headquarters, of creating an international military executive to provide for day-to-day development of joint military plans.

It is a new experience for the United States to send military missions and assistance to Europe and for American military officers to have to play the role of military instructors to their European professional colleagues. What is probably new for any power is the detailed peacetime coalition military planning, which now rests on the firm basis of twenty-five years of the most intimate Anglo-American collaboration, in the combined operations of World War II and in a variety of postwar military activities. Intimate coalition military planning takes place through the three-member Standing Group of NATO and through international staffs under three co-equal military commanders: the Supreme Commander, Allied Forces Europe (SACEUR), at SHAPE, near Paris; the Supreme Allied Commander Atlantic (SACLANT), with headquarters at Norfolk, Virginia; and the Commander in Chief, Channel Command (CINCHAN), with headquarters at Portsmouth, England. The senior military officers of the United States and all its allies seem to be almost continuously crossing and re-crossing the Atlantic in the interest of united Western defense. The creation of a rudimentary central executive in the NATO organization, both civilian and military, carries forward the concept of continuous and immediately available coalition military power to a point never before attained in peacetime. It is this that gives meaning to the NATO objective of developing a strategy fairly described as deterrent.

Finally, there are new substantive kinds of American military representation outside Europe, which have arisen from the character of internal war and subversion. These generally take the form of assistance to strengthen the internal security of weak nations and to exploit the capacity of their military forces for contributing to economic and political stability and growth.

Types of Military Representation

Force, Psychological Operations, and Troop-Community Relations

In war as in peace, sovereign states through their chosen representatives continually exchange messages—intimations of purpose and of the firmness with which the purposes will be supported. In war, the "message" is communicated partly by hurling bits of metal through the air. The contrast between the war and peace situations can easily be overstated, however, for purposeless displays of force are as sterile in their consequences as diplomacy unsupported by the ability or will to enforce it. In the "no war, no peace" situation of the present era, pious exhortation is particularly pointless. Force, then, has a role to play whether the guns are silent or whether they speak. In the same way, both diplomatic and propagandistic messages have a role to play in war *and* peace, as long as they are underlined by the existence of force.

In a sense, American forces stationed abroad represent the United States more than do the personnel of whom we traditionally think as our military representatives. The foreign policy of the United States must be promoted and maintained by a continuing and changing combination of constraint, inducement, and free negotiation. One thinks of armed forces as representing the element of constraint and of diplomacy as representing the element of negotiation. But the opposite may sometimes be true. A diplomatic communication can take the form of an ultimatum, and a visit of naval units to some foreign port may be a gesture of friendship. Every change in the composition, deployment, or level of our armed forces that becomes known to a foreign government communicates to that government something about United States policy, American intentions, and the degree of firmness with which those intentions are to be promoted.

When Theodore Roosevelt sent the White Fleet around the world, he obviously meant a new image of American power to be fixed in the minds of foreign rulers. As long as the United States maintains a token force in Berlin or sends military units along the *autobahn* in and out of that city, it advertises to the world that free Berlin cannot be incorporated into the Soviet realm without the probability of Soviet-American war.

Today, the communication of such messages by military means is not left to a chance idea of Teddy Roosevelt's but is systematically governed by what Pentagon planners call "psychological operations." Guided by foreign-policy objectives and by broad military strategic considerations, psychological operations planners both in Washington and in the major commands abroad seek to derive psychological dividends from existing military assets and ongoing military activities. Such influences often emanate from the "message" character of forces in being. These messages may be highly coercive or quite friendly. Characteristically, they take such forms as fleet visits and demonstrations of strategic air or ground mobility by long nonstop flights and rapid overseas deployments, as well as by disaster relief operations and other missions of mercy. The complexity of the military structure, its diversity of functions and commands, is such that by no means all such operations derive from the single motive of the message. Psychological operations frequently consist merely of publicly interpreting the act or influencing its performance in its details.

Such informal yet fundamental representation is not limited to manifestations of force. To a large degree, it has come to include the influence of the soldier as an individual abroad. As a result of our sizable overseas deployments, literally millions of foreign peoples have come to picture the "typical" American through personal observation of our soldiers. Because of his numbers and the duration of his stay, the soldier has the potential, both for good and for bad, to create such images far more than our government-to-government representatives or our hurried tourists.

Characteristically, American troops tend to associate rather closely with local peoples wherever they serve. This is less true of married personnel, who tend to bring America with them and live a kind of "compound" life. Nonetheless, close social contact has been marked in most areas of the world where American troops have been stationed. Indeed, never before has so extensive intercultural contact taken place, save on the basis of empire. And in the environment of empire, the characteristic superior-inferior relationship, particularly in an age when public opinion was an insignificant factor, produced a simpler set of problems.

Formerly, nations formed their policies toward others on the basis of limited knowledge about them gathered by painstaking intelligence operations. Today, nations like West Germany, where the American soldier is in effect a permanent resident, inevitably form their policies in the context of first-hand impressions about American values and character, however incomplete or *un*representative these may be. The consequences of such associations for American interests, therefore, can hardly be ignored. Indeed, they have not been ignored by the armed forces, which, from the first days when American NATO troops were deployed to Europe, have taken measures to exploit the positive and arrest the negative effects of association.

Wherever American forces serve, the natural American tendency to participate in benevolent nonmilitary activities has grown autonomously, and their number and variety defy cataloguing. Upon such local initiatives, major commanders have superimposed planning, direction, and control. In Europe, the efforts to systematize contacts have had a positive rationale in the desire of psychological-operations planners to serve specific American policies, and a negative one of minimizing frictions that might impede the military mission.

Both the positive and negative aspects of American behavior and military actions abroad are normally treated and planned under the rubric of troop-community relations. The positive activities have entailed initiative and imagination; among a wide variety, a few examples may suffice. In West Germany, each year "Operation Kinderlift" transports West Berlin children by military aircraft to visit friends, relatives, and American families in

West Germany. In Austria, where medical practice is to treat certain respiratory diseases by exposure to rare atmosphere, the ill are commonly taken in American aircraft for "medical flights." In the Christmas season, particularly in Germany and Italy, the Commander in Chief of U.S. Forces in Europe conducts a massive food distribution program; delivery is in military vehicles, and military personnel participate in related ceremonies; naval forces under the Commander in Chief for the Eastern Atlantic and Mediterranean even deliver the food to Italian and Greek islands on warships, complete with ceremonial shore visits; while in Italy, the Italian equivalent of Santa Claus lands on village squares by helicopter and distributes toys. For many years, American military commands operated German youth organizations, constructing camping and other recreational facilities and organizing activities. The Armed Forces also participate actively in disaster relief, as, for example, following the Dutch floods of 1953 and the Po Valley flood of 1954. More recently, U.S. military forces played a key role in the rescue and rehabilitation operations after the earthquake that largely destroyed Skoplje, Yugoslavia, and in the earthquake at Agadir.

To believe that such positive psychological operations serve American foreign policies is very much an act of faith, since scholarship still knows little of how foreign public attitudes are shaped and still less of how they can be effectively brought to bear upon the policy decisions their governments make. Very likely this varies according to the élite structure of different countries and is most strong in those countries where the power of governmental leaders to act is habitually circumscribed and guided by a strongly based public opinion.

Now, the execution of psychological operations and troop-community relations cannot in itself be construed as a "representative" duty, for the larger part of such activities does not depend upon negotiative or advisory contacts between U.S. military representatives and host countries.

But the approval and the coordination of many of them does depend upon such contacts. Thus, "negative" activities designed to prevent incidents between troops and host-country civilians are frequently handled through binational Troop–Community Relations Committees. In France, a committee representing the French Defense Ministry and the U.S. Embassy is active in resolving frictions. Again, the host country participates actively in carrying out the "Operation Kinderlift" and Christmas food distribution program. For these programs, extensive binational staff and operational coordination and planning are required. The execution of disaster relief operations imposes on the top military staffs in each country—MAAG's, attachés and major military commands—the need to work with a wide range of cabinet-level agencies in the stricken country. Thus, we see that the proliferation of American psychological operations and troop–community relations activities has greatly increased the tasks of military representation and fostered the growth in the size of our military staffs abroad.

The European experience in psychological operations and troop-community relations has been applied as a matter of course in the less developed areas, but, as we shall see, the problems of security and modernization in the less stable areas such as Southeast Asia necessitated the development of far more novel military means of action and influence.

Coalition Planning

Every American officer who serves in an international command represents the United States in very real and specific ways. Today, most service abroad is under coalition command, and coalition problems are the American officer's bread and butter, although only at the level of combined (international) headquarters are the international contacts frequent. In Europe alone, there are about ten such headquarters. The character of the officer's representation reflects a combination of his American cultural background, the specific American politico-military perspectives that comprise his professional training, and the international flavor his viewpoint takes on because of job experience and job loyalty. The first two influences normally predominate, but we can recall an American four-star general cautioning his American subordinates to overcome their national biases and, "whenever JCS [Joint Chiefs of Staff] directives allow," to interpret their planning tasks so as to strengthen NATO authority. Coalition officers work on international teams, and their intimate day-to-day influence on foreign colleagues can be more meaningful and durable than any other form of military representation. And, too, the perspectives they themselves derive from this association can importantly shape the character of their representation as they rise to higher positions of responsibility.

The highest form of coalition representation is, of course, that of the senior American officer commanding an international headquarters. His duties are often as much diplomatic as military. The tasks facing Eisenhower, Gruenther, or Norstad, for example, in allocating key commands by nationality, in exhorting adequate contributions of national forces, and in urging adequate military draft legislation were as much diplomatic as military. (The general problem of military representation in international commands is discussed in Chapter 5 by Ben Moore.) The point to make here is that in a period of protracted military effort, multinational commands require our senior officers to have a high degree of political understanding.

Mutual Security and Military Representation Abroad

The United States maintains Military Assistance Advisory Groups (MAAG's) to carry out its military assistance functions abroad in about sixty-five nations. It provides minor military assistance to another twenty states where MAAG's are not maintained. This program thus embraces more countries than any other military activity save the attaché program; in numbers, the officer representatives on MAAG's exceed the attachés by at least ten to one. More than 9,000 military personnel (4,000 officers and 5,000 enlisted men) serve in MAAG's abroad, of whom about 7,000 perform training functions and another 2,300 advisory and administrative tasks. Typically, the head of a MAAG mission is a general or flag officer, and the senior officer of each service has diplomatic status. There have been indications from the Office of the Secretary of Defense that the MAAG's, as well as United States military headquarters abroad, have passed their peak in size and that significant reductions will be made as part of a general retrenchment reflecting modifications in United States foreign policy. We hazard the guess that, if so, these will not be permanent, but simply reflect a low point in the cycle of international tension.

The essential purposes of the Military Assistance Program as prescribed in the still-valid wording of the early legislation (the Mutual Defense Assistance Act of 1949 and the Mutual Security Act of 1951) were to make direct contributions of military end-items (vehicles, guns, etc.) to countries whose defense served our interests, and to provide training in their maintenance and use. With respect to countries crucial to our defense, the military-assistance function gradually broadened out of necessity to assure general combat readiness. Training even in the use of individual end-items can be sizable, as in the training of complete crews to man United States warships transferred to foreign navies. Since the publication of the Report of the Draper Committee, which, in 1958–59, at President Eisenhower's direction, reviewed the entire military assistance program, the Department of Defense has required that, as a collateral aim, the military assistance program encourage the use of indigenous forces in public works and other activities helpful to economic development.

This corollary interest was recognized, for example, in the Summary Presentation to the Congress of the Mutual Defense and Assistance Programs for Fiscal Year 1964, which points out the contribution of its training programs through "civic action and public safety programs which stress the civic responsibility of indigenous military forces . . . and contribute to economic and social development." In reality, however, the Military Assistance Program remains essentially focused on military training.

The Military Assistance Program grew out of the Greek-Turkish Aid Program, the "Truman Doctrine," by which the United States took over from the United Kingdom the obligation to bolster the defenses of those countries in the face of Soviet pressure. Since the early 1950's, when economic assistance became a relatively permanent arm of United States policy, the Military Assistance Program has been budgeted and planned as a coordinate part of our over-all assistance and supervised by the civilian aid agency. The main categories of over-all assistance throughout the 1950's included economic and technical assistance, military assistance, and defense support. In 1961, the categories of aid were fundamentally redefined. Military assistance was retained and confirmed by a separate Congressional Act; defense support, however, was eliminated. Defense support was assistance to strengthen the economic base of countries that had assumed the burdens of military preparedness through bilateral agreement with the United States. In the absence of defense support, their economies would be retarded or unbalanced. In 1961, all projects in the defense support category were absorbed into one or the other of the new aid categories of development loans and grants, and supporting assistance. Defense support had always been difficult to define, since some projects made contributions to economic development and others to military security. In 1964, supporting assistance was grouped along with the categories of military assistance and the contingency fund under the rubric of strategic assistance. It included economic aid to support a military burden and assistance either in return for the granting of base rights to prevent emergency economic instability or as an alternative to exclusive economic dependence on Sino-Soviet aid.

Military and Nonmilitary Considerations

In the first years after World War II, United States foreign aid was primarily nonmilitary. As a result of the Korean War, the major rearmament of the United States, and the build-up of NATO, military assistance greatly exceeded economic aid between 1950 and 1954, reaching a peak of almost $6 billion a year. Since then it has never exceeded $2 billion a year, averaging through the remainder of the decade about half the total aid budget and in later years constituting about one-third. (*See* chart, "Trend of Appropriations of Foreign Assistance," p. 149.)

As the aid budget continues to rise, it has been devoted more and more to economic development. Both in proportion to the cost of supporting United States forces and in absolute terms, military assistance has declined far more rapidly.

Meanwhile, the regional emphasis in military assistance shifted drastically (as it already had in economic aid). The initial cross-over point occurred in 1957 when more than 50 per cent went to the less developed countries; in 1963, 75 per cent went to areas other than Japan and Europe. Within the underdeveloped areas of the world, it has been sharply concentrated as well. In 1963, more than two-thirds of military assistance was going to nine underdeveloped countries. At the same time, the *number* of countries receiving assistance rose to 66. This has meant a vast multiplication in the numbers of military representatives who had to be trained for service in exotic areas. This, of course, reflects a shift in the security threat: in the 1960's, Europe's strength rapidly increased, while the other areas, notably the Far East, which received almost half of United States military assistance, became severely threatened by both aggression and subversion. The Middle East, including Pakistan, received well over 25 per cent of the military-assistance funds, while Europe's share declined to 15 per cent or less (9 per cent, if one deducts the United States contribution to the NATO infrastructure rather than to other countries). It is worth recalling, as we take note of this fundamental shift, that the United States had by the early 1960's contributed some $18 billion in military assistance to NATO allies. Moreover, the United States continued to bear by far the largest share of the costs of construction, maintenance, and operation of the NATO infrastructure. The U.S. share of operations and maintenance costs is about 23 per cent. Our share of construction was about 44 per cent, but that program had neared completion by the early 1960's. In addition, assistance to NATO continued in a new form: the contribution of technological knowledge enabling European countries to produce for themselves material engineered in the United States.

As the regional emphasis in military assistance has shifted, the character of the aid has changed even more. While countries (like Greece and Turkey) facing Warsaw Pact nations continue to require the paraphernalia of modern conventional war, most Asian countries require less sophisticated equipment, and some require the very special weaponry to suppress internal guerrilla warfare. Perhaps the most interesting and instructive example of the need for less sophisticated weapons is India, the newest recipient of military aid, which began receiving emergency deliveries of light weapons in November, 1962. Indeed, India has become one of the nine key countries receiving most of the military-assistance funds.

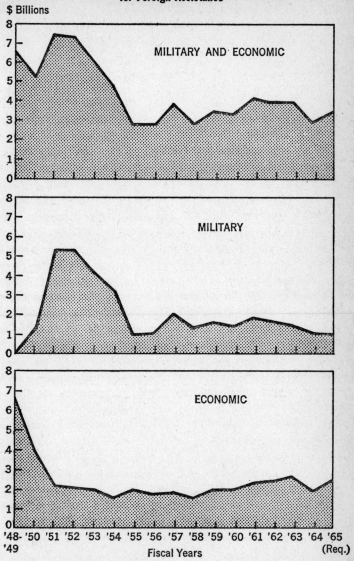

TREND OF APPROPRIATIONS*
for Foreign Assistance

$ Billions

MILITARY AND ECONOMIC

MILITARY

ECONOMIC

'48-'49 '50 '51 '52 '53 '54 '55 '56 '57 '58 '59 '60 '61 '62 '63 '64 '65 (Req.)

Fiscal Years

*Adjusted for Transfers and Other Receipts, Excludes Reappropriations and Excludes Military sales receipts, in FY1964 included $5.3 million in loan accounts not available for obligation.

For Thailand and Vietnam, the emphasis has in recent years been on weapons useful for the suppression of internal subversion and guerrilla warfare.

The Supervision and Management of Military Assistance

The intermixture of military and nonmilitary considerations in foreign aid has been clear from the beginning and makes necessary close coordination of military-aid and other overseas programs, both in Washington and within the embassies abroad. For example, in the Offshore Procurement of Military Assistance Program equipment, the United States Ambassador to Italy succeeded in 1955 in cancelling purchases from factories whose unions were Communist-controlled, an action that caused many workers to change their union membership. Similarly in Vietnam, economic- and military-assistance planning are coordinated by the ambassador to insure that both serve the strategic object of breaking the hold of the Communist Viet Cong upon the countryside.

Significant efforts to strengthen and clarify the policy control, general supervision, and detailed management of the Military Assistance Program have been made since 1959, when action was initiated to carry out the major recommendations of the Draper Committee Report. In that year, the Department of Defense moved to improve administration of the program, notably through long-range planning and closer integration of military assistance with United States and allied defense planning. Two years later, the Foreign Assistance Act of 1961 did much to clarify the means for effectively coordinating military assistance with foreign policy. Not only was the Secretary of State assigned responsibility for the "continuous supervision and general direction" of military assistance, which he carries out mainly by delegation to the foreign-aid administrator; it was also made his responsibility to decide whether there should be a military assistance program for a particular country and what its size should be.

This seems to suggest that while the Secretary of Defense can (and must) recommend what share of the American defense mission should be performed by means of military assistance, and to what countries, his recommendation can be overruled by the Secretary of State. This clarification of their respective responsibilities probably does not settle the problem of differing perspectives, but at least the Congress should be better informed than in the past as to the basis of their respective judgments. The Secretary of Defense will largely base his on strategic concepts and defense plans, the Secretary of State on political evaluations concerning the reliability of allies or the possibility of favorably influencing the uncommitted. Such distinctions tend to become blurred, however, because of the extent of interdepartmental coordination at the working level and the awareness of senior defense officials of political and economic considerations. Thus, Secretary McNamara, in testifying before Congress in 1963 on the Defense Department study of aid to India, remarked that:

> Political and economic factors, including India's efforts to help itself and reduce the vulnerability of the sub-continent by contributing to the resolution of Indo-Pakistan differences, will be given due consideration in arriving at our final recommendations to the President.

A source of continuing difficulty, however, which is not readily apparent, was built into recent legislation. The Mutual Security Act of 1959 and the Foreign Assistance Act of 1961 required that programming and budgeting procedures be established to insure that the Military Assistance Program would "come into direct competition for financial support with other activities and programs of the Department of Defense." The Department of Defense carried this out by introducing a planning system that integrated the determination of military-assistance needs with the over-all military plans that are the basis for establishing the needs of the American forces. However, in compliance with the same Act, military-assistance requirements are coordinated with economic-assistance programs to insure consistency with economic criteria and political objectives, and the economic-assistance and military-assistance programs' budgets are then presented to Congress in one budget package by the AID Administrator. There has been criticism from Congress that the MAP has not been included in the Department of Defense budget. Present Executive procedure has in effect rightly placed the Military Assistance Program in competition with both the United States force requirements and economic assistance, although the first of these are decided in the Pentagon, not in the Congress. Clearly, the Congress prefers the simpler task of reconciling domestic versus foreign military requirements to the more intricate task of reconciling them with political and economic purposes as well. What the Congress now wants seems to contradict the original Congressional intent expressed in the same legislation that the Secretary of State should exercise continuous supervision over military-assistance programs. Nonetheless, President Johnson decided in 1964 to comply with Congressional wishes and incorporate military-assistance costs into the Department of Defense budget.

Planning and Programming Within the Defense Department

Organization of military assistance within the Department of Defense reflects both the intention to keep to a minimum differences of political and military judgment and an effort to streamline management. Within the Office of the Assistant Secretary of Defense for International Security Affairs is located the Office of Military Assistance. This is important, since the Assistant Secretary (whose staff, incidentally, includes representation from the Department of State) handles all national-security and other politico-military matters and can thus insure consistency of military assistance with political purposes. The Office of Military Assistance is headed by a Director, usually a very senior officer (four-star rank), who directs and supervises all Defense Department aspects of military assistance, State Department policy control being the main function excluded.

Sharing in the planning and supervision of military assistance with this office are two overseas organizations, the Unified Commands and the Country Teams. Almost all MAAG's are grouped under the direction of either the Commander-in-Chief Europe (whose responsibility includes North Africa), Commander-in-Chief South (for Latin America), Commander-in-Chief Pacific, or Commander-in-Chief Middle East, Africa and South Asia. It is the job of these commanders to coordinate military-assistance plans with plans for their area and to see that Washington directives concerning military assistance are carried out. The Unified Commanders play a particularly vital role in comparing gross requirements of the nations within their command areas in order to identify net deficiencies that will have to be met through military assistance rather than self-help.

The Country Team is a committee of officers in the U.S. embassy in each country, headed by the Ambassador, and including the Chief of the Operations Mission of the AID agency, the Chief of the Military Assistance Advisory Group, and the Public Affairs Officer. Its purpose is to insure at the field level the consistency between foreign policies and military assistance that State Department policy guidance and review is intended to provide in Washington.

The Unified Commanders and the Country Teams, in coordination with the three military departments, are required to prepare five-year time-phased military-assistance plans and to develop from them annual programs and budgets for submission to the Congress. This planning process is time-consuming and complex. Basic guidance as to political and economic objectives is provided by the National Security Council, the Department of State, and a Mutual Security Objectives Plan prepared by the Joint Chiefs of Staff. For the five-year plans, a Basic Planning Document is then formulated setting forth the guide-lines and order of magnitude of forces within which to plan. The Unified Commanders, drawing together MAAG recommendations, then submit detailed military-assistance proposals and incorporate them in their long-range military plans. Working closely with the Office of Military Assistance, the military departments then check out the pricing, availability, and procurement aspects, which are reviewed again by the Secretary of Defense and the Assistant Secretary for International Security Affairs from the political and economic points of view. A formal review is conducted in coordination with other departments and agencies. The Joint Chiefs of Staff, in preparing the Mutual Security Objectives Plan and reviewing the Unified Commanders' plans, provide advice and review from a strategic viewpoint. Based on these five-year plans, the annual military-assistance budget is prepared, using a similar cycle of guidance, recommendations and review (see chart, "Military Assistance Screening Process," p. 156).

In preparing his country plan, the MAAG representative in effect acts as an arbitrator among the requests of the recipient country, his own professional judgment, and the restraints imposed by higher headquarters. His planning duties include advising the recipient country while it prepares its list of desired end-items and advising higher commands on the recipient's capacity to use the equipment requested.

Large as the annual appropriations for military assistance are, they are much smaller than they would be if foreign governments were given all the items for which they asked. The screening process is, indeed, elaborate, and, while it is generally considered tight by those who participate in it, there is no assurance that the Secretary of Defense, the AID Administrator, the Director of the Bureau of the Budget, or the President may not cut the allocations even further, for reasons that go beyond military determinations of need. Once the budgetary ceilings are imposed, the planning stages must be repeated. New planning guidance is provided the subordinate headquarters, and they submit revised plans conforming to the budgetary guide-lines imposed.

Seven to eight months normally elapse before the first item is shipped or the first contract placed, and it may be another two years before some more complex end-items finally reach the recipient country. Thus, from the first request by a recipient country to the receipt of the last approved item, more than three years may have elapsed. This suggests how great are the requirements for foresight and advance planning that fall upon our military representatives abroad and on the officials in Washington to whom they report, and how complex and finely adjusted must be the administrative mechanism through which they operate. Their collective task in organizing data for Congressional judgment on the need for a military-assistance program whose effectiveness may not be felt for two or three years is a difficult one. However, it is precisely because a future war would probably not permit the United States or its allies time to mobilize that this protracted preparedness effort must be made to meet crises as yet only dimly perceived.

Offshore Procurement

Not all the funds appropriated by Congress for matériel under the military-assistance programs are for goods produced in the United States. Some of the money is spent overseas under the Offshore Procurement Program. When an item can be purchased more cheaply or delivered more promptly from abroad, or when it assists in developing an overseas mobilization base, contracts may be placed for offshore procurement. The greatest amount of money has been spent under this program in France, with Great Britain and Italy ranking second and third.

Military Missions and "Special-Name Missions"

In Latin America, there are about a dozen American single-service military missions that long pre-date the MAAG's. The tasks of all these missions pertain to training, though the character of the training varies from country to country. Mission representatives act as advisers to general staffs, teach in service schools, or act as training advisers. After the Military Assistance Program was established, the United States concluded special agreements with the Latin American countries where these missions existed to permit the assignment of MAAG duties to the missions in addition to their training responsibilities.

The military-assistance organizations in Greece, the Philippine Islands, Saudi Arabia, Thailand, and Turkey also have designations other than MAAG. The Greek mission, for example, is called the Joint United States Military Assistance Group. These variations are due simply to the laws or special agreements under which they were first established. Their functions and control are exactly the same as the MAAG's.

The Military Attaché

Historically, the ambitious career officer has not sought assignment as an attaché. However, this duty has been sought by officers with a flair for military intelligence, languages, and refined living, so the development of an effective group of attachés has not

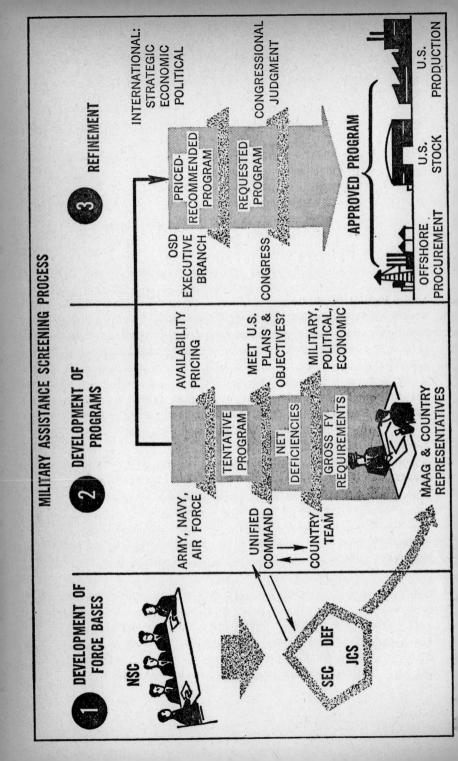

MILITARY ASSISTANCE SCREENING PROCESS

1 DEVELOPMENT OF FORCE BASES

NSC

SEC DEF
JCS

2 DEVELOPMENT OF PROGRAMS

ARMY, NAVY, AIR FORCE

UNIFIED COMMAND
COUNTRY TEAM

AVAILABILITY PRICING

TENTATIVE PROGRAM

MEET U.S. PLANS & OBJECTIVES?

NET DEFICIENCIES

MILITARY, POLITICAL, ECONOMIC

GROSS FY REQUIREMENTS

MAAG & COUNTRY REPRESENTATIVES

3 REFINEMENT

INTERNATIONAL:
STRATEGIC
ECONOMIC
POLITICAL

CONGRESSIONAL JUDGMENT

OSD
EXECUTIVE BRANCH

PRICED-RECOMMENDED PROGRAM

CONGRESS

REQUESTED PROGRAM

APPROVED PROGRAM

OFFSHORE PROCUREMENT

U.S. STOCK

U.S. PRODUCTION

been prevented. The fact is, though, that the attaché positions were not regarded as plums, particularly by the majority of officers who lacked both interest and private incomes. Furthermore, since the American intelligence system as a whole operated on a shoestring, most officers did not regard attaché duty as important.

Since World War II, the entire American intelligence service has been put on a highly professional basis, and military intelligence has shared in this revolution. The Central Intelligence Agency, the Bureau of Intelligence and Research of the State Department (both formed after World War II), and the intelligence divisions of the military services grew apace, in both close coordination and competition. The creation of a Defense Intelligence Agency in 1961, while not applauded everywhere within the military services, was but one tribute to the new exalted status of military intelligence.

In this environment, military attaché duty came to be regarded as highly important. The process of selection and the perquisites that go with it have both professionalized the duty and made it more attractive; it is now possible for the most able officers to be made available for the duty and to be content to participate. Attaché duty still is not compulsory. But where the initiative for the assignment once rested entirely with the individual, selection of officers who have not volunteered is now often made by the "career managers" to insure fulfillment of the best professional qualifications, and the uninterested officer must in such cases take specific action if he wishes to decline the choice. The senior attaché of each service must today be a War College graduate, and the education, social adaptability, and responsibility of the officers and their wives are criteria for selection as well. Once the man is selected, he is carefully schooled: he is sent to language school for intensive study; he also receives four months' training at the Defense Intelligence School, which serves to stimulate not only his intellectual curiosity but his understanding of how he can be most effective in gathering information. Once on station, he is not financially inhibited from doing an effective job. Where once military men believed the scale of supplementary allowances allotted to the Department of State more generous than theirs, they know that the situation is now reversed. Attachés receive liberal entertainment and maintenance allowances, a source of envy and dissatisfaction to many State Department personnel.

The attaché's duties are invariably both representative and reportorial. But how he carries them out, particularly the reporting functions, varies drastically, depending on whether he is serving in a Communist or free-world nation.

In a Communist country, the attaché's "hosts" tell him nothing. Only rarely will he be allowed to observe maneuvers, visit military bases, or even travel in large areas of the countryside. Information about military units is almost never available in the press. Yet he must collect information about military capabilities and weaknesses, including information about industrial contributions to military strength, the communications and transportation systems, and key military personnel. His task is therefore a difficult one. He can perform it only by painstakingly accumulating small shreds of evidence. He is aided in the task, however, by the possibility of pooling evidence with the attachés from embassies of other free-world countries. Furthermore, there are areas of overlapping intelligence responsibilities and knowledge among United States agencies. For example, while the Department of State is responsible for gathering over-all economic information, the military attachés collect economic data of direct military concern. It is possible to share and compare much of this information.

In non-Communist nations, the military attaché has precisely the same reporting mission: to determine military capabilities and weakness. But access to military facilities is far less restricted, data is available in publications, and it is often possible to establish close informal relations with staff officers of the host country, which eases the collection process. Among allied nations, the exchange of information is, of course, formalized and relatively comprehensive.

In all countries, the military attaché also performs ceremonial representative duties on behalf of the ambassador. The cocktail and dinner circuit, although in part ceremonial, affords the attaché opportunities to gather tidbits of information. Even in Communist posts, he is occasionally able to exploit differences among the bloc countries, increasingly so as Soviet control over the bloc has loosened.

The military attaché is responsible not only to his intelligence superiors in the Pentagon, but to the ambassador as well. The latter can assign him reporting as well as ceremonial tasks. In instances of conflict, he must comply with the ambassador's orders, at the same time notifying his military superiors of the conflict. However, military attachés are selected for their tact, and relations with ambassadors are normally cooperative and congenial.

An important restraint on the attaché's performance is the limited size of his staff. The representatives of the three services in any one embassy together seldom add up to more than five or six. Where there is a MAAG, its size affords a greater potential access to information, but this source is sometimes not fully tapped, either because MAAG personnel lack intelligence training, since such work naturally comes second to the performance of the MAAG mission, or because extensive use of MAAG personnel for such purposes might be an obstacle to performance of military-assistance inspection duties. MAAG's, however, have a substantial justification for openly requesting certain kinds of information, since foreign governments cannot obtain military assistance from the United States without indicating the deficiencies they hope this assistance will meet.

One may well ask, therefore, why it is necessary to keep military attachés in any capital in which a MAAG is operating. One answer is that it is up to the attaché to get, if he can, a whole picture of the military capabilities of the country. Officers assigned to the MAAG are entitled to ask only for information needed to evaluate requests for military assistance. Equally important, the MAAG is temporary, while the attaché remains as long as diplomatic relations between the United States and that nation exist. We are reminded of the impermanence of MAAG's by the termination of the mission to Cuba in March, 1958, and by Cambodia's cancellation of military assistance late in 1963.

There are about 400 military officers now serving as military attachés. Slightly less than half of these are assigned by the Department of the Army.

Attaché service is not a career line, nor is there any special effort to assign men who have specialized in intelligence problems. There are two reasons for not setting up a specialized career pattern: first, only a man who has had fairly recent command responsibilities and a working knowledge of the most recent developments in military technology and doctrine is likely to be efficient in evaluating the units of a foreign country's armed forces that he is permitted to inspect; secondly, an attaché is likely to be unable to win the confidence of the best professional officers of the country where he is stationed, and to gain the additional knowledge that comes from having won that confidence, unless he can impress them with the fact that he, too, is a real professional. These reasons, of course, are less applicable to service in Communist countries, where a good case can be made for the advantages of language and espionage skills. However, such values are probably offset by the fact that career specialists would soon become known to host countries and easily made expendable by exposure techniques, in which the Communists are quite adept.

COUNTERINSURGENCY FORCES

Just as psychological operations and troop-community relations have led to enlarged functions for our military staffs in Europe, so have the MAAG's in certain Asian countries exposed to Communist military pressure had to broaden their responsibilities because of new and unprecedented military functions. Of these, counterinsurgency and civic action are the most significant.

In earlier times, counterinsurgency forces would more properly have been thought of simply as a special kind of troops rather than as military representatives. This was before American forces trained in counterinsurgency assumed important advisory roles in Vietnam, Thailand, and Laos as well as responsibilities for training foreign personnel. Formed in 1952 as the Special Forces Groups, these troops were originally trained to land behind enemy lines in wartime in order to train native personnel in guerrilla and resistance activities. Their doctrine during the early 1950's was based on World War II experience; it spurned the idea that guerrilla action should be political in technique and aimed instead at utmost military efficiency, designed simply to support the military objectives of conventional American forces.

When the United States in 1954 took over the French commitment to protect Vietnam, Laos, and Cambodia against Communist guerrilla incursions, American Special Forces personnel became advisers on how to fight guerrillas; this made sense since some of the tactics of guerrilla and of counterguerrilla action are quite similar. In the process, they began the hard task of absorbing the knowledge the British had acquired in Kenya and Malaya, the French in Indochina and Algeria, and the Filipinos at home. They began to acquire a new appreciation for the necessity of wooing the villagers (upon whom guerrillas rely for food and intelligence) and of urging upon governments the measures of protection and reform that would win their allegiance. In coping with the basic task of severing the ties between villagers and Communists, they have had to acquire skills of tact and diplomacy and to deal with the essentially political problem of alleviating concrete grievances. Much of the conceptual development of the politico-strategic framework for counterinsurgency has fallen, indeed, not on guerrilla-warfare specialists but upon military psychological-operations planners, State Department policy-makers, and a new coterie of interested scholars.

Meanwhile, Special Forces personnel began to train significant numbers of foreign troops in guerrilla and counterguerrilla warfare, and in Vietnam to engage selectively in combat alongside native troops. Special Forces personnel had long been skilled in a variety of the rudimentary skills needed to live "off the land." These include certain crafts useful to village life, such as making ammunition, minor surgery, sanitation measures, improvised construction, and water-source location. They soon found themselves performing services for the peasants that well served the political aim of winning over the countryside. As other military organizations began to build a more comprehensive approach to the problems of economic development and modernization, Special Warfare personnel were able to contribute to such operations in situations where active guerrilla warfare demanded their combat skills. As it became clear that counterinsurgency was not simply a combat task, it was found necessary to augment Special Forces units with psychological-operations and civic-action personnel, as well as to adopt concepts developed by the latter.

When so augmented and used in a counterinsurgency role, Special Forces units are known as Special Action Forces. There are about 5,000 Special Forces and Special Action troops. Those not engaged in training and advisory functions in crisis areas are based at Fort Bragg, North Carolina, and Bad Tolz, Germany, and in Okinawa and the Canal Zone.

CIVIC ACTION

Civic action is one of the newest (and yet in a sense one of the oldest) forms of military activity. In the bureaucratic language of the budgetary presentation to the Congress, it consists of "joint military-economic projects, such as construction of roads, communications and sanitation facilities, public health and vocational education programs, which are designed to strengthen the civilian economy and improve the living conditions of the people. Local armed forces, supported by military assistance, provide the labor and, as necessary, AID finances the materials." With equal formality but a different departmental perspective, the Department of Defense, according to its 1963 manual, *Military Assistance Program Information and Guidance,* considers civic action to be "the use of foreign military and paramilitary forces on projects useful to the local population in fields . . . which cultivate social and economic improvement." In the informal language of Major General Edward Lansdale, USAF, Retired, who has done by far the most to nurse civic action to maturity, it is, "almost any action which makes the soldier a brother of the people, as well as their protector." In the language of the scholar, it is the use of modernized military élites of less developed countries to participate in the process of nation-building, a process that not only diverts these dynamic military elements from less healthy pursuits to constructive tasks but integrates them into their society and substitutes in the minds of their peoples new and sympathetic images for stereotypes of arbitrary authority.

In what sense has civic action modified the representational tasks of American forces? It has vastly broadened the negotiative and advisory functions of the MAAG's, because significant numbers of civic-action personnel advise and train foreign military personnel to perform unaccustomed nonmilitary tasks. Furthermore, our civic-action officers and enlisted men themselves serve with the military personnel of host countries in positions that bring them into influential contact with the local populace and communities.

The tasks in which they serve include construction and irrigation projects and low-cost economic development plans, as well as programs to assist in detribalization, inculcating a sense of national identity, sponsoring youth activities, and developing community spirit. All these nation-building activities have political implications of great sensitivity and inevitably give rise to innumerable day-to-day problems requiring intimate and frequent work with the governmental staffs of host countries, both civilian and military. And many of the problems that arise are of deep and fundamental import, requiring the closest coordination between the MAAG and the American Embassy staff.

For all these reasons the new instrument of civic action merits detailed examination.

The concept of civic action is remarkably simple. The instructive aspect for assessing the representative role of American officers has been not the basic concept but the demonstrated capacity to organize, find the necessary skills and funds, and obtain the blessings of the United States and the host countries to undertake this novel activity. Like most simple ideas, it was not always so simple as it now seems. It took officers of experience and imagination, interested in things beyond the purely military, to recognize that the armed forces of less developed countries had certain advantages—such as discipline, organizational skill, a high moral code, and technical aptitudes—that could be turned to tasks of economic and political modernization. In many societies, great differences in the level of skill exist between the enlisted man and his civilian counterpart. In Pakistan, for example, 90 per cent of the soldiers can read in a country where average literacy is 20 per cent. Such practical needs as literacy, a disciplined attitude, ambition, and the desire for individual fulfillment through recognition are essential to the modernization of underdeveloped states. The peoples of many of these states are, in basic respects, living in the thirteenth or fourteenth century. Their demands for liberty and equality and the material trappings of the twentieth century can only be self-defeating if the habits that go with them are not acquired.

Recently, a growing group of scholars has added new depth to our understanding of the changing political role of the military profession in such societies. Lucian Pye, for example, has pointed out that as the officer class of underdeveloped countries has shifted from "line" to staff duties, in order to plan for the adjustment of the armed forces to a point where it can incorporate technical skills and equipment, he has inevitably become truly modern in his outlook, and this transformation has elevated his class to the highest levels of society, even in cultures that formerly accorded the lowest status to the military.

It is worth reminding ourselves that the development of this new function has required energy, patience, and imagination on the part of innovating military thinkers. Such initiatives typify the rapidly changing foci of the American Armed Forces.

Origins and Evolution of Civic Action

The notion of civic action as an American task existed in World War II in both psychological-warfare and military-government operations, which had as their purpose the restoration of civil order. American military forces were also extensively used for nonmilitary, chiefly economic, purposes during the Korean War. Its immediate lineage as a cold war instrumentality can, however, best be traced to its use by the Philippine Government to defeat the Hukbalahap insurrections.* Philippine Secretary of National Defense Magsaysay made of civic action an important counterguerrilla concept when he established a Civil Affairs Division and conducted a psychological and economic campaign to wean the villagers from the Communist-led Hukbalahaps and to win over the 'Huks' themselves. Besides assisting them in modernizing their villages, he resettled significant numbers on virgin farmland, using as his operative agency the military-directed Economic Development Corps. It is reported that General (then Lieutenant Colonel) Lansdale, who assisted in this program, coined the term "civic action" in this period. The Philippine example was soon emulated in Burma, Malaya, Laos, and Vietnam. Vietnam, for example, employed its army most effectively beginning in 1954 to re-establish administrative control and to carry out reconstruction in the war-torn border area below the 17th Parallel. As the Draper Committee put it, "In

* For this citation, as well as for much of the factual background on civic action, we are indebted to Harry F. Walterhouse, *A Time to Build: Military Civic Action: Medium for Economic Development and Social Reform* (Columbia, South Carolina: R. L. Bryan, for the University of South Carolina, 1965).

connection with the 'pacification' of newly liberated areas in such countries as the Philippines, Burma, Laos, and Vietnam, the military was the principal tool on which newly formed governments depended not only for establishment of law and order but for civic leadership, local improvements, and development of virgin areas for settlement."

Meanwhile, a number of Latin American countries had seen the value of their military forces as instruments of economic development. Bolivia is a notable example. A drastic socio-economic revolution was begun in 1952, and the country has since used virtually all its military units in productive activities. The army operates a commercial airline, engages in farming, and, since 1955, has directed a Colonial Division to open up Bolivia's eastern territories. Since 1958, this program has been supported by the Department of Defense, with the cooperation of the AID agency. In 1962, the colonization of Bolivia's virgin lands was even placed under the directorship of an American officer.

Civil Affairs and Civic Action

The United States entered the field of civic action largely under the initiative of the Directorate of Civil Affairs, a staff agency of the Department of the Army. This office was re-activated during the Korean War, having been inactive since World War II. With a World War II tradition of similar work and a large reserve strong in the skills of public administration, it soon assumed an interest in civic action, concentrating on it particularly after the impetus and support provided in 1958–59 by the Draper Committee.

The Directorate of Civil Affairs played a significant role in civic action in the Far East. From the experience gained in such countries as Laos and Vietnam, its interest then turned to Latin America. The first United States–sponsored civic action in Latin America got under way in Guatemala in 1960. At the request of President Ydigoras and with the support of the American Ambassador, a civic-action team was dispatched from the United States. It was combined with a Guatemalan team, and very shortly had turned the Guatemalan army to entirely new tasks: building schools, hospitals, and roads, and conducting community-education programs.

By 1963, American specialists, in coordination with Guatemalan civic-action personnel, had prepared and launched a plan to develop the Peten area, a major region of the country.

President Kennedy gave civic action his personal support, and it gained significant official stature with the approval and publication of an National Security Council directive on *Civic Action and Counter-insurgency.*

Combining American Resources for Civic Action

The launching of a civic-action program in Ecuador requiring both MAP and AID funds established the precedent for joint MAP-AID civic-action programs that has since become standard for projects which the Defense Department cannot finance alone. Reportedly, there was initial concern within the AID agency that civic action by the Armed Forces might impinge on AID responsibilities. But the compartmentalization of military, economic, and political functions in recent years has proved impracticable and wasteful in a wide variety of national-security tasks. In the field of civic action, the solution appears to be the careful definition of areas of legitimate interest and of necessary interdepartmental coordination.

There have been problems of coordinating civic action within the military services as well. In Vietnam, where a huge Military Assistance and Advisory Command focuses on the vital struggle to crush the Vietcong, the use of military civic-action detachments has had in turn to be accommodated to the larger strategic concepts (which, from time to time, have had to be changed) jointly developed by the State Department and Joint Chiefs of Staff.

Essentially, military civic action as a part of counterinsurgency has drawn on three strands of military thought and experience: the public-administration and political-modernization perspective of Civil Affairs, the political communications (propaganda) perspective of Psychological Operations, and the "win village support by practical deeds" approach of Special Forces. The result is an experience in informal representative activity at the popular level that should prove invaluable for future American efforts to deal with the problems of revolutionary or unstable societies.

By 1964, United States Civic Action was supporting programs in more than forty countries, not only in Asia and Latin America, but among the new states of Africa as well. In many, the programs are planned entirely by American military personnel in collaboration with host countries; in a few, permanent American civic-action advisers have been assigned. Larger programs are jointly planned with the Agency for International Development and their budgets prepared in that agency. To support this enlarged program, civic action is taught in a number of military schools attended by both American and foreign personnel. Indeed, the military-service schools are an important source of leadership in representative duties.

It is important to take note of the possible difficulties where such modernizing activities are conducted only by military personnel. It is likely that for some years to come the armed forces of underdeveloped countries will play a large role in the process and will therefore be "in politics" whether they wish it or not. If there is a solution to the problem of insuring that military leadership does not inherit the role of political leadership and so defeat their very object of modernization, it would seem to lie not in cutting back military efforts in civic action, but in developing equivalent programs for training civilian political leaders for these countries.

It is too early to judge the effectiveness of civic action. It undertakes to perform a kind of function that, at its broadest, amounts to nation-building. American foreign aid for economic development has been engaged in similar activities, more extensively to be sure, for a number of years without approaching the stage of clarity and hopefulness. We can expect that civic action will have its conceptual and administrative problems as well. It is encouraging, nonetheless, that the military services are approaching the task in an orderly way: research to clarify the function is actually under way within the Combat Development Command, which concentrates on the development of doctrine.

Administrative Control of Counterinsurgency Forces and Civic-Action Teams

The structure for representation within which counterinsurgency and civic-action advisers and detachments operate varies. In most countries, they are administered as part of the Military Assistance Advisory Group. However, where large-scale American military efforts exist (including deployment of combat units) to support threatened countries, as in Taiwan and Vietnam, Military Defense Commands or Military Assistance Commands are established, embracing both assistance and operational functions. In such cases, the counterinsurgency and civic-action functions come under the Defense Commander. Whatever the staff structure for managing counterinsurgency and civic action, the representative tasks that derive from the extensive ramifications of these two functions are uncustomary ones for the typical staff officer, and they add significantly to the number of his representative duties, the volume of his work, and his need of military schooling.

The presence of American troops abroad also involves a number of representative duties which, because of their unglamorous character, receive little public notice. These include the negotiations pertaining to the legal status of American forces on foreign soil, the many claims and criminal actions that must be settled according to the rules of Status of Forces Agreement negotiated with foreign countries, property occupancy and damage problems, arrangements governing American construction on foreign soil, and purchasing arrangements for the local supplying of American forces. In each country, one service is designated as "country representative" to perform these duties, usually by augmenting one of its overseas headquarters. The effective performance of such duties requires knowledge of local laws and customs as well as an appreciation of foreign viewpoints in matters of law, commerce, and industry. Detailed discussion of such matters is beyond the scope of this essay, but any survey of military representation abroad that did not take note of these activities would be incomplete.

Schools and Training for Representation Abroad

What have the Armed Forces been doing to provide our military personnel with the skills needed to perform the wide range of representative duties demanded in the fields of coalition planning, military assistance, attaché duty, counterinsurgency and civic action? All require in some degree education that goes beyond military professionalism narrowly defined.

Although the record is by no means unblemished, the military services have done surprisingly well in meeting these new educational challenges, for military schools are as a matter of course staffed and their curriculums continually re-shaped to meet new skill requirements. It is the exception that a soldier, sailor, or airman enters upon a new career-line or special assignment without schooling. Indeed, the career officer commonly spends one-third or more of his professional life in school. Moreover, military schools today are almost as active in educating foreign as American personnel, usually in the same schools. The importance of the military schools, long recognized within the military services, since 1961 has been given even greater attention with the creation of the position of Deputy Assistant Secretary of Defense for Education.

The Military Assistance Training Program

The Military Assistance Training Program, long an established part of the Mutual Security Program, has performed a staggering task in training foreign personnel at approximately 150 American military schools. By the mid-1960's, the number trained in the United States approached 180,000, while almost 60,000 had been trained at American military schools abroad. This far exceeds the number trained under all American civilian programs, such as the Fulbright program. However, this education is virtually limited to technical training in the use of military end-items, even though those charged with the direction of the program have formally acknowledged the obligation to support civic action, public works, and economic development. Despite this acknowledgment, a recent study by Charles Windle and T. R. Vallance states:

> The Military Assistance Training Program consists of an extensive national effort with considerable political, social, and economic implications as well as military ones. It is suggested that the policies guiding the conduct of this program have not kept pace with changes in international relations and foreign policy objectives.*

* "Optimizing Military Assistance Training," *World Politics*, October, 1962, pp. 91–107.

This is consistent with earlier findings of the Draper Committee.

It is incidentally worth noting that this bias toward narrowly technical training for foreign officers, no doubt natural in the purely technical schools, is reflected in the education of both foreign and American officers at the lower and middle range of schools. The so-called branch schools and General Staff Colleges concentrate on military doctrine, and the officer is not introduced to the political, social, and economic considerations bearing on his duties until he reaches the War College level. By this time many, probably a majority, of officers have already served as military representatives under the handicap of a very limited outlook. Moreover, foreign officers seldom have the opportunity to study such factors except in those American schools that specialize in extra-military subjects, such as the Civil Affairs School. Among the five American War Colleges, only the Naval War College admits foreign officers. The essentially military doctrinal courses of the Command and Staff Colleges, though perhaps suited to their American middle-level official clientele, are in essential respects unsuited to the foreign officers. Many foreign officers reach top positions in their own armed forces or government at a comparatively early age, having acquired in our middle-level schools the needed staff training, but without the broad political and strategic training that is taught only at the War Colleges. The omission of such training deprives the foreign officer of insights into American concepts of politics, law, and social responsibility. The foreign officer therefore often proves politically naive or ruthlessly insensitive to the political needs of his country. Although the United States does not admit foreign students to most of its war colleges, it does compensate to a degree by aiding many countries in establishing their own National War Colleges. In any event, it is clear that the Military Assistance Training Program has served importantly to strengthen the military defenses of many countries, despite the deficiencies we have alluded to.

An exception to the technical orientation is the Military Assistance Institute; unlike the other schooling provided under the Military Assistance Training Program, it is not intended for foreign personnel but for Americans taking up MAAG duties. Practically all American personnel taking up key MAAG assignments attend this school, which is supervised by the Department of Defense, privately operated, and has about 1,100 graduates each year. It deals with the specialized aspects of military assistance within a broadly political and strategic framework. It provides orientation not only in the operations of the MAAG system but in the political structure of countries of assignment and the United States' broad security responsibilities.

The Special Warfare and Civil Affairs Schools

The Special Warfare School and the Civil Affairs School are two among a variety of specialized service schools which conduct courses both for American and for foreign military personnel. The Special Warfare School, located at Fort Bragg, North Carolina, emphasizes psychological operations, guerrilla warfare, and counter-insurgency, while the Civil Affairs School, located at Fort Gordon, Georgia, emphasizes public administration. Both schools, however, teach a special course in civic action (for both American and foreign service men), and their student bodies have many overlapping interests.

The Inter-American and NATO Defense Colleges

These two schools are similar in that they both support collective security organizations (OAS and NATO). However, the Inter-American Defense College is operated by the United States, while control of the NATO College is truly multinational. The orientation of these two schools is also quite different. The NATO Defense College focuses entirely on collective security coalition planning. The Inter-American Defense College, while it also deals with these subjects, concentrates heavily on civic action and the tasks of political modernization. Its student body is predominantly Latin American, and much of its instruction is in Spanish.

Mention should also be made of the United States Army School of the Americas and the United States Air Force School for Latin America, both in the Canal Zone. The first of these now provides instruction in the principles and administration of civic action, in addition to more traditional courses. The latter provides important training in preventive medicine, aimed at bringing such assistance to remote areas. The student bodies are entirely Latin American, all instruction is in Spanish, and the focus is upon the improvement of internal security.

The Defense Intelligence School

Attendance at a four-month course at the Defense Intelligence School in Washington is mandatory for all prospective military attachés. The curriculum ranges widely over the field of national security, as well as intelligence and the attaché's representative duties. Because much of the material taught is sensitive, the school is not open to foreign students. Interestingly, however, wives of students are permitted to attend lectures.

The schools we have so far discussed reveal the degree to which new forms of military representation or the increased peacetime importance of old forms (such as attaché duty) are reflected in new patterns of education. It is worth noting that where American and foreign officers are taught together, strong associations are formed that help effective future performance of representative functions, as these officers meet in later assignments. It is not insignificant that President Park of South Korea and ex-Premier Qassim of Iraq are numbered among such graduates. Moreover, where foreign officers are present, American officers have the opportunity to develop empathy, tolerance, and knowledge that can serve them well in future representative tasks.

Even in many of the schools not attended by foreigners, American military personnel are able to acquire a breadth of knowledge that equips them to appreciate the political and strategic role which military power plays. There is, however, insufficient consistency among schools, and the typical officer is not exposed to the knowledge needed for representative duties early enough in his career. The better schools exercise little direct influence upon the curriculums of the others—except in the Air Force, where many are grouped on one military base under the immediate direction of a single officer whose primary mission is educational.

So far we have described only the specialized service schools.

The capacity of American officers does not rest alone on specialized schooling, however. The more senior representatives (Lieutenant Colonel and above), particularly in coalition planning, MAAG, and attaché work derive their broadest perspectives and qualities for such work from training in the War Colleges, a subject we shall now discuss in the context of their military characteristics.

Characteristics of Senior Military Representatives

The United States has traveled a long way since the day in the 1870's when General Sherman moved the headquarters of the Army from Washington to St. Louis in order to keep the Army out of politics. By moving it to St. Louis, he kept it free to concentrate on what was to be its main task during the next decade or two, the pacification of the West and of its Indian inhabitants. An army so separated from the center of national policy-making was perforce separated from international politics. There was no premium placed on curiosity about either foreign military establishments or foreign policy.

War Colleges and the General Staff

The turn of the century, however, saw a rapid reorientation. The writings of Admiral Mahan, dissatisfaction with the conduct of our armed forces in the Spanish-American War, the entry of the United States into the high politics of the world, particularly in the Far East, and the reforming zeal of Elihu Root in the War Department—all these combined to effect a revolution in the organization of our armed forces and in the professional training of those who were to make military policy. The first decade of the twentieth century saw the Army War College established, parallel to the Naval War College that had been established in the 1880's. It also saw the emergence of a General Staff system. There was no comparable development of a General Staff in the Navy, but the Navy General Board had by 1903 already laid down a long-range building program based on an over-all analysis of the United States' position in world affairs.

What is important for the purposes of our discussion is not how accurate this analysis was but that it shows that for more than 50 years, our military men have regarded it as their professional responsibility to relate recommendations regarding military policy to the political objectives of U.S. foreign policy. The role of the war college in this development is critical, since its curriculum deals more broadly with military problems than the more technical intermediate and lower staff schools.

Until the 1930's, however, war plans were not normally developed on the assumption that the United States would be part of a military alliance including European great powers and operating on the rimlands of Europe and Asia. World War I was seen as an exceptional period. It was only after there was general recognition that the United States would normally have to be a member of a transoceanic alliance that training began to reflect the need for staff officers capable of engaging in coalition military planning.

Lieutenant-General Sir Frederick Morgan, who, as Chief of Staff of the then unchosen Supreme Allied Commander, was charged with planning the Normandy landings, writes in his *Overture to Overlord* that before 1939, "there could hardly have been a single case of a United States Army officer, other than the official attaché, paying more than a formal courtesy visit to any military units or establishments in Europe." His American deputy, Brigadier General Ray Barker, was almost unique in that he "had all his life spent much of his leave in England." As we look back on nearly twenty-five years of combined operations and intimate joint planning, it is well to remember how recently it is that our military establishment has developed the men capable of military planning for an effective coalition.

Without the prior development of the various war colleges, it is difficult to see how our military men could have risen so quickly to their new politico-military responsibilities. While conventional diplomacy was and still is described as an "art," and one that a gifted amateur can best learn on the job, the professional military man came to recognize that staff work, including the kind that must be done abroad, is essential and therefore professionally respectable and appropriate for professional training. The war-college structure was naturally broadened to include the Army Industrial

College (renamed after unification the Industrial College of the Armed Forces), the Air War College, and the National War College.

The National War College has assumed particular importance for interdepartmental coordination abroad, since the student body includes forty representatives of civilian branches of the government and the remaining ninety represent the three military services in equal numbers. The study of international relations looms especially large in its curriculum—indeed, it has played an increasingly large role in all the service war colleges. Finally, the NATO Defense College, mentioned earlier, symbolized the expectation that coalition military planning and operations are continuing tasks for the American military.

The five war colleges set the tone for the intellectual life of the armed services and particularly of those officers with a share in making military policy. Specific training for service on combined or joint staffs, however, comes in an intermediate training institution, the Armed Forces Staff College, set up at Norfolk, Virginia, in 1946.

The armed services have to be staffed at all times so as to avoid being understaffed in war. This is particularly true of the Army, which undergoes especially large expansion in numbers during war, even large-scale limited war. This means that, except in crisis periods, it is efficient to plan military careers so that much of an officer's career, especially if he is marked for promotion to policy-making levels, may be spent in school. Under these circumstances, once the need for a given skill is recognized and an efficient way of developing that skill is discovered, it is relatively easy for the armed services to equip themselves with the new skill.

According to sample surveys made for the Department of Defense in 1962, 7.4 per cent of Army officers held the Master of Arts degree and 3 per cent the doctorate or Ll.B. degree. The equivalent figures for the Air Force were 7 per cent and 2.3 per cent. According to the Deputy Assistant Secretary of Defense for Education, about 70 per cent of the 1964 class of the United States Military Academy entered graduate school upon graduation, 40 per cent of these in the social sciences. These figures indicate a major growth in higher military education since World War II, particularly since most graduate degrees are now sponsored and financed by the services. This advanced social-science training of a small group of younger officers should make them valuable both in Pentagon staff work in foreign military affairs and in military representation abroad.

Whether or not this training program, in service schools and civilian universities, sets a standard the Department of State should be permitted to emulate, no one suggests that our professional military ought to have less training for policy jobs in order to prevent an overmilitarization of our foreign policy. On the other hand, the need for civilians who understand the problems of the military is at least as great as the need for soldiers who comprehend the problems of statesmen, diplomats, and industrial mobilizers. This need is qualitatively well met by the National War College, but not in numbers sufficient to the need. The growth of interest and research in military policy in the universities may eventually help, but bringing a larger number of professional diplomats and civil servants into the war colleges could probably meet the existing need more quickly.

Overseas Experience

In an earlier period, the Navy showed more concern with world politics than the Army. By 1964, the Army had been maintaining forces abroad on a large scale for nearly twenty-three years. It also had the responsibility for the government of Germany and Japan. Among the three services, it probably has the largest reservoir of men with experience and understanding of the types of problems in which political and military considerations are mingled.

So substantial a proportion of the young military officer's service today is spent in overseas assignment that it would be unusual for a man selected to be a senior military representative not to have previously served abroad in some representative capacity. From the point of view, therefore, of both training and experience, he is likely to be well equipped for such service.

Attitudes Toward Staff-Type Assignments

Military men go where they are sent; unlike civilian government employees who may feel free to return to their businesses or law practices or universities when the novelty wears off or the going gets rough, military men are "in for the duration" and must be prepared to live with the consequences of their decisions. Good military representation requires qualities additional to those expected of every professional officer, however, and must depend on representational duties being made sufficiently attractive so that the better officers do not try to avoid them.

It has now become a requirement that any officer who hopes to reach the higher grades seek out staff work and representational duties. Indeed, senior officers have been officially enjoined to work in such novel fields as counterinsurgency; prior service on a joint staff is mandatory for promotion to General or Flag Officer rank. On the other hand, long service in fields other than war planning and command duty can be costly to an officer's career. Furthermore, an able and ambitious officer may be apprehensive about an assignment that is regarded as abnormal, one in which performance is difficult to evaluate by promotion boards or in which the officer's efficiency report is written by a civilian superior.

Before turning to consider what the special characteristics of the military representative are, let us examine some of those that are frequently attributed to officers. The military officer is taught to be thorough, to discover what the "facts" are, and to act promptly. The assumptions that things are either so or not so, either black or white, and that it is a virtue to act promptly are proper ones wherever inaction is worse than any proposed alternative of action. Men of action will regard a given objective as desirable or undesirable, and many military men find themselves impatient with their civilian colleagues who equivocate or hesitate. It is in truth difficult to make clear military plans on the basis of cloudy policymaking.

If preparedness is a good thing, then, at the moment of crisis, the military man who finds his country something less than absolutely prepared is likely to counsel the civilian political leader to give him more time. But if the decision is made to fight, then political limitations on the conduct of war may appear to him as proof of the politician's "characteristic" deviousness, vacillation, or infirmity of purpose. He may qualify his advice to his civilian superiors by prefacing it with the phrase, "speaking from a purely military point of view." This may be anything from an assertion of monopoly of insight on his part or an advance denial of responsibility in case his recommendation is ignored, to a real modesty regarding the limits of his contribution in a complex situation in which the military factor is only one of many.

The civilian is sometimes said to be a horizontal paper-shuffler, while the soldier is a vertical paper-shuffler. The soldier gives orders and takes orders; he asks for advice and receives recommendations from his subordinates and he gives advice and makes recommendations to his superiors. The civilian, on the other hand, may be less conscious of hierarchy and lines of authority. In his horizontal consultations, he may, in the eyes of his military colleagues, even verge on being indiscreet.

The military man is likely to want to base all his plans on the most serious contingency, while the civilian will want to "keep the future open" and delay as long as possible a choice that involves acceptance of the most serious contingency as the only one for which plans should be made. The same sort of consideration may lead the military man to oppose any dispersal of the nation's main striking power to accomplish some intermediate foreign-policy objective. To him, tying down military force in "penny packets" at various trouble spots around the world may only permit the main opponent to deal with American force in detail.

For the purpose of the present analysis, however, it is not the characteristics of professional military officers in general but the characteristics of a rather small group of staff-type officers that are important. It is probably true that the staff officer or military representative abroad, with long contacts at policy-making levels with complex and stubborn problems, finds it easier than most officers to see the virtue of letting time and inaction occasionally work for him, of horizontal paper-shuffling, of sometimes paying a modest military price to increase the chance of a major political gain. On the other hand, even when he has learned to restrain his compulsion to act, he is likely to retain a willingness to act that makes him a healthy member of a policy-making team. Furthermore, the military man's respect for order, protocol, and the virtues of courtesy add to his effectiveness as a representative of his country. So, of course, does his professional military expertise if he is negotiating on a problem that calls it into play.

The American traditional opposition to a separate staff officer corps is firm, but it has not prevented the emergence on a wholly informal basis of a staff officer type. There is a fairly small group of devoted officers who find staff work challenging, who are prepared to accept unique assignments, whatever the implications for their whole career, and who generally seem either to know each other or know of each other. Where the position is not one that requires a senior officer, perhaps for protocol or prestige reasons, this group of officers, some of them fairly junior in rank, have a key role in military representation, especially in NATO activities.

The group of officers who are used in negotiating and representative capacities have one advantage over their civilian colleagues. They are likely to be dealing with foreign military officers whose training and experience parallel their own. They have come to accept the absolute necessity of combined military effort in a way that some of their political superiors have as yet not quite felt and understood. Where it is a matter of indifference from the Washington point of view whether some item is negotiated through civilian or military channels, there may sometimes be cases in which agreement can be reached much more expeditiously and satisfactorily if American military officers who know their foreign opposite numbers quite well are given the task of negotiating.

In two respects, existing practice regarding "the military foreign service," if that name is permissible to describe the American military representatives abroad, anticipated the recommendations made by the Wriston Committee for the improvement of American diplomacy. Separate career programs have not been set up for the Pentagon and for military missions abroad, as have so long been the case for the Department of State and its Foreign Service Officers. Military officers for Washington and foreign assignments are drawn from the same pool, and the same type of preparation and skills are thought desirable for work on coalition and foreign military affairs wherever the work is done. Also, the practice of the military departments in professional schooling goes further than even the most radical proposals for a more professional Foreign Service.

So far, we have discussed the problem of military representation as if it consisted solely of finding the right men to execute the right policy. This assumption is reasonable in the case of the military attaché whose task is fairly clearly defined, but the Military Assistance Program, civic action, and counter-insurgency have raised a number of additional problems. Whatever the policy is and however capable such representatives are, that policy ought to be transmitted to them and to their civilian colleagues abroad in terms that are both clear and consistent if they are to be effective representatives.

Efforts to Coordinate in Washington

Although the President's constitutional powers are ample to assure clear and coherent policy if they are fully exercised, the size and ponderousness of the Washington governmental machine, the traditional weakness of the Cabinet as an instrument of coordination and the traditional independence of the executive departments means that interdepartmental differences tend to remain unsettled until they reach the Cabinet or White House level. The President's time to attend to detailed matters being limited, only major differences can be sent up to him for final decision. Minor differences, including differences of interpretation of major decisions, may remain unresolved until they become inflamed.

Unity of policy is further threatened by the vigilance of Congressional committees in questioning the President's departmental subordinates and in exploiting their right to military advice by the Joint Chiefs of Staff. Interdepartmental and interservice differences that have been finally and painfully settled may be opened up again if Congressmen, in their questioning, drive a wedge between the public positions of the President and his subordinates.

As a Cabinet-level committee, the National Security Council is a major device for minimizing the built-in causes of friction in the politico-military field. So is the Bureau of the Budget, as a Presidential staff agency operating on a government-wide basis.

Since the abolition of the Operations Coordinating Board in 1961, new means for coordinating the execution of policy abroad have had to be created. The so-called Task Forces then became the main mechanisms for overseeing the execution of policies approved by the President. (The names for these expediting devices vary from one administration to another. The Task Force is an interdepartmental committee usually headed by a State Department official of the Assistant Secretary level, to concentrate on a specific, urgent policy area such as Berlin or Vietnam.) A similar but more high-powered mechanism used in the Kennedy and Johnson administrations was the interdepartmental committee at the Cabinet level, known as the Special Group (Counterinsurgency), which provided the guidance to develop for threatened countries a so-called Internal Defense Policy. This committee was used to sharpen the forces of all military and nonmilitary instrumentalities assisting countries in defeating guerrilla warfare.

Foreign policy, military policy, defense mobilization policy, and financial policy are, through these devices, supposed to be kept in harmony. The International Security Affairs Committee and a host of other more informal interdepartmental committees are meanwhile expected to adjust interdepartmental questions that can be settled at working levels. Coordination is particularly difficult where different departments and services have resources as well as needs for similar representational tasks such as intelligence or information collection. Within the military services, the creation of a Defense Intelligence Agency has made possible some streamlining and economy in the allocation to the different services of the kinds of intelligence each should collect.

All this coordinating machinery simplifies the problem, but it does not eliminate it. In fact, the more perfect the State–Defense–AID agency coordination in the foreign-aid program and the more perfect the government-wide coordination of budgetary policy, the greater the chance of a direct confrontation between those who want to increase appropriations to alleviate problems of foreign policy and those who want to reduce them to ease problems of domestic policy.

Similarly, the more perfect the coordination within the Department of Defense, the harder it may be to achieve coordination in the field among the members of the country team if it involves overturning or modifying a decision by the Joint Chiefs of Staff. The corporate conception of the JCS implies that modification of JCS policy must be on a corporate basis, too. If the issue is not large enough or clear enough to be passed up to the Cabinet for reconsideration, this particular rigidity may be decisive.

Agreement on a Central Strategic Concept

The problem of coordination in Washington is intimately related to the problem of an agreed central strategic concept. The military man, who believes that detailed military planning is possible only on the basis of clear policy, applies this doctrine to combined military planning. This, he would say, presupposes a consensus on the central strategic concept. Without a clear and agreed statement of policy to which both he and his foreign opposite number can continuously refer, their discussions bog down at every point. To cite a hypothetical example, the question of how extensively a German division ought to be equipped with self-propelled weapons can hardly be discussed unless an agreed central strategic concept indicates how far afield the division may be expected to operate and in how mobile a war.

Of course, if the United States finds itself unable to agree with its allies on the central strategic concept because there is no agreement within the American Government, the consequences are even worse. Problems accumulate in the field that can only be finally settled by having top officials of the allied governments come to Washington or our senior officials go abroad. Frequent visits at ministerial levels may sometimes be evidence of the lack of a clearly defined central strategic concept.

This is also evident in the tendency of foreign military representatives in Washington to go over the heads of American military representatives abroad—particularly respecting NATO matters, since two permanent subordinate organizations of the top-level

NATO Military Committee are in permanent residence: the Standing Group—NATO's executive military committee of American, British and French representatives; and the Military Representatives Committee, which comprises the deputies to the members of the Military Committee, representing all NATO countries except Iceland, which has no armed forces.

It is evident from all we have said that the scope of military representation has continually broadened in recent years, and that there is little likelihood that the nature or size of military representation will become static. The military services are constantly striving to revise strategic doctrines and broaden military education in the effort to keep abreast of new opportunities for the exercise of politically meaningful military representation abroad. Particularly where this representation involves nonmilitary considerations, and it usually does, an effective performance cannot be judged by military criteria alone. It must also be judged on the way it is coordinated with nonmilitary representative activities, recognizing that coordination can be useful only to the degree it is guided by clear national strategic concepts.

5. *American Representation to International and Multilateral Organizations*

BEN T. MOORE

THE GROWTH OF AMERICAN PARTICIPATION IN INTERNATIONAL ORGANIZATIONS

No branch of diplomacy has grown more rapidly since World War II than what is loosely called "multilateral diplomacy." Under this omnibus title fall the activities of thirty-four international and regional organizations in which the United States is a member, and numerous commissions, agencies, and committees affiliated with one or more of these organizations.

The burden of United States representation in international organizations today is, then, considerable. In the year 1963 alone, these organizations and their affiliates held 547 conferences and meetings, the bulk of them overseas. The U.S. Government authorized overseas travel for 2,200 civil servants and 383 "public members" from outside the government to attend these conferences and meetings as accredited representatives of the United States. While the burden falls heaviest on the State Department (819 accredited conference representatives in 1963), virtually every department of government has its share. The Agriculture Department sent 271 official participants to international conferences in 1963; the Agency for International Development, 152; the Commerce Department, 151; the Defense Department, 113; and so on. Multilateral diplomacy today is a government-wide operation, employing virtually all the skills and talents available in the government.

In addition, an increasing number of representatives from various walks of public life are also recruited. A meeting of the World Health Organization, for example, typically will find on the United States delegation a health officer from one of the state governments, a member of the executive board of the American Medical Association, and a leading medical-school administrator. The American labor movement participates regularly in both the government and the workers' delegations to the annual International Labor Conference. The United States Delegation to the United Nations General Assembly has since the war included leading men and women from a variety of political, social, and economic organizations, besides members of Congress. Scientists drawn from virtually all disciplines are regularly accredited as United States representatives to a host of international and multilateral diplomatic gatherings.

The range of multilateral diplomacy covers key security organizations—like NATO, SEATO, and CENTO; a growing number of important organizations concerned with economic policy, trade, money, and development—like GATT, OECD, the World Bank, and the International Monetary Fund; and a galaxy of "technical" organizations concerned with cooperation in every important field of technology and social intercourse—from water pollution to human rights, from coal production to the status of women, from problems of the cocoa leaf to civil liability in the case of accidents involving atomic radiation. These organizations are established by famous treaties or little known informal agreements. Membership varies widely from the almost world-wide roster of the U.N. to a three-power treaty organization like ANZUS (Australia, New Zealand, and the United States). Some are highly organized, with a strong secretariat; others have no permanent organization and meet only infrequently.

Whatever their character, providing effective representation to these organizations constitutes a major problem in the conduct of American foreign relations. Moreover, the emergence of the

United States as a leading world power has resulted in much more intensive American participation. Before World War I, international organizations were almost entirely technical in their functions, designed largely to facilitate technical aspects of trade and commercial relations. The United States joined those in which it was interested, particularly the International Union of American States, the forerunner of the present Organization of American States. In the interwar period came the first attempt to establish a world security organization—the League of Nations. Following her traditional policy of isolation, the United States refused to become a member, although she later established a small liaison office in Geneva.

With the collapse of isolation as a national policy in World War II, the tide of American participation in international organizations began to flow strongly. The character of this participation is very different from that envisaged by those who planned the postwar organization of the world during the war years. They expected that the United States would concentrate her participation in the U.N. and its subsidiary and affiliated organizations. The U.N. continues to absorb a large share of American energies in this field, but the breakdown of great-power cooperation with the Soviet Union after the war made it impossible for the U.N. to ensure world security as its proponents had expected. The United States began to look more and more to regional alliances as a means of strengthening her security. And the intractability of postwar economic problems prevented the International Monetary Fund and other U.N. organs from effecting the world-wide system of trade and payments for which the wartime plans had provided. Regional systems of economic integration and cooperation like the European Economic Community (Common Market) and the Latin American Free Trade Association (LAFTA) developed without American membership, although these bodies were often of great importance to the United States and required high-level representation. Lastly, as modern technology has continued to shrink our world, the scope and activities of the technical organizations—such as those dealing with civil aviation, communications, weather, shipping, internationally traded commodities, fishing and whaling, to mention only a few of the more important—have greatly increased.

Again using conferences as a measure of activity, the Organization for Economic Cooperation and Development (OECD) in Paris was the most active single agency in the American fiscal year 1964, holding more than 140 separate meetings at which the United States Government was officially represented, plus a large number of additional meetings attended by representatives of our permanent delegation. Turning to another region, the organizations that go to make up the Inter-American system—notably the Organization of American States (OAS) and its economic arm, the Inter-American Economic and Social Council and its affiliated committees—held fifty conferences. In terms of man-hours of representation, the United Nations family of agencies, commissions and committees is by far the most demanding: altogether the United States was represented officially at 265 U.N. conferences and meetings in 1963.

But conferences are only one measure of the activity that goes on under the heading of multilateral diplomacy. The 1964 Foreign Service List shows 233 officers, including fourteen ambassadors, concerned with permanent liaison and representation with one or more international or regional organizations. The United States Mission to the North Atlantic Treaty Organization and European Regional Organizations (USRO) in Paris has a permanent staff of eighty-three, including two ambassadors (one for NATO and one for OECD). The United States Mission to the European Office of the United Nations and other International Organizations in Geneva has a staff of fifty-four, including three ambassadors (one in charge of the semi-permanent disarmament negotiations, one in charge of the Kennedy Round of tariff negotiations being conducted by GATT, and one as chief of mission). The United States Mission to the United Nations in New York has a staff of forty-six, including five ambassadors. A staff of twelve supports the United States Ambassador at the United States Mission to the Organization of American States (OAS) in Washington. Another staff of twenty-nine serves the United States Ambassador at the United States Mission to the European Community in Brussels. There are smaller missions in Paris for

Major International Organizations in which the United States Maintains Membership

ANZUS	Australia, New Zealand, United States Council
CENTO	Central Treaty Organization
ECA	Economic Commission for Africa
ECAFE	Economic Commission for Asia and the Far East
ECE	Economic Commission for Europe
ECLA	Economic Commission for Latin America
ECOSOC	Economic and Social Council
FAO	Food and Agriculture Organization of the United Nations
GATT	General Agreement on Tariffs and Trade
IAEA	International Atomic Energy Agency
IA-ECOSOC	Inter-American Economic and Social Council
IBRD	International Bank for Reconstruction and Development
ICAO	International Civil Aviation Organization
ICEM	Inter-Governmental Committee for European Migration
ICJ	International Court of Justice
ICSU	International Council of Scientific Unions
IFC	International Finance Corporation
ILO	International Labor Organization
IMCO	Inter-Governmental Maritime Consultative Organization
IMF	International Monetary Fund
INTERPOL	International Criminal Police Organization
ITU	International Telecommunication Union
NATO	North Atlantic Treaty Organization
OAS	Organization of American States
OECD	Organization for Economic Cooperation and Development
PAHO	Pan American Health Organization
SEATO	Southeast Asia Treaty Organization
SPC	South Pacific Commission
UNESCO	United Nations Educational, Scientific and Cultural Organization
UNGA	United Nations General Assembly
UNICEF	United Nations International Children's Emergency Fund
UPU	Universal Postal Union
WHO	World Health Organization
WMO	World Meteorological Organization

MAJOR INTERNATIONAL ORGANIZATIONS IN WHICH THE
UNITED STATES IS NOT A MEMBER BUT MAINTAINS
AN INTEREST

Arab League
Bank for International Settlements
Colombo Plan
Commonwealth of Nations
Council of Europe
Council for Mutual Economic Aid (members of Soviet bloc)
European Atomic Energy Community
European Coal and Steel Community
European Council for Nuclear Research
European Economic Community
European Free Trade Association
International Bureau of Education
Latin American Free Trade Association
Northern Council
Organization of Central American States
Western European Union

UNESCO, in Vienna for the International Atomic Energy Agency
(IAEA), and in Rome for the Food and Agriculture Organization (FAO), plus selected liaison officers assigned to the
headquarters of the U.N. regional commissions in Santiago (the
Economic Commission for Latin America [ECLA]), Addis Ababa
(the Economic Commission for Africa [ECA]), and Bangkok
(the Economic Commission for the Far East [ECAFE]).

Finally, to backstop this representation in Washington and to
prepare for conferences and meetings, there is a large bureaucracy
in the State Department and in the departments of Commerce,
Labor, HEW, and Agriculture. It is not possible to give with any
precision the magnitude of man-hours in Washington that are
devoted to multilateral diplomacy, because much of the work
makes up only a portion of the duties of the officers involved, but
it is considerable. The Bureau of International Organization
Affairs in the State Department alone has a staff of 167 working
full-time on these matters, and there are offices of regional affairs
in all the State Department regional bureaus. Both the Labor
Department and the Agriculture Department (the Foreign Agri-

cultural Service) have sizable full-time staffs working on international organization work, as does the Department of Health, Education and Welfare.

The Growth and Change of American Interests in Multilateral Diplomacy

The proliferation of international and regional organizations reflects many different interests inside and outside of the government. The degree of official government interest varies considerably from organization to organization and, from time to time, within an organization. The interests of other countries and domestic interests within the United States, not normally associated with foreign policy, have also influenced the pattern of multilateral diplomacy. To appreciate the varied demands for effective representation, it may be helpful to review briefly the wide and shifting range of interests involved.

Right after World War II, the U.N.'s regional commission in Europe, the Economic Commission for Europe (ECE), was a key instrument in our European policy. Initially, the ECE absorbed the work of the committees and organizations concerned with European recovery and reconstruction, which grew out of allied cooperation during the war. This was the brief period when it was hoped that the Soviet Union and its satellites would cooperate in the manifold tasks of European recovery. Accordingly, the United States established a high-level mission to ECE and actively recruited competent people to serve on the ECE secretariat.

While the ECE secretariat became for a time one of the strongest and most useful sources of competent research on European economic matters, the organization itself quickly degenerated into a propaganda forum between the West and the Russians. With the start of the Marshall Plan, United States interest shifted abruptly to Paris and along with it most of the United States' multilateral diplomatic effort. From early 1948 to the present, Western interest in ECE has been desultory, except in the technical committees (coal, steel, electric power, etc.), where interest has been kept alive by a desire to keep in touch with technical developments in Eastern Europe. Political interest in ECE, however, has waned to the point where a single Foreign Service Officer maintains our representational duties in Geneva, backstopped only by part-time work by a few officers in the State and Commerce departments.

It is quite possible that ECE will again become important to the United States as an instrument of multilateral diplomacy in the near future. Together with the General Agreement on Tariffs and Trade (GATT), it is the logical forum in which to try to reconcile East-West trade policies; in fact, a committee for that purpose was established in 1963 with United States support. There is perhaps somewhat more interest among the nations of Western Europe than in Washington in using ECE as a forum for such purposes. In any case, the structure of the organization has remained in operation without interruption. In 1963, there were thirty separate meetings of ECE and its committees at which the United States was represented.

A similar ebb and flow of interest can be traced in other, more important international organizations. Multilateral diplomacy in the realm of military security has probably received the most serious attention from the United States since the war. The hope implicit in the Charter of the United Nations, that Russia and the United States could keep the peace by coming to sufficient agreement on outstanding problems, was short lived, and United States interest in multilateral security diplomacy quickly shifted to instruments of regional cooperation. Through the North Atlantic Treaty Organization (NATO) first, then the South East Asia Treaty Organization (SEATO) and the Central Treaty Organization (CENTO), the United States in the 1950's exercised multilateral diplomacy with vigor and imagination, while there was little serious interest in the U.N. as a security organization.

But by 1960 even here there was a noticeable change. The crisis in the Congo, followed swiftly by a crisis in Cyprus, gave rise to a new interest in the possibilities of the U.N. as a peacekeeping organization, while the combination of growing *détente* with the Russians and the rise of nationalism in France under De Gaulle and in other countries under their new leaders weakened somewhat the effectiveness of the regional security organizations. Of all the areas of multilateral diplomacy, this is the one most in flux today.

The most elaborate and successful exercise of multilateral diplomacy began with the Marshall Plan and continues today in the policies of the Johnson Administration designed to bring about an Atlantic partnership of nations, in which vital decisions affecting not just defense, but also the strength and health of the economies of the Atlantic nations and their relations with less developed countries are truly shared. With considerable persistence, the United States has encouraged as many free countries of Europe as were willing to unite in an association that goes well beyond other international organizations in the intimacy and durability of the relations among member states. The Europeans themselves have designated their grouping a "Community," in order to distinguish it from the organizations that preserve more carefully the formal principles of national sovereignty and independence. Because Europeans felt compelled to build this Community functionally, in stages, by integrating successively more important aspects of their common life, the United States has found itself supporting first the European Coal and Steel Community (ECSC) and later the European Economic and Atomic Energy Communities (Common Market and Euratom)—all designed to knit together the economies of the six member states into a single market and economic union.

The founders of these communities (notably Jean Monnet of France) set themselves as a goal nothing less than a United States of Europe in which a common foreign policy and defense would be added to the common market. This conception has been challenged by another Frenchman, General de Gaulle, who has put forward as an alternative a "Europe of States" which would preserve national sovereignty and resist American predominance. In pursuit of this goal, General de Gaulle has pressed the development of a national "force de frappe," or striking force of nuclear weapons, vetoed the admission of Britain to the Common Market, and evolved a set of independent foreign-policy initiatives.

Undoubtedly, De Gaulle has been responsible for some of the shifts and ambiguities that have affected the twin policies of European Union and Atlantic Partnership, but he did not create the fundamental problems and dilemmas that confront the multi-lateral diplomacy of Europe and the United States, and they will continue after he has left the international stage. NATO has been struggling with the difficulties of adapting an alliance to the impact of nuclear weapons for some years. The multilateral force (MLF), a plan for surface vessels armed with nuclear rockets and manned by crews from several NATO countries, is not the first initiative designed to deal with this problem; nor will it be the last, at least in the form in which it was proposed by President Kennedy at his meeting with Prime Minister Macmillan at Nassau in December, 1962. The rise of the Common Market adversely affected the Organization for Economic Cooperation (OEEC) which had served so well in the Marshall Plan. Although Britain was moving toward a decision to apply for membership in the Common Market, the United States felt compelled to revive the OEEC, to transform it into the Organization for Economic Cooperation and Development (OECD), and, along with Canada, to become a full member, because she recognized the inevitability of a long period of transition before economic problems could be dealt with by an equal partnership of the European Community and the United States.

The European states and the United States are both fully committed to multilateral diplomacy. The Six have relied almost entirely on this new diplomatic technique to develop their own institutions, and the United States has established a large mission headed by an ambassador in Brussels to maintain close diplomatic contact with the European Community, of which she is *not* a member, as well as an even larger mission in Paris headed by two ambassadors to negotiate in NATO and OECD, in both of which she participates actively as a member. If Europe presses forward with the creation of an effective union, this situation will change fundamentally. Relations within the Community will become more like the political bargaining which goes on among regions, states, and other institutions and interests within a federal system; external relations will be more akin to the familiar diplomacy of a single nation. Similarly, the United States will find herself less involved in the complexities of multilateral diplomacy in her relations with a Community that progressively seeks to evolve a unified European foreign policy.

The trend was illustrated by the tariff negotiations between the United States and the Common Market known as the Kennedy Round, which got under way formally in May, 1964. The Treaty of Rome gives the European Commission in Brussels authority to negotiate trade arrangements, including tariff reductions, for the Common Market with outside countries. Accordingly, American representatives have found themselves negotiating with Commission members under the auspices of GATT in Geneva and elsewhere as though the latter were trade officials of a single country. Nevertheless, each of the countries in the Community still has an important influence on the negotiating positions the Commission takes; the United States representatives have at times sought to negotiate bilaterally with France, Germany, or others of the Six in order to bring influence to bear on the common European position and thus achieve a diplomatic bargain more acceptable to the American view. This American effort to go behind the Commission has been criticized in Europe as incompatible with the principles of Atlantic partnership, and, in a sense, the charge is correct; but until the Europeans achieve a unity in which the American multilateral diplomat finds few interstices in which he can exercise his skills, the relationship will continue to be mixed. The President would no doubt welcome a single European with both authority and responsibility to whom he can confide his view of the great problems of the Alliance with some hope that a joint bilateral agreement would bring resolution of some of them. In this sense, the United States has been seeking to relieve herself of some of the difficulties of multilateral diplomacy by her support of European union and Atlantic partnership. As long as the prolonged transition continues, however, multilateral diplomacy will continue to play an important role in this region.

Probably the most ambitious exercise ever undertaken in the name of multilateral diplomacy is the Alliance for Progress. The Punta del Este Charter drawn up in August, 1961, pledges the nations of the inter-American system to seek together, *inter alia*, the following objectives:

1. To assure a ". . . rate of economic growth . . . not less than 2.5 per cent per capita per year. . . ."
2. To assure a ". . . more equitable distribution of national income. . . ."
3. "To accelerate the process of . . . industrialization. . . ."
4. "To encourage . . . agrarian reform. . . ."
5. "To eliminate adult illiteracy . . . and by 1970 assure . . . access to six years of primary education for each school age child. . . ."
6. "To increase life expectancy at birth by a minimum of five years. . . ."
7. "To maintain stable price levels. . . ."
8. To strengthen existing agreements on economic integration.
9. ". . . To prevent harmful effects of excessive fluctuation in foreign exchange earnings derived from exports of primary products. . . ."

The multilateral machinery designed to help reach these objectives includes the OAS, the Inter-American Development Bank and the Economic Commission for Latin America, a regional organization of the UN. In addition, a panel of nine high-level experts ("The Committee of Nine") was appointed to review and comment on the development plans of the Latin American republics.

The Alliance was not two years old before new machinery of multilateral diplomacy was deemed necessary. Following critical reports on the lack of progress in the Alliance by ex-Presidents Kubitschek of Brazil and Lleras Camargo of Colombia, the Inter-American Economic and Social Council in the fall of 1963 approved an Inter-American Committee on the Alliance for Progress (called CIAP, after the Spanish initials). CIAP is modeled on the OEEC of Marshall Plan days and, like the OEEC before it, has as its main task to make recommendations on the division of Alliance funds among Alliance members. CIAP and OEEC will provide analysts of the future with excellent material for a comparative study of multilateral diplomacy in two very different regions of the world.

In trade policy, multilateral diplomacy has been the rule ever since Cordell Hull's reciprocal trade policy was launched in 1934. After the failure of the International Trade Organization at Havana in 1947, the United States adopted the General Agreement on Tariffs and Trade (GATT) as its chosen instrument. GATT is not strictly speaking an organization at all; it is an international agreement to which the United States accords only provisional adherence. The Congress has consistently opposed ratifying GATT or approving an official international secretariat to administer the treaty. Nonetheless, GATT functions as an international organization and has an active, if unofficial, secretariat in Geneva, supported in part by annual appropriation by the Congress. The committees established to refine and interpret GATT have, since the war, set the rules that govern the multilateral trading world. GATT has been the vehicle under which periodic rounds of tariff reductions have been negotiated among the nations that adhere to the treaty.

As with other international organizations, GATT is under great pressures to change. Among less developed countries in recent years, the treaty has gained the reputation of being the charter for a "rich man's" trading club. Much of the agitation that led to the United Nations Conference on Trade and Development in the spring of 1964 stemmed from a widespread feeling on the part of key developing countries like Brazil, the United Arab Republic, India, and Yugoslavia that the GATT rules governing world trade ought radically to be revised in favor of the poorer nations. Despite the fact that by 1964 nearly seventy nations had adhered to GATT in one way or another, including virtually all the important trading nations, rich and poor, outside of the Sino-Soviet bloc, less developed countries in general have displayed a marked lack of enthusiasm for the treaty. As a minimum, they have indicated interest in setting up within the framework of the United Nations supplementary forums for discussing trade; at a maximum, some countries want to absorb GATT in a new trade organization within the U.N. framework.

In the years immediately ahead, the efficiency of GATT as an instrument of multilateral diplomacy will be severely tested, not only by the demands of the poor countries, but also by a growing divergence within the West over the advantages and disadvantages of classic multilateral trade policies. A great deal will depend on the success of the Kennedy Round of tariff negotiations. If it leads to important concessions to the poor countries, it is possible that the move to create a competing U.N. trade organization will wane. If a solid agreement between the Common Market and the United States can be reached, it is possible that there will be a period of renewed faith in conventional multilateral trade policies in the West. In any case, GATT, one of the oldest instruments of multilateral diplomacy, is being tested as never before.

The most rapid inflation of international organizations has taken place within the United Nations framework, as a result of the rapid increase in U.N. membership, drawn largely from the continents of Asia and Africa. Between 1954 and 1964, U.N. membership grew from 60 to 113 nations. In that time, the U.N. ceased to be primarily a forum for competition between the United States and the Soviet Union and became instead primarily a forum in which the new nations of Africa, Asia, and Latin America—some new in fact, others new in spirit—express their accummulated resentments and frustrations.

The United States, as the largest contributor to all U.N. activities, has been put increasingly on the defensive in U.N. debates as a direct result of the increase in U.N. membership. As the racial policies of South Africa and Southern Rhodesia and the colonial policies of Portugal have become the major continuing political issues debated in the General Assembly and Security Council, the United States has been progressively squeezed between its interest in preserving constitutional procedures and its desires to provide some legitimate redress in these cases for the less developed countries. In these and related matters, actions taken in the U.N. have an increasing impact on the formulation of United States policy. In fact, they have brought about something close to a constitutional crisis within the U.N.

Simultaneously, the newer U.N. members are developing an almost proprietary interest in the U.N. as an instrument for accelerating economic and social change. Most of the money and most of the manpower the U.N. employs are devoted to work connected with economic and social development. The new nations would dramatically increase both the scope and the intensity of this work. Specifically, they would create new U.N. organizations in trade, industry, and development finance.

For its part, United States interest in the U.N. as an instrument of development diplomacy has increased somewhat with the decline in Congressional support for our own foreign-aid program. Our interest has centered on the Bretton Woods institutions—the International Monetary Fund (IMF) and the World Bank, with its affiliates, the International Development Association and the International Finance Corporation. For the first decade of their existence, both the IMF and the World Bank proved totally inadequate to the tasks set out for them in their charters. But gradually they have come into their own—the IMF with the restoration of currency convertibility in 1960 and the World Bank, after becoming accepted as a borrower in the private capital markets of Europe and North America and after having fashioned one of the most effective techniques for administering development aid employed anywhere in the world today.

The U.N. itself and the major Specialized Agencies have so far proved less effective as instruments of development diplomacy. The major Specialized Agencies—International Labor Organization (ILO); Food and Agriculture Organization (FAO); World Health Organization (WHO); and the U.N. Educational, Scientific, and Cultural Organization (UNESCO)—were not created as operating organizations but rather as pseudo-universities in which specialists from member governments met together to exchange information and experience and to conduct modest programs of research. Today, however, each is called upon to administer operating programs of technical assistance in three score or more countries.

The United States has been very active in promoting and financing the various technical-assistance activities of the U.N. In particular, the United States was the prime mover behind the formation of the U.N. Expanded Program of Technical Assistance (EPTA) and the UN Special Fund, which together provide to the Specialized Agencies most of the technical experts and funds spent on technical assistance and training work, including the 300-odd "pre-investment" surveys financed by the Special Fund.

The attempted transformation of the U.N. system from a place to talk into a place to work has been beset by acute administrative and jurisdictional problems and by a severe shortage of competent personnel. Nonetheless, the U.N. does have certain advantages as an administrator of technical assistance. The fact that it is very often the preferred instrument of the new nations, preoccupied with their new sovereignty, is important. Also, the U.N. can draw on 113 countries for talent, which is potentially a very great advantage. The task of the U.N. as an instrument of development diplomacy in the years ahead is to realize these potentialities in the face of insistent demands from the newer nations to establish new organizations and new functions far beyond its administrative capacity.

Not even a brief review of the various instruments of multilateral diplomacy in use today would be complete without mention of the expanding diplomatic role of the scientist. More and more international cooperation has become a *sine qua non* for realizing the advantages of new advances in science. This is particularly true where weather and communications satellites are involved. Among the most complex exercises in multilateral diplomacy today are the efforts to establish a single, global communications satellite system and the program of the World Meteorological Organization to establish a "world weather watch."

The American scientist, in his role as a diplomat, is also deeply involved in political matters. This is particularly true in the case of disarmament negotiations where the range of possible actions depends so much on agreement about the range of scientific possibilities for detection and verification. The scientist *cum* diplomat is also appearing more and more in multilateral forums concerned with economic development, as one of many searching for the ways and means to help less developed countries engineer an escape from the vicious circle of their poverty.

The scientist may represent his country on the Science Committees of NATO or OECD or in any of a large number of United Nations organizations and committees. His presence in the ranks of multilateral diplomats is a major reason for the recent, very rapid increase in United States interest in this form of diplomacy. But just as the economist and the lawyer and the Foreign Service officer must acquire new skills and talents in order to be effective representatives in international organizations, so the scientist must be more than a scientist.

Characteristic Tasks of Multilateral Diplomacy

The tasks of representing the United States in the various organs of multilateral diplomacy are as varied and complex as are the interests involved. These tasks may entail operating responsibilities, as was the case with the OEEC in Marshall Plan days and is the case in U.N. peacekeeping operations. They may entail consultations on issues of fundamental policy importance, as is true in NATO and OECD. They may entail practical negotiations, as when the adherents to GATT gather to negotiate tariff reductions. They may entail propagandistic confrontations with the Russians or representatives of the developing countries, as is often true in U.N. debates. They may, on the other hand, involve complex approaches to agreement with the Russians, as in the case of the disarmament negotiations or the simultaneous launching of a Soviet-American weather satellite as the prelude to the World Meteorological Organization's "world weather watch" program.

More often than not, these tasks are immensely complicated. One only has to consider the diplomacy of the Congo crisis. Here, the United States, together with the Secretary General of the U.N., had to provide leadership in recruiting, supplying, and financing an international army and, simultaneously, recruiting, supplying, and financing a skeleton government for a country that had been granted independence without having acquired the means to maintain a minimum of order. To undertake this task, a drastic reshuffling of bureaucracies in Washington, with branches at U.N. headquarters in New York, in Brussels, and in Léopoldville was required. Every major administrative decision had to have at least the acquiescence of the U.N. Secretariat and the sovereign governments of Belgium and the Congo. Every legislative decision had to be referred to the Security Council or the General Assembly. The diplomatic exercise was conducted in the full glare of publicity and under an especially watchful Congressional eye.

Or, to take a smaller example, consider the task of the State

Department representatives charged with negotiating the construction of a global satellite communications system, in which the participants may include our own "private" Communications Satellite Corporation, the state-owned communications agencies of Western Europe, the Soviet Government, and the other nations of the world who have a right to some consideration in the allocation of available radio frequencies.

These varied and complex diplomatic tasks have a few characteristics in common. The unique fact confronting an American representative to an international organization is that he is negotiating with more than one country. Instead of facing the sufficiently difficult task of reconciling the views of two countries—his own and the other—he must find ways of reaching agreement among a variety of national interests that often conflict with one another, as well as with his own country's interest.

The representative must, therefore, be familiar with the problems and positions of all the countries with which he deals, and be able to tailor his own nation's interest to appeal to these various parties. Often, as in most U.N. debates, useful agreement is not possible and the exercise of multilateral diplomacy is dissipated in meaningless resolutions. But the ritual is nonetheless extremely demanding on the United States representative. And when, as in the case of who should pick up what part of the bill for a peacekeeping operation, a hard agreement cannot be avoided, the stamina of the multilateral diplomat and his supporting bureaucracy is often strained to the point of physical exhaustion.

Some tasks of multilateral representation are made easier because the United States is the largest contributor to or because the Russians are not participants in the given organization. Thus, U.S. representation on the Executive Board of the World Bank traditionally has been more ceremonial than anything else. But more often the size and power of the United States makes representation even more difficult as other, smaller countries band together to force the United States and its allies to move to a different position. This is often true when it comes to budget questions within the U.N. and its Specialized Agencies. With ten or so countries paying 80 or even 90 per cent of the bill yet having only one vote apiece, the remaining 100-odd countries can hardly be expected not to exercise their preponderent voting power on occasion. One of the outstanding tasks of U.S. representatives to U.N. organizations today is to overcome this disadvantage in ways that preserve the useful functions of the organizations concerned.

One of the first tasks of the United States representative to an international organization is to know the prevailing pattern of influence in it. Some countries have more influence than others and can be useful, or the reverse, in persuading other members to accept a given position or compromise. It is usually important to identify these key countries and to consult them informally in advance of a negotiation. If their positions coincide with the American one, or can be adjusted so as to reach a compromise, this may make the negotiation of agreements with the other countries relatively easy.

Prior informal consultation with other less influential members is often helpful. An informal exchange of views in the corridors of an international organization can often be more effective in reaching a consensus than the more formal statements in the meetings themselves. Sometimes, an effort to present the American view to a large part of the membership can help to modify the opposition of a key country. Sometimes, elaborate consultations among governments will take place before a large and important conference; occasionally, a smaller organization such as OECD or its Development Assistance Committee is used as a forum for consultation in advance of a large U.N. meeting such as the U.N. Conference on Trade and Development. Instruction through the usual diplomatic channels to nations participating in a conference is also often helpful.

Prior consultation with other delegations to U.N. meetings is always essential for the United States representatives. More and more, bloc voting among nations from the same region has become the rule in the U.N.; fewer and fewer votes are changed in formal debate. This means that the United States representative has to be alert in his lobbying and "pulse-taking" in order to influence the caucuses of the Latin Americans and the Afro-Asians before the regional "line" is set. United States delegations to the General Assembly typically carry a dozen or more Foreign Service "liaison" officers to keep in constant touch with the members of the regional caucuses.

Very often, however, the lobbying exercise must be conducted by one or two officers on their own. For example, one of the first and routine tasks of any United States representative to a conference or meeting of a U.N. Specialized Agency is to assure himself that action will not be taken to change the representation of China. If, as is the usual case, there is only one State Department representative on hand, he must be sufficiently familiar with the organization to know the necessary minimum number of delegations or individuals on whom the question of action or no action depends. Obviously, no one man can lobby 113 delegations.

In these and other circumstances, the secretariats are often the key to the protection of United States interests. In most international organizations today, the secretariats, or "executives," wield a considerable power both to initiate and to block action. Typically, it is the secretariats that are masters of and advisers on all procedural matters. Very often, they supply texts of resolutions to delegations on request as well as "planting" resolutions of their own. Secretariats vary in their prestige and in their willingness to support United States positions; within the U.N., they are all governed by Articles 100 and 101 of the Charter, which command impartiality from the International Civil Service. However, secretariats, like the delegations they serve, develop attitudes and feelings of "sovereignty" and therefore inevitably become agents of diplomacy to which the United States representative must pay close attention.

The typical United States representative to an international organization must be both a writer and a speaker, as well as a lobbyist in the corridors. He must be a master of timing, for *when* he speaks may often have as much effect as *what* he says. He must be expert on Robert's *Rules of Order*, preferably on the special procedural provisions of his organization, if only to provide some check on the secretariat that will provide this expertise to most other delegations. He must be able to form and to lead caucuses of like-minded delegations, usually caucuses of Western allies, but sometimes caucuses drawn from other regions where there is a momentary identity of their interests and ours. He must, above all, display keen judgment as a negotiator, for there is a time to vote "yes," a time to vote "no," a time to "abstain," and even a time to be among the absent.

Very often, the United States representatives will have to act either without instructions or in the face of conflicting instructions from home. The "backstopping" bureaucracy in Washington may involve so many different offices and departments that quick responses to requests for instructions are impossible. There may be jurisdictional disputes among Washington departments which cause the bureaucracy deliberately or tacitly to leave the representative in a quandary. In these cases, he must become an advocate of his actions. He must create a detailed record that may be praised or ignored, but may also serve as ground for an *ex post facto* censure.

Most United States delegations to international organizations today represent at least a composite of departmental interests in Washington and often include articulate spokesmen of domestic interests with a voice in Congress as well. Delegations to OECD usually represent a mixture of State, AID, and Treasury interests. The United States delegation to big conferences like the U.N. Conference on Trade and Development at Geneva in 1964 may well include fairly high-level representatives from State, Treasury, Commerce, Agriculture, Labor, and AID. In these circumstances, the delegation itself is sometimes a source of controversy and dissension, and the chairman requires the skill of an experienced Washington bureaucrat as well as the new skills of multilateral diplomacy.

The inclusion on United States delegations of prominent persons from special-interest groups is particularly common in the case of U.N. meetings. To the professional practitioner of multilateral diplomacy, the "public member" (sometimes a Congressman) can be a great help. After all, the United States is a pluralistic society, and it is quite proper to employ a wealth of private talent along with public talent in American diplomatic efforts. But the tasks of representation are complicated when prominent persons outside of the government are recruited. They are likely to be less restrained by political considerations of interest to the government. And they are tempted to advocate too zealously their own special concerns, failing to take into account the fact that the United States Government often pays the largest share of the budgets of multilateral organizations and therefore must somehow weigh the competing claims of each domestic interest group against the total national investment.

Finally, multilateral diplomacy often attracts far more public attention than does conventional diplomacy. The American delegation, even to an organization like NATO, must always have its eye on public opinion. Meetings of these organizations often make news in and of themselves, necessitating some public-relations attention even when the agenda is not newsworthy. And when the subject under discussion is sensitive, great care must be taken. For example, the negotiations leading to the NATO agreement on the status of forces stationed abroad determined the jurisdiction of foreign nations over American soldiers who break the law in the country in which they serve. Naturally, the American negotiators and those who have supervised the agreement's implementation have had to be keenly aware of public opinion back home.

Many, if not most, U.N. debates are carried on in the full glare of publicity and this often requires from the United States representative the skills of an accomplished actor. This is particularly true when the sole objective is effectively to propagandize against the Communists or effectively to defend a key United States policy —whether it be our race relations or a blockade of Cuba.

The growth of international organizations has done much to remove the cloak of secrecy from diplomacy and to increase the interest and curiosity about foreign affairs that has characterized public opinion here and abroad since World War II. The American public particularly is aware as never before that we live today in uncomfortable intimacy with other nations often professing divergent interests. This new awareness has certainly contributed importantly to the creation of a fairly solid public consensus behind the basic tenets of our foreign policy in recent years.

The Special Tasks of Atlantic Diplomacy

By far the most important and successful exercises in multilateral diplomacy since World War II were those concerned with the recovery and integration of Western Europe. The success of these exercises led the United States, under the Kennedy and Johnson administrations, to seek an Atlantic partnership, which, in the words of the late President Kennedy, "would have the resources and the resourcefulness with which to share as equals the burdens of leadership" in all the great enterprises the West must undertake to assure its security and prosperity.

In spite of the difficulties of the past two years, President Kennedy's vision of an Atlantic partnership remains a fundamental goal of American policy. And many of those who are pursuing this goal are doing so with the skills of multilateral diplomacy that were first learned in the days of the Marshall Plan. Their success is likely to determine in large measure whether multilateral diplomacy continues to grow in importance in United States policy or to wane in favor of a return to more conventional diplomatic methods.

Two of the major institutional elements of Atlantic partnership were to be NATO and the Organization for Economic Cooperation and Development (OECD, a direct descendant of the OEEC). Each institution grew up in the 1940's and 1950's with a more limited goal—the recovery, security, and integration of Western Europe. Each had a period of brilliant success followed by a period of "hard times." The tasks of United States representation in NATO and OEEC in their formative years set the pattern that is followed in multilateral Atlantic diplomacy today. The Office of the United States Special Representative in Europe (OSR) of Marshall Plan days has become the United States Mission to the North Atlantic Treaty Organization and European Regional Organizations (USRO). During the Marshall Plan, the Economic Cooperation Administration chose to deal with the Europeans largely through the OEEC, even though the United States was not a member.

The first objective of the Marshall Plan was, of course, to raise production and exports so that Europe could become self-supporting again. For this purpose it was necessary to decide how much aid each country would receive, since this largely determined its level of imports and had an important effect on its production. In the first year of the program, ECA made the decision itself,

Membership of European and Western Organizations

	North Atlantic Treaty Organization NATO	Organization for Economic Cooperation and Development OECD	Western European Union WEU	Council of Europe CE	*European Communities* European Economic Community (Common Market) EEC	European Coal and Steel Community ECSC	European Atomic Energy Community Euratom	European Free Trade Association EFTA
Austria		x		x				x
Belgium	x	x	x	x	x	x	x	
Canada	x	x						
Cyprus				x				
Denmark	x	x		x				x
France	x	x	x	x	x	x	x	
Federal Republic of Germany	x	x	x	x	x	x	x	
Greece	x	x		x	*			
Ireland		x		x				
Italy	x	x	x	x	x	x	x	
Japan		x						
Luxembourg	x	x	x	x	x	x	x	
Netherlands	x	x	x	x	x	x	x	
Norway	x	x		x				x
Portugal	x	x						x
Spain		x						
Sweden		x		x				x
Switzerland		x		x				x
Turkey	x	x		x	*			
United Kingdom	x	x	x	x				x
United States	x	x						
Iceland	*	*		*				
Finland								*

* Associate Member

based on information received from the countries. In subsequent years, the OEEC was given increasing responsibility for the division of aid, taking it over completely in 1950. Instead of negotiating separately with each country, ECA instructed OSR to notify OEEC of the total amount of aid available for the year. The negotiations then took place among the European countries within OEEC. OSR was very much in the picture, of course, but its staff tried to facilitate agreement from the background.

The ECA decided to throw this great responsibility on OEEC because it wanted to strengthen the organization and thereby promote European economic integration. The ultimate goal was defined by Mr. Paul Hoffman, in a speech to the OEEC Council of Ministers in October, 1949, as the creation of a large single market. His speech—a major pronouncement of American foreign policy, although the State Department had only a few hours to review it—was the opening gambit in a long and complex negotiation between the United States and the European representatives in OEEC. It was given maximum publicity in an effort to build up public support and to influence governments. And it illustrated the then new technique of sending Washington figures of Cabinet rank to European meetings at the ministerial level so as to emphasize American views. Indeed, in dealing with the OEEC, OSR faced a continuing problem: the positions it took involved such important policies that officials from ECA headquarters in Washington were continually coming to Paris to participate in the negotiations.

In negotiating the European Payments Union, OSR came up against still other problems. It was impossible to set up the EPU without Great Britain's agreement. Yet the British could not participate unless they could find a way to link the EPU with the sterling area. Consequently, alongside its complicated negotiations in OEEC, which were completely entangled with the problem of programming American aid, OSR was obliged simultaneously to conduct a series of difficult discussions with the British Treasury that led in the end to a supplementary bilateral agreement between Britain and ECA, under which Britain was later reimbursed for part of her EPU deficit. Furthermore, OSR discovered that not only was the State Department interested in its activities but also

the Treasury Department. For it was negotiating a financial arrangement with a regional organization that would inevitably have a
most profound effect on the International Monetary Fund and
American policies in that organization, for which the Treasury was
responsible. Yet no senior Treasury official participated in the
negotiations.

About half-way through the Marshall Plan, Americans became
more aware of the underlying weaknesses in the European economy, solutions to which could be approached directly as well as
through broadening the market. The cartel structure of European
industry could still function in a larger market. The low-wage, high-
cost philosophy of many European industrialists could be attacked
directly as well as indirectly through the impact of the market.
And productivity was a problem of management and know-how as
well as competition. So OSR undertook to encourage OEEC to
initiate new activities dealing with these problems. The OEEC
delegates sat down to consider anti-trust agreements of various
degrees of stringency or vagueness, with OSR hastily summoning
experts in American anti-trust law from Washington to advise
them. This enterprise produced few anti-cartel laws, but it did
increase European awareness of the economic burdens imposed by
restraint of trade. More significant were the OEEC discussions
over the problem of increasing productivity, which added another
OEEC subsidiary to those already in existence—the European
Productivity Agency. This organization was financed in large part
with Marshall Plan funds set aside under a Senate amendment for
the purpose of encouraging increased productivity and higher wages.
It was the American expectation that, after some initial help, the
Europeans would take up the responsibility for financing the
Agency and keep it going themselves.

This broad range of representational activities intertwined with
operating functions imposed a tremendous staffing problem on
OSR. It was met largely by observing the same principle the ECA
followed throughout its organization at home and abroad—recruiting personnel from outside the government on a temporary basis.
OSR grew to be a very large organization. The qualifications required of its staff ranged from the highest level of diplomatic
experience to experts in insecticides and the labor practices of the

ladies' garment industry. Many of these people were actually needed to represent the United States in meetings of the OEEC or its innumerable committees and subordinate organs. They carried on many negotiations with OEEC delegations outside the conference room. Faced with a complex operation, the OSR organization tended to be complicated too. There were country, commodity, and functional offices in great profusion.

The OSR staff included many men of outstanding ability. Their great accomplishments in solving problems without precedent are now a matter of historical record. In assembling a mission that was presumed to be temporary, it is not surprising that difficulties were encountered. The staff certainly became too large. In meeting after meeting of the OEEC, the American group would be much the largest, although the United States was not a member of the organization. The Europeans in Paris began to complain politely of the "American presence." The turnover among the very able businessmen was heavy. Relations with other delegations were not always handled with the greatest tact. But apart from the U.N., which presented a different problem, this was the first American immersion in that new phenomenon of diplomacy, multilateral negotiation through a more or less permanent international organization.

NATO was as a more or less conventional military alliance until the onset of the Korean War. Then its character changed radically. Its members decided to create an integrated NATO army with a unified command to defend the European continent against invasion. The United States had been the strong but somewhat distant member of the alliance; she now assumed leadership of the heretofore leaderless effort to build a NATO deterrent to invasion, provided her leading general officer as Supreme Commander of the NATO forces in Europe, and found herself intimately involved in a complex effort to persuade the Europeans to increase their defense forces from inside an organization in which she was theoretically only one of twelve members, each with independent control over its own defense establishment.

These responsibilities confronted our representatives to NATO with many unprecedented problems as well as some that were familiar from the OEEC experience. No coalition had ever before achieved a unified command in time of peace, however uneasy.

American officers served alongside their counterparts from other countries in a command that was responsible to NATO rather than national defense establishments. Thus, the Pentagon faced new personnel problems in assigning officers to a type of duty they had never experienced in peace. Some officers could adapt themselves to the psychological requirements of an international command; others could not. Some were worried about the effect of the "taint" of internationalism on their careers. Nevertheless, SHAPE developed morale and efficiency to such an extent that it became a strong factor in the negotiations within NATO alongside the international secretariat.

This secretariat posed personnel problems for the Foreign Service similar to those presented to the Defense Department by the NATO commands. Unlike the U.N. secretariats, which are staffed by permanent officials, NATO depends on member countries to contribute officials to staff its secretariat. These officers rotate in and out of NATO on assignment just as diplomatic officers do at any post. But an American officer assigned to the NATO international staff has no immediate superior to review his work and report his performance to the State Department. Furthermore, he is confronted with a confusing problem of loyalties. Is he to use his international position directly to further the interests of the United States or should he consider only the interests of the alliance as a whole? These assignments have not been considered particularly attractive by career officers, and the United States has not pulled its share of the load in contributing to the NATO international staff.

An integrated force and command logically led to an agreed strategy. But here a dilemma appeared. The countries had given the Supreme Commander full authority over the forces which they were willing to assign to him. But they were not willing—indeed they were constitutionally unable—to give the NATO Council authority to declare war. After years of negotiation on the problem of how to decide when commanders should be given the power to declare war or even to give an alert, NATO is still wrestling with the difficulties. Strategic planning was difficult enough. The Standing Group, consisting of the chiefs of staff of the United States, Britain, and France, might decide that some territory would have to be given up to permit a shortening of defense lines and an effective stand along defensible terrain. But the small country whose territory was to be abandoned could not possibly agree to such a strategic plan. Defense ministers and foreign offices both became deeply involved in these problems.

Perhaps most difficult of all, the forces assigned to NATO were always inadequate to meet the requirements the military planners set. Throughout its history, NATO has struggled to reconcile military requirements with the limited resources its members are willing to provide in manpower and equipment. Here, NATO impinged upon touchy domestic issues—such as the length of military service and the level of taxes needed to meet defense budgets. Treasury and finance ministers were concerned, as well as defense departments and foreign offices.

The NATO annual review is a triumph of ingenious organization as a device to reconcile a modern coalition's needs for intimate association with sovereign national control over sensitive domestic decisions. In essence, it requires simultaneous consideration of national defense plans and budgets in fifteen capitals and at NATO headquarters in Paris. As the decisions about manpower, units, supplies, and budgets are arrived at in the capitals, the programs are spread on the green tables at NATO, where each country, the International Staff, and the Commands make their comments and recommendations. The members take into account the results of these sessions in determining their firm domestic programs. American and Canadian aid programs, either in the form of direct transfers of equipment from North America or of procurement in Europe for the account of a NATO country, are included in the process.

This annual review has been more successful in influencing the composition of national defense budgets than in determining their level. Member countries have shied away from anything that appears to commit them to devote a fixed proportion of their resources to NATO defense—or in the NATO jargon, "burden-sharing." Only for the NATO-controlled airfields, pipelines, and communications systems on the Continent, known by the French term "infrastructure," has it been possible to agree on percentage shares of the cost to be borne by each country. And this was possible only after long and arduous negotiations, often at the ministerial level.

Staffing a mission that can carry on negotiations of this character, as well as the many other complicated activities of NATO, has put a great strain on American resources of personnel. A few officers in the State Department and other departments have painfully become experts in the NATO annual review. But the strength of the American Government is very thin in this field and that of other NATO members even thinner. The combination of necessary skills—economic analysis, military understanding, budgetary competence, negotiating ability—is an unlikely one. Officers who show competence in this peculiar art are likely to be held longer on the NATO circuit than may be good for their careers.

To some extent, it has been possible to meet the needs of American representation to NATO by assigning specialists from Washington to a particular meeting. Committees on wartime shipping problems, commodity problems, security, labor mobility, and many other matters have been staffed in this manner.

Flexibility in personnel has been needed also to meet the staff requirements of the semi-annual ministerial meetings of the organization. At the most important of these conferences, the meeting in Paris in December, tradition calls for representation of each member country by three cabinet-level officers—the ministers of foreign affairs, defense, and finance (treasury). In recent years, attendance of the finance ministers has been irregular, indicating, perhaps, a decline in the impact of NATO on national budgets. The other conference in the spring is normally attended only by foreign ministers. The United States delegation has in the past included four: the Administrator of AID has also been a member. Each Cabinet member brings with him a group of advisers from Washington and adds to the delegation certain staff members of the American mission to NATO. The extent of the negotiations actually carried on during the meetings depends on whether the permanent delegations have been able to reach agreement beforehand. If they have had to leave important issues to be settled by the ministers, there are usually informal meetings between the principal members in an effort to settle differences outside the regular sessions, which are ordinarily reserved for the routine business of approving documents or for general exchange of views. Frequently, the American cabinet officers use the occasion to negotiate with their colleagues on matters far removed from NATO business.

Keeping track of a meeting of this size and scope requires special expertise in itself. There are only a handful of senior officers of the State Department who are sufficiently familiar with NATO procedures, with the many personalities who may be encountered, and with the broad subject matter of the many individual meetings they must attend to coordinate the American delegation at a NATO conference.

If both NATO and OEEC had been abandoned in 1960, they would have remained the outstanding examples of multilateral diplomacy in the post-war period—indeed, in any period. Given limited and well-defined objectives—the creation of a strong and unified European economy and a workable, Atlantic defense system—both institutions performed their complicated tasks with historic effect. Once the objectives of the organizations become less limited, less susceptible to achievement within a given time period, it was inevitable that the tasks of multilateral diplomacy would be less productive.

The OEEC became the OECD in December, 1961. The United States and Canada agreed to join the new organization along with nineteen other charter members, including all the countries of Western Europe. (In 1964, Japan was added as the twenty-first member.) Along with the broader membership went broader goals, geared to American ideas of Atlantic partnership. Specifically the OECD membership declared their aims to be (1) "the achievement of the highest sustainable economic growth and employment . . . while maintaining financial stability"; (2) "to contribute to sound economic expansion in member as well as non-member countries"; and (3) "to contribute to the expansion of world trade." These broad goals were to be served by agreeing not to a program of operations but to a series of formal consultations on a broad range of policy matters including internal economic policies. As an earnest of their intentions, the assembled ministers of the twenty original OECD nations, at their first meeting in December, 1961, pledged themselves to achieve together a growth target of 50 per cent in real gross national product during the decade 1960–70.

The OECD has continued many of the consultative functions of the old OEEC and added some new ones. An annual review of the economic situation in each member nation is conducted by OECD as it was by OEEC. So are studies of broad economic trends. Several times a year, OECD's Economic Policy Committee attracts high officials from member governments, carrying on a practice started in Marshall Plan days. Perhaps OECD's greatest success has been to provide a forum for the monetary authorities of member governments to meet regularly and privately to the end of strengthening international monetary stability.

There are regular OECD consultative committees on trade and payments; agriculture and fisheries; industry and energy; science, technology and education; and nuclear energy. The task of representation at these meetings is simpler than it was in the days of the OEEC, since OECD does not have any operational program comparable to OEEC's. However, the effect is to develop the possibility of closer working relations in the years to come. Through its committees, OECD is bringing together the relevant bureaucracies of the Atlantic nations at regular intervals to discuss their common problems.

The closest OECD comes to having an operational responsibility is in the matter of aid to less developed countries. OECD's Development Advisory Committee (DAC) does not disburse funds itself nor does it determine the division of aid funds in any way. It does, however, provide a forum for consulting on and coordinating aid policies in general and in regard to specific countries. It has been the forum for serious and practical negotiations among the various consortiums of nations aiding countries such as India, Pakistan, Turkey, and the Congo. It has been the primary focus of American efforts to persuade Europe to carry a greater share of the general foreign-aid burden. And here again, DAC provides the possibility in the future of a forum for negotiating a truly coordinated Western policy towards less developed countries and for overseeing the works of that policy.

It cannot be denied that the success of the Common Market has hampered the development of OECD as it was originally conceived. It was probably inevitable in any case that after the signing of the Treaty of Rome in 1957 the nations of Europe would become introspective—would concentrate on the complex and exciting problems of unifying their economies, at the expense of building an Atlantic partnership. General de Gaulle's appeal to a new European nationalism increased Europe's tendency to assert an independent role, but the tendency was there all along. Like OECD, NATO has suffered as a consequence.

The future of NATO today is very much in doubt. While American support has never wavered, the strategic situation is changing all the time and the French seem to be abandoning the organization. De Gaulle's insistence on an independent French nuclear deterrent hits at the heart of NATO by denying the possibility of a truly multilateral strategic force. While NATO remains on "the alert" in the defense of the West in Germany, the organization has been less and less able to function as a joint military staff charged with keeping strategy up to date with technical and political developments. Even when two members, Greece and Turkey, became embroiled over Cyprus, NATO was unable to act and had to yield to the U.N.

To a limited extent, NATO has established itself as a forum for useful political consultation. However, the same trends that prevented the development of OECD have seriously crippled NATO. Nonetheless, its past successes and its very existence today give to the United States a "presence" in Western European affairs through which the idea of Atlantic partnership can be kept alive. If representation at NATO today is full of frustrations and inaction, it remains nonetheless a key task in American diplomacy. Through the idea of a multilateral force, American diplomacy is keeping alive the possibility of a joint Western deterrent. Whatever its future, the MLF will have served as a useful exercise in multilateral diplomacy.

PROBLEMS OF REPRESENTATION IN THE FUTURE

The United States has had enough experience with the various instruments of multilateral diplomacy to suggest some qualifications about its use. The successes of OEEC and NATO in their early days suggest that where there is a well-defined and limited objective shared by allies, multilateral diplomacy provides unique opportunities for carrying forward a program of operations. It does not follow, however, that this is true where very broad objectives are sought, as is the case with the Alliance for Progress. While the new Inter-American Committee for the Alliance may become a useful innovation, it will be difficult for it to prove itself as OEEC did, simply because the objectives of the Alliance are so broad as to make the establishment of meaningful timetables very difficult.

It is probably significant too, that OECD and NATO as consultative organizations have failed to engender among their participants the *esprit de corps* they had as operating organizations. Effective consultation depends again on a set of agreed policy objectives. As Western Europe has become preoccupied with its own Community and as the Sino-Soviet bloc has dissolved from a "monolith" into a montage of competing Communist interests, multilateral diplomacy among the Atlantic nations in politico-military affairs has naturally encountered difficulties.

However, it remains a major objective of United States policy to hold out to our Western European allies some alternative to a future under French or American hegemony. The aim of encouraging the nations of Europe to preserve the vigor of their nationalities, but to do so by discarding the traditional trappings of nationalism, remains a matter of prime interest to United States foreign policy. For this reason alone, our representation in and to various kinds of Atlantic or European organizations is certain to command top priority in the allocation of diplomatic skills and resources.

Likewise, the ever-increasing demands on the West of the less developed countries of Asia, Africa, and Latin America makes necessary at least the pursuit of a common and coordinated Western policy toward these countries. It is unlikely that the West will revert to policies of spheres-of-influence in its relations with the less developed world. The challenges of development and of the political ambitions and resentments that leaders of these developing countries have are common challenges to all Western nations, if for no other reason than that they derive so much from the impact of Western ideas and achievements in the past. Fashioning a common Western policy to meet these common challenges is certainly a task that will require constant and imaginative exercise in multilateral Atlantic diplomacy for as far ahead as one can see.

Finally, it is very likely that the economic problems of the Western nations—both domestic and international—will continue to command multilateral action and consultation. This is particularly true in the field of monetary policy; the "key currency" system, in which the world's trade and investment were financed on the basis of reserves in gold, dollars, and sterling is certain to become even less adequate in the future than it is today. Multilateral action to amend or replace this system is likely to provide the multilateral diplomat with one of his greatest challenges in the years ahead.

Similarly, unless there is to be a complete failure of diplomacy in trade, leading to a retreat into bilateralism, trade policy will continue to be worked out through the instruments of multilateral diplomacy. Whether Atlantic cooperation will grow in the areas of domestic fiscal policies is more problematical. But the very fact that the habit of consulting on these matters has been formed, first through OEEC and now through OECD, suggests that the Atlantic nations will continue at least to explore opportunities for new multilateral diplomatic action.

The future of the U.N. system as an effective instrument of multilateral diplomacy is most cloudy. The U.N. has grown so rapidly that it is undergoing a series of crises—a constitutional crisis, an organizational crisis, and most of all an administrative and financial crisis. Alone among U.N. organizations, the IMF and the World Bank have established themselves as important and solid institutions for the exercise of diplomacy.

In its peacekeeping roles in Cyprus, the Congo, and the Gaza strip, the U.N. has performed functions for which there has been no substitute organization ready, willing, and able to act. But it does not follow that therefore the U.N. will flourish in this new role. The administrative and financial arrangements necessary to mount a U.N. peacekeeping operation are so complex that these considerations, in and of themselves, make for caution in predicting future actions. Furthermore, the U.N. cannot for long function as an effective security force without substantial support from the major powers. The U.N. can never have more authority than the great powers are willing to give it. It is doubtful that in the fore-seeable future there will be sufficient identity of interest among the great powers to develop a permanent peacekeeping capacity within the U.N. It is at least possible, in fact, that recent experi-ence in the Congo and Cyprus will make the great powers less, rather than more, willing to use the U.N. in this way.

The future of the U.N. as an agent of development diplomacy, or of "nation-building," is likewise uncertain. Pressed on the one hand by its new members' insistent demands for more and better services, and squeezed on the other by a desperate shortage of trained administrative talent, the U.N. family of organizations is certain to pass through some very difficult years in the immediate future.

In addition, while new U.N. members are insistent on more and better services, their delegates have all too often chosen to couch their demands in political terms which usually preclude agreement. This is true even in the more technical Specialized Agencies, and perhaps it is inevitable, since in many countries today, particularly in Africa, the doctor, or economist, or educator is almost auto-matically a political leader as well, so thin is the class of educated men and women. However, unless new U.N. members can dis-criminate between demands for development assistance and de-mands for redress against real or imagined injustice in the past, they are likely to prevent the development of the very organiza-tions that, typically, are their chosen instruments when it comes to all kinds of "foreign aid."

United States participation in the U.N. family of organizations has received less serious professional attention in the policy coun-cils of the State Department than any other branch of multilateral diplomacy. Foreign Service Officers have tended to avoid service concerned with U.N. affairs on the grounds that it is a professional dead end. Outside of a small group of highly dedicated men and women, United States participation in U.N. affairs has been very largely the province of appointees drawn directly from domestic politics or from various special interest groups. As a result there has often been a lack of clarity of purpose behind our policies in the U.N. There has been a tendency to let the mere existence of a U.N. organization dictate policy. As a result much of the official effort that goes into United States representation in the U.N. has an artificial and wasteful character.

This is a serious problem, affecting not only multilateral diplomacy in the U.N. but potentially affecting other branches of the art. Clarity of purpose is more important than organization. To make multilateral diplomacy effective, we must keep our eye firmly fixed on the fundamental purposes of American foreign policy and try to adapt the organizations to these, rather than the other way round. The pragmatic approach to matters of organization is an American characteristic, but the present state of multilateral diplomacy suggests that pragmatism is slipping over into confusion.

Whatever the future of the international organizations, it seems likely that there will continue to be many of them and that the United States will be represented. The personnel requirements will be heavy. Some of the problems are familiar and are not limited to the framework of representation to the international organizations as such. However, a clearer recognition that staffing these delegations is a continuing requirement that needs to be more effectively integrated into our personnel policies should be helpful.

When the organization is a technical one without broader functions, representation can be provided by assigning competent personnel with the appropriate technical experience. These assignments should be distinguished from those to be filled by officials in the career overseas service. A specialist in wheat culture from the Department of Agriculture who may be a member of the American delegation to negotiate an international wheat agreement is not likely to be looking forward to a career representing the United States overseas. He will consider an assignment of this type temporary even if it takes him overseas for several years; he will expect to return to the Department of Agriculture to pursue his specialty. As long as those responsible for the assignments are clear as to their character, there is no serious problem. It is important, however, that these officers have the necessary representational qualifications as well as the technical skills. Sometimes organizations with broad functions will require experts—for example, the NATO delegation may need a security officer with technical training of the type normally available only in the Department of Justice. The career principles involved are similar, and arrangements have been made between State and Justice to handle the assignments reasonably well.

The more difficult problem is the need for specialized personnel who would normally look forward to a career in overseas representation. As we have seen, representation to international organizations requires many officers with knowledge of economic, legal, military, and information problems. If these officers are to be treated equitably, they must be given the same opportunities to advance to more general responsibilities as the officer with political and diplomatic experience. The problem is the same in principle as the one considered in the separate papers on military, economic, and information representation. But the organizations complicate it because they expand the range of skills required. They tend to blur the line between the career technician and the career overseas representative. For example, our participation in the International Civil Aviation Organization requires us to staff a small permanent delegation in Montreal with experts in this field. Since the State Department has maintained a small group of Civil Air Attachés in key embassies abroad, it has until recently assumed the main responsibility for staffing the Montreal office. The Civil Aeronautics Board in the Department of Commerce has become increasingly interested in the staffing arrangements for the ICAO and the trend appears to be in the direction of greater CAB responsibility. This may have an important effect on the career outlook of those officers in State with experience in civil aviation. There is need for clear lines of responsibility and for an opening to the top for demonstrated ability for both types of personnel in their different careers.

An assignment to represent the United States at an international organization is still too often considered to have a hampering effect on the career of an officer, either military or civilian. This is less true in the case of the Atlantic or European organizations than it is in the case of the U.N. But, in both cases, the prevailing attitudes should be changed by making certain that the importance of such representation is understood throughout the services and that good performance in these difficult assignments is rewarded in career terms.

The problem of assigning able American representatives to international secretariats requires special attention. In many organizations, United States interests are best preserved through a strong secretariat. In the U.N. particularly, Americans are very underrepresented on the secretariats, and those who do serve often must work under great handicaps because the need to observe "adequate geographical representation" often conflicts with efficient merit promotions and efficient administrative policies. In 1963, an advisory committee to the State Department's Bureau of International Organization Affairs recommended a number of policy changes and the establishment of a special recruiting unit to increase the number and caliber of Americans serving on international organization secretariats, but the report has not yet been fully implemented. The British, Dutch, and French governments have done a great deal to recruit their citizens to serve on international secretariats and have provided special inducements for them to do so. The United States could learn much from this experience.

The possibilities of rotation of assignment also need more aggressive application. Personnel with experience in a mission to a regional organization can often greatly strengthen an embassy to one of the members of that organization, and *vice versa*. Officers with experience in the European regional organization can be useful in U.N. delegations. Flexibility in the use of personnel is, as we have seen, absolutely essential if American responsibilities to these bodies are to be met.

Most important of all, there needs to be more emphasis on training. The growing recognition that assignments to the defense colleges are an excellent way of training officers for service in the missions to organizations concerned with security problems is a step in the right direction. The number of civilians attending the National War College should be increased. And the very small number of officers now studying at the Imperial Defense College, the Canadian Defense College, and the NATO Defense College could be enlarged by a policy of greater reciprocity in accepting allied nationals at the American institutions.

Training in the techniques of multilateral diplomacy is likely to continue to be a matter of learning more by doing than by studying. But more information on the international organizations could be included in the regular training programs with advantage.

Finally there is a need to mobilize the growing number of high-level, noncareer individuals with experience in these organizations. Some technique should be developed for tapping the great experience and wisdom of the men who have served or are now serving in NATO, the U.N., or OECD to strengthen present American representation in this difficult but important area of our foreign relations.

6. The Coordination of Overseas Representation

LINCOLN GORDON

It will be evident from the earlier chapters of this volume that overseas representation during World War II and after has posed innumerable opportunities for conflict, duplication, and overlapping, for clashes of personality, and for discord in policy. The need for coordination seems self-evident, a need considered in this chapter at the three levels of action—in foreign countries, in regional areas, and in Washington.

In considering this problem, however, it should always be borne in mind that coordination is not the only goal. Other objectives may override that of harmony for its own sake. Policies must be implemented and programs fulfilled to the satisfaction not only of the Chief Executive but also of a host of Washington agencies, organized interest groups in the American public, the Congress, and the public at large. Excessive emphasis on coordination in a merely formal or mechanical sense may mean the multiplication of clearances and the dead weight of numberless committees, or the imposition of stultifying uniform personnel systems to the point where policy becomes frustrated by the very attempt to secure harmony. There is, perhaps, even some inherent conflict between the objectives of effective action and of coordination as an end in itself. The first requirement is the clear definition and communication of policy; if that requirement is not fulfilled, coordinating machinery may be worse than useless.

POINTS OF POSSIBLE CONFLICT

Reviewing the postwar history of foreign-affairs administration and overseas representation as a whole, it is difficult to discern any consistent pattern or line of evolution. As in the case of all administrative developments, individual personalities and the immediate urgency of particular programs certainly have played as large a part as any self-conscious effort at rational organization. Nonetheless, there do repeatedly emerge a number of characteristic points of conflict around which the problem of coordination is focused.

Among the various agencies of government, for example, there is the chronic potential conflict between the Department of State and the overseas interests of agencies whose primary concerns are domestic—the Treasury, the departments of Agriculture, Commerce, and Labor, the Atomic Energy Commission, and, one might perhaps add, the Department of Defense and the military services. Then there is the question of temporary or permanent special foreign-affairs agencies for program operations. There are the internal problems of State Department organization, difficult enough in themselves and greatly magnified if one tries to have the Department cover the whole field of nonmilitary foreign affairs. And there exists in any case a problem of Washington coordination, with the chronic question whether it can be performed by the State Department alone, by interdepartmental committees, by the President without a special staff, or by special arrangements in the President's Executive Office or in the White House staff.

Overseas, the problem of multiple agencies concerned with foreign affairs creates parallel potential conflicts. Should each such agency have its own representatives abroad or should the State Department serve as agent overseas for all of them? Can a career service cover all types of civilian employees overseas? If there are separate personnel systems, how are they to be related, and what are the problems of status, discrimination, and effective working relationships? Are special purpose programs to be handled by special missions, or by specially trained and recruited officers in the diplomatic missions, or can they be entrusted to a broadened complement of regular embassy officers? If there are special missions or semi-independent groups of special program experts, what is to be their relationship with the ambassadors and regular embassy officers?

With respect to regional organizations and representation in international organizations, how can the United States' viewpoints and negotiations thus conducted be harmonized with its bilateral relations? If special regional organizations, especially of the "theater command" type, are created, potential conflicts arise both with individual country missions and with Washington. In international agencies of specialized character, is the leading voice for the United States always to be provided by the State Department, or should it come from the functional agency most closely concerned? Or should the United States be represented by multi-agency teams, as has become customary in NATO?

COORDINATION AT THE COUNTRY LEVEL

The Role of the Ambassador

Responsibility for coordination of overseas representation at the country level is centered on the ambassador. What are the tasks faced by a conscientious ambassador who is placed in charge of a medium-sized or large American mission to a country participating in the whole range of the United States' foreign operations?

The ambassador has many official duties, of course, which he must perform in person. He must establish and maintain contact with the head of state, the head of the government, the foreign minister, and other principal cabinet members. If he is assigned to a democratic country with opposition political parties, he must know the leaders of the opposition who may take office. He must come to know the American press corps stationed in the country and the press corps of the country itself. He must exchange formal visits with other ambassadors, entertain and be entertained by the rest of the diplomatic corps. The local American business community and other resident Americans of influence must be among his acquaintances. His range of contacts must extend beyond the official sphere to all types of leaders—in business, in the labor unions, among religious, civic, and educational institutions, agriculture, and other circles. He is called on for a variety of speeches, some purely ceremonial but many of substance bearing on the country's relations with the United States. He must travel widely in the country, learn of its internal problems, and meet leading citizens outside the capital city. If he can command the language of the country, his influence will be multiplied many times over.

The ambassador's function of representation is further magnified by today's ease of travel and the resulting large number of visiting Americans. Many of them expect at least to see the ambassador and preferably to be entertained by him. This is true, of course, of Senators and Congressmen and of Washington officials from many departments; it is also true of many private citizens. The ambassador must also facilitate their contacts with the country's government.

While much of the burden of day-to-day negotiation will be carried by his staff, the ambassador himself must take personal part in bilateral negotiations that reach the cabinet level. To perform his duties effectively, he must spend a good deal of time keeping informed. This may mean reading hundreds of cablegrams and despatches each week going in and out of his mission, seeing the local press, keeping abreast of news from home, and drawing information from his innumerable personal contacts of all kinds, as well as from his own staff. He must be prepared, often at very short notice, to return to Washington for consultation and perhaps for testimony before Congressional committees.

This extraordinarily diverse range of personal functions is in addition to his responsibilities for coordinating the work of American representatives in the country. In sheer variety and demand on time and energy, although of course not in responsibility for decision, the ambassadorial task is perhaps comparable only to the Presidency. It can be properly carried out only by highly capable individuals, backed by effective and well-organized staff support.

The Country-Level Organization

What sort of staff support will the typical embassy offer to the ambassador? He will have a political section, manned with Foreign Service Officers recruited under the 1946 legislation. They will assume most of the burden of contacts with the Foreign

Office below the cabinet level, general negotiation, and political reporting. There will be a larger economic section, probably manned in part with former reserve or departmental officers incorporated into the expanded Foreign Service under the Wriston reforms. Some of the economic officers will not be on the State Department payroll and will have special responsibilities to and channels of communication with other agencies in Washington. There may be a Treasury representative; there will certainly be an agricultural attaché.

The staff will include a consular section, with units not only in the capital but also in other major centers in the country. This will also be manned primarily by old-line Foreign Service Officers. While many of its duties are routine, they include dealing with visa applications and handling the problems of American citizens in difficulty—both sensitive areas in relations with the country, which may require the ambassador's personal attention from time to time. In a large country, the consulates may also have important local political and economic reporting and representational functions. For housekeeping support, the mission will have an administrative section dealing with office space and housing, personnel administration, security, the embassy budget, local transportation, and the special personnel problems of local citizens employed by the embassy.

The remaining civilian officials will be organized in missions at least partly independent of the embassy proper. There may be a very sizable United States Information Service group, with total personnel perhaps rivaling that of the embassy itself and with representatives in all major cities. Its chief will serve as the public-relations officer of the ambassador, helping to draft his speeches, maintaining effective relations with the press and other information media, and advising on public relations generally. He will also be the head of a substantial operating program to inform the country's citizens about the United States and its policies, to report home on public opinion in the country, and to carry out the State Department's educational exchange and cultural programs. Then there may be an Agency for International Development mission, conducting many negotiations on the technical aspects of assistance programs and supervising a considerable body of American technical personnel in various parts of the country. The AID group may or may not be integrated with the economic section of the embassy. There will be also a semi-independent group of intelligence officers.

On the military side, the ambassador will have on his immediate staff attachés from each of the three services and a group of officers dealing directly with the military services of the country. There may also be a semi-independent Military Assistance Advisory Group, with its responsibilities for providing equipment and military training. Finally, if there are American military installations in the country, they will be in charge of a senior military officer with large groups of subordinate officers and enlisted men, whose presence in the country adds a major additional dimension to the ambassador's coordinating responsibilities.

The functions and supporting staffs so far described are all concerned with bilateral relations between the country and the United States. If the capital happens also to be the headquarters of a regional international organization, the ambassador must have at least some contact with the permanent American delegation there. In any case, he must be knowledgeable on regional as well as national issues and be prepared to deal with them in bilateral negotiations and in conferences with his colleagues in the other countries of the region as well as in Washington.

The Task of Coordination

The task of coordination at the country level is to keep this large and diverse bundle of activities and staffs working together harmoniously and in accord with the basic lines of American policy toward the country. As executive tasks go, the number of persons involved in foreign representation in any country is not very large, but the variety and complexity of functions, and the sensitivity inherent in international relations, pose a problem of effective coordination wholly out of proportion to these mere numbers.

The task of resolving this problem rests squarely with the ambassador. In diplomatic form, he is the President's personal representative to the head of the state, and he is theoretically senior in rank even to the Vice President or the Secretary of State when they visit the country. Apart from this position of unquestioned seniority, he has a special coordinating charter, which now takes the form of President Kennedy's circular letter of May 29, 1961, addressed to all United States ambassadors. This document is of such cardinal importance to the coordination of overseas representation that it is quoted here in full:

DEAR MR. AMBASSADOR:

Please accept my best wishes for the successful accomplishment of your mission. As the personal representative of the President of the United States in ———, you are part of a memorable tradition which began with Benjamin Franklin and Thomas Jefferson, and which has included many of our most distinguished citizens.

We are living in a critical moment in history. Powerful destructive forces are challenging the universal values which, for centuries, have inspired men of good will in all parts of the world.

If we are to make progress toward a prosperous community of nations in a world of peace, the United States must exercise the most affirmative and responsible leadership. Beyond our shores, this leadership, in large measure, must be provided by our ambassadors and their staffs.

I have asked you to represent our Government in ——— because I am confident that you have the ability, dedication, and experience. The purpose of this letter is to define guidelines which I hope may be helpful to you.

The practice of modern diplomacy requires a close understanding not only of governments but also of people, their cultures and institutions. Therefore, I hope that you will plan your work so that you may have the time to travel extensively outside the nation's capital. Only in this way can you develop the close, personal associations that go beyond official diplomatic circles and maintain a sympathetic and accurate understanding of all segments of the country.

Moreover, the improved understanding which is so essential to a more peaceful and rational world is a two-way street. It is our task not only to understand what motivates others, but to give them a better understanding of what motivates us.

Many persons in ——— who have never visited the United States, receive their principal impressions of our nation through their contact with Americans who come to their country either as private citizens or as government employees.

Therefore, the manner in which you and your staff personally conduct yourselves is of the utmost importance. This applies to the way in which you carry out your official duties and to the attitudes you and they bring to day-to-day contacts and associations.

It is an essential part of your task to create a climate of dignified, dedicated understanding, cooperation, and service in and around the Embassy.

In regard to your personal authority and responsibility, I shall count on you to oversee and coordinate all the activities of the United States Government in ————.

You are in charge of the entire United States Diplomatic Mission, and I shall expect you to supervise all of its operations. The Mission includes not only the personnel of the Department of State and the Foreign Service, but also the representatives of all other United States agencies which have programs or activities in ————. I shall give you full support and backing in carrying out your assignment.

Needless to say, the representatives of other agencies are expected to communicate directly with their offices here in Washington, and in the event of a decision by you in which they do not concur, they may ask to have the decision reviewed by a higher authority in Washington.

However, it is their responsibility to keep you fully informed of their views and activities and to abide by your decisions unless in some particular instance you and they are notified to the contrary.

If in your judgment individual members of the Mission are not functioning effectively, you should take whatever action you feel may be required, reporting the circumstances, of course, to the Department of State.

In case the departure from————of any individual member of the Mission is indicated in your judgment, I shall expect you to make the decision and see that it is carried into effect. Such instances I am confident will be rare.

Now one word about your relations to the military. As you know, the United States Diplomatic Mission includes Service Attachés, Military Assistance Advisory Groups, and other Military components attached to the Mission. It does not, however, include United States military forces operating in the field where such forces are under the command of a United States area military commander.

The line of authority to these forces runs from me, to the Secretary of Defense, to the Joint Chiefs of Staff in Washington and to the area commander in the field.

Although this means that the chief of the American Diplomatic Mission is not in the line of military command, nevertheless, as Chief of Mission, you should work closely with the appropriate area military commander to assure the full exchange of information. If it is your opinion that activities by the United States military forces may adversely affect our over-all relations with the people or government of ————, you should promptly discuss the matter with the military commander and, if necessary, request a decision by higher authority.

I have informed all heads of departments and agencies of the Government of the responsibilities of the chiefs of American Diplomatic Missions for our combined operations abroad, and I have asked them to instruct their representatives in the field accordingly.

As you know, your own lines of communication as Chief of Mission run through the Department of State.

Let me close with an expression of confidence in you personally and the earnest hope that your efforts may help strengthen our relations with both the Government and the people of ————. I am sure that you will make a major contribution to the cause of world peace and understanding.

Good luck and my warmest regards,

Sincerely,

[Signed] John F. Kennedy*

This is a sweeping assignment of coordinating authority. It is the culminating step in a series of statutory provisions, executive orders, and Presidential directives issued during the postwar years. The clear trend in the succession of documents has been toward increasing authority for the ambassador, not merely as coordinator but as active leader of the whole array of official American activities in his country of assignment.†

---

* Paragraphs 16 and 17 were omitted from letters sent to ambassadors in countries in which there were no United States military forces under an area military commander.

† This evolution is well documented in the booklet entitled *The Ambassador and the Problem of Coordination*, prepared by the Historical Studies Division

It is especially significant that the Kennedy letter, unlike earlier directives, refers to the ambassador's authority and responsibility to "oversee" and "supervise," as well as to "coordinate." Since the diplomatic mission includes attachés on the payrolls of various civilian and military agencies, as well as semi-autonomous AID, USIS, and military-assistance missions, this comes close to making the ambassador a civilian theater commander for American official activities in the country concerned—a Presidential representative for the overseas policy direction of many functions which are backstopped by agencies in Washington other than the Department of State.

Since, however, the ambassador is on the payroll of the State Department and receives his instructions from or through the Secretary of State, this arrangement necessarily requires sensitive handling of the relations with other agencies by the State Department at home and by the ambassador abroad. There will be noted the explicit safeguards in the Kennedy letter of the right of other agencies to communicate with their overseas representatives, and the right of the latter to request Washington review of ambassadorial decisions from which they dissent.

In practice as well as theory, the trend has been toward greater acceptance of broad ambassadorial responsibility. There have been occasional exceptions, some of them highly publicized, involving economic or intelligence officers functioning independently from and at variance with the views of the ambassadors concerned. Such cases, however, have been resolved in favor of ambassadorial authority. The resulting situation is in sharp contrast to the wartime conditions when various independent missions conducted their affairs in total disregard even of the ambassador's existence, to say nothing of his authority. The oral and written testimony of many ambassadors to the Senate Subcommittee on National Security Staffing and Operations makes clear with near unanimity that ambassadorial supremacy is generally recognized.

The powerful sanction of demanding the withdrawal of any American official who is *persona non grata* to an ambassador is

---

of the State Department for the Senate Subcommittee on National Security Staffing and Operations, and published by the U.S. Government Printing Office in July, 1963.

very rarely used, but its existence is an important reinforcement to the ambassador's rank and prestige. More important, as the operating programs have come to be increasingly important in international relations, ambassadors have in fact developed a keen interest in their conduct and taken an active part, with the specialized officers concerned, in the development of their programs and policies.

Integrated Embassies or Specialized Missions?

Until comparatively recently, it was taken for granted that special program operations overseas required special missions to administer them. During World War II, these were wholly independent of the embassies, and there were many cases of severe friction. At the close of the war, it was generally agreed that this was not a happy experience and that it should be avoided in all but overriding emergencies. Nonetheless, the postwar relief missions were also established on an independent basis and the first special aid mission to Greece was established apart from the embassy and even from ambassadorial control. In the case of the ECA, as Chapter 1 has shown, the emphasis was on independent missions but with special provisions for exchange of information and suspensive veto by the ambassador. The Point IV missions were originally established on a semi-independent basis; this pattern exists today with the missions for economic and technical assistance, for military assistance, and for information and educational exchange.

The main impetus for independent specialized missions results from the fact that in Washington, responsibility is placed in independent agencies, and they naturally desire to be served abroad by their own men. Assuming that there are independent program agencies in Washington, however, could not the embassies nonetheless be so organized and staffed as to serve all their purposes? Or are there overriding advantages in the specialized mission as a type of organization?

There are certainly many arguments in favor of the latter arrangement. If private citizens from other walks of life are desired to direct individual country operations, it may be easier to attract them if they are given the rank and prestige of mission chiefs than if they are merely senior officers in an elaborate embassy hierarchy. Separate missions lend themselves to flexible staffing and budgetary procedures and to varying degrees of devolution of authority as desired by the home agencies. It is also sometimes argued that specialized missions can have greater freedom of action in dealing with governments and private groups abroad, on the theory that they can take locally unpopular positions or exert pressures that would be impossible or embarrassing for an embassy in view of the basic tradition of noninterference in another country's sovereign affairs.

This latter point, however, seems largely illusory. In the eyes of foreign governments and peoples, the United States has one and not many faces. Private citizens, of course, can do things that government officials can not, but if resentment is aroused by official pressures or activities, it is unlikely to be assuaged because the pressure comes from a special mission rather than an embassy. Divergence of approach among various American representatives is more likely to cause confusion as to what the United States really wants, or to give the foreign country an opportunity to drive wedges between the several agencies.

Moreover, independent missions may cause not only frictions but also sheer inefficiencies in operation. Neat functional lines cannot in practice be drawn between their various areas of responsibility. In the case of the ECA, it was not long before its country staffs were involved in serious overlaps or outright competition with the economic reporting and general informational activities of the embassies. In seeking the disposal of agricultural surpluses, areas of overlap immediately develop with the economic- and technical-aid programs, and even occasionally with the military-aid program, with general economic policy relationships, with the field of public relations, and with the broad concerns of political relationships and cold-war strategy. Examples could be multiplied.

Moreover, work loads in various segments of the official family fluctuate a good deal, and the ability to spread assignments can mean substantial savings in manpower and make for a far more harmonious and effective working team. A fully integrated embassy organization, in which all civilian personnel, regardless of payroll status, are in a direct command hierarchy headed by the ambassador, offers the best prospect of maximum working efficiency and effective country-level coordination.

Apart from purely administrative considerations, the exigencies of the cold war tend to draw more tightly together the diplomatic, political, military, economic, informational, and cultural activities of the United States in each country. Whatever may be the merits of the "theater command" idea as applied to regions, there are certainly some real advantages in adopting this concept in individual country representation. The emphasis is on *command* and not merely *coordination*, and the trend has been in this direction, as shown above.

Should this line of thought be carried to its logical conclusion—the abolition of specialized independent missions at the country level? The military missions are probably an unavoidable exception, in view of their necessarily specialized personnel system and the deeply rooted principles of the military chain of command. On the civilian side, however, the question is whether the advantages of complete embassy integration can be secured without sacrificing the very real advantages—in personnel selection and administrative flexibility—of the specialized missions. This depends largely on the personnel systems applied to representation overseas for the manifold activities in which the United States Government is now involved.

The postwar development of staffing arrangements for our expanding overseas representation has been described in Chapter 1. It will be recalled that, despite the effort to create a unified Foreign Service for the old-line agencies, the Treasury and Agricultural departments have had separate overseas representation for some time, and there is endemic pressure from other agencies to follow these examples. The newer overseas operating agencies have their own staffing systems.

From the viewpoint of effective integration of official activities, these arrangements leave much to be desired. The simple solution would appear to be to broaden the Foreign Service further to accommodate all civilian needs. Short of this, the Herter Committee recommendations for a "family of compatible services" would go a long way in the same direction. It should be noted that the Herter Committee also recommended the incorporation of overseas Treasury and Agriculture personnel into the Foreign Service.

The advantages of such a development would be many. The chronic inequities and frictions inherent in the operation of several personnel systems in a single foreign capital would be removed at the source. Such tendencies as still persist for political officers to regard their colleagues as second-class citizens would be greatly weakened. Above all, a broadened service would be likely to generate in embassies a genuine attitude, in place of the lip service that is still all too common, of serving the interests of the government as a whole.

On the answer to the question of the broadened personnel system probably depends the feasibility of developing genuinely integrated embassies. It is true that, during the last several years, practical integration in economic affairs has been accomplished at many posts, despite the multiplicity of payrolls; and officers of the departments of State, Commerce, Agriculture, Labor, the Treasury, and AID have worked smoothly together as single teams. In some cases, moreover, the administrative sections of the embassies have been given the responsibility of providing housekeeping services for non–State Department personnel. These are, however, inherently uneasy arrangements, largely dependent for their success on individual leadership and good personal relations.

REGIONAL COORDINATION

One consequence of rapid technological advance in transportation, communications, and military weapons has been to increase the relative importance in international relations of problems of a regional character. This is by no means a wholly new development, as the long record of pan-American cooperation makes clear. During the postwar period, however, its importance has greatly expanded, and the new American role of leadership in the free world has led to active participation in regional organizations in almost all parts of the globe.

The regional factor is especially marked in collective-security arrangements. Although the cold war is global in scope, the organizations designed to bolster the free world's physical defenses are almost all regional in character: NATO, SEATO, CENTO, and ANZUS. Certain outstanding international political issues, moreover, are essentially regional in character: a leading example is the Arab-Israeli conflict. The Pan-American Union has been replaced by the much more far-reaching Organization of American States.

In the economic field, likewise, while there are major global interests reflected in the United Nations, the International Bank and Monetary Fund, and the General Agreement on Tariffs and Trade, much attention has also been given to promoting cooperation on a regional basis. The United States is a full member of the U.N. regional Economic Commissions for Europe, Asia and the Far East, Latin America, and Africa. We are also active members of the Organization for Economic Cooperation and Development and the Inter-American Development Bank, and we maintain special relations with the European Economic Community and the Central American organizations for economic integration. In South and Southeast Asia, we are likewise members of the Colombo Plan Organization for promoting economic development. And with the broadening of Western Hemisphere cooperation in the economic and social fields, we have become a leading member of the Inter-American Committee on the Alliance for Progress.

This enhanced importance of regionalism has naturally been reflected in the arrangements for United States overseas representation. Individual country representatives have had to become informed on and able to deal with regional problems and to be in close touch with their opposite numbers in other countries of the region. Permanent delegations have had to be established wherever we participate actively in regional organizations. And there has been some experimentation in the establishment of offices abroad concerned solely with regional interests and charged with coordinating country representation on regional matters.

Coordination at the regional level has two dimensions. For any given function or program, there is a problem of geographical coordination among the individual countries concerned. On a region-wide basis, there may also be a problem of interfunctional or inter-agency coordination.

Regional Coordination of Single Functions

In Washington, the regional factor in foreign affairs is often emphasized by making geographical areas the basis of headquarters organization. This has been true for many decades of the political offices in the State Department. Since the reorganization of 1949, the principal units of the Department have been geographical bureaus headed by Assistant Secretaries. Within the bureaus of European and American Republic Affairs, the unusual importance of regional interests is reflected in special offices of regional affairs. And in the defense organizations, regional theater commands have become the principal elements of our military structure overseas.

Both the State Department and other agencies concerned with foreign representation have also developed the device of periodic regional conferences. At such conferences, there is assembled a group of ambassadors and top political officers, or economic officers, or information officers, labor officers, etc., from a regionally associated group of countries, together with senior Washington officials concerned with their area and specialty. Such conferences serve three purposes. They bring the overseas representatives up to date on Washington thinking and prospective action through personal contact that even the best communications systems cannot match. They provide to each country group both the opportunity and the impulse to be informed on the problems of neighboring countries. They focus the attention of country representatives on regional policy issues and develop recommended courses of governmental action from a regional point of view.

Under this arrangement, however, the only officers concerned with region-wide matters are in Washington, and there is no provision for regional coordination on a continuing basis. In the European Recovery Program, an effort was made to go beyond this, through establishing a regional headquarters in Paris with substantial authority over the ECA's country missions. The Office of the Special Representative in Europe was far more than an American delegation to the OEEC. In many ways, it was closer to a theater command organization. It had delegated to it much of the budgetary and personnel control of the country missions, and it served as a channel between Washington and the missions on many policy and program matters. Moreover, because of the program's heavy emphasis on European cooperation, integration, and joint programming, the office carried the regional-conference device to unusual lengths. In the program's most active phase, scarcely a week went by when, at the Hotel Talleyrand in Paris, there were not assembled program, trade, finance, industry, agriculture, information, productivity, and other special officers from the ECA missions to the seventeen participating countries.

There is much controversy over the merits of this ECA experiment. The triangular arrangement of Washington, Paris, and country-level organizations certainly engendered a good deal of jurisdictional conflict. On the other hand, it played a major part in giving the program a European-wide character and in enhancing the role of the OEEC. Without it, the entire effort might have become a mere congeries of bilateral programs, with the results simply added up from time to time for presentational purposes. Moreover, it brought about a close concerting of American negotiation with European government representatives in the OEEC and in the national capitals. The ECA record was superior in this regard to the experience during the first years of NATO, when our delegation in London had no coordinating authority with respect to the country missions. This weakness was later somewhat remedied by the formal terms of reference issued to our North Atlantic Council Deputy in 1951, and more strongly by establishing the post of the President's Special Representative in Europe in 1952.

Other experiments in regional coordination of single functions include the Joint American Military Advisory Group, which supervised the various country military-assistance and training programs in Europe, and a short-lived and not too successful roving ambassadorship in the Middle East in the early 1950's. An analogous, but not too clearly defined, example in 1953–54 was the assignment of an ambassador who, in addition to representing the United States in the Schuman Plan and the interim commission for the European Defense Community, was responsible for coordinating American efforts to secure ratification of the EDC Treaty in the countries concerned.

Theater Command versus *Regional Cooperation*

The high-water mark of efforts to organize American representation overseas in regional patterns was the Office of the President's Special Representative in Europe in 1952–53. In this office, geographical and functional coordinating responsibilities were combined: it not only inherited the old ECA Paris headquarters' relations with country economic missions, but also included representation to NATO, coordination of U.S. positions on the defense programs of the European NATO countries, military offshore-procurement policy, and defense-strategy questions as related to NATO. So wide a charter and range of interests necessarily extended to the very broadest issues of general foreign policy that were relevant to matters of European interest, especially European military and economic cooperation and integration. During its brief existence, this office was an important center of regional initiative in the whole complex of West European developments.

It was the closest approach to a genuine theater-command concept in any of our overseas civilian offices. Despite its many and important accomplishments, it generated the same kinds of jurisdictional frictions and resistance the ECA Paris headquarters had experienced, but magnified several times because of its all-inclusive functional scope. This was especially true on the political side, in relations with country embassies. Individual ambassadors were neither ready nor willing to accept a regional Presidential representative in the chain of command between them and Washington. Nor was such a concept acceptable to the State Department itself, which was never too pleased with having a regional Presidential representative reporting to the Secretaries of Defense and Treasury and to the Director for Mutual Security as well as to the Secretary of State—and therefore, perhaps, in the final analysis answerable only to the President.

For these reasons, the formal terms of reference for the Paris regional office never fully embodied the idea of a political theater command. To the extent that its practical operations approached this status, it built up tensions that tended to undermine even its coordinating role. It was often accused of assuming responsibility for bilateral negotiations that individual country embassies regarded as wholly within their own jurisdictions. This was especially the case in France, where its physical presence encouraged the government to negotiate directly with it rather than through the regular embassy. To some extent, the conflict was inherent in the very existence of a strong regional office, since at that time almost all matters of defense and economic policy at issue between the European nations and the United States contained major, if not predominant, regional elements.

In these circumstances, only a vigorous reconfirmation of its authority under Presidential direction could have maintained the position of the regional office. This was not forthcoming from the Truman Administration, and in 1953 the Eisenhower Administration took prompt action to reduce the size and authority of the Paris regional office. It was reshaped into a U.S. Mission to NATO and European Regional Organizations (USRO), and it was expressly debarred from having "any supervisory powers over the U.S. country teams of Europe." The bitterness of jurisdictional antagonism aroused by the previous arrangements can be seen in the wording of the final paragraph of the Presidentially approved memorandum reorganizing the office: "The members of USRO will not (repeat not) initiate directly with officials of other governments, except for those governments' representatives on the multilateral organization, any item of United States business."

In the internal organization of USRO, however, some degree of inter-functional coordination was retained despite the almost vehement rejection of geographical coordination. Under its Chief, who was given ambassadorial rank and who reported to, and only to, the State Department, there were political, defense, economic, and financial sections. Their heads were appointed by the Departments of State and Defense, the Foreign Operations Administration, and the Treasury respectively, but they were to report to their respective agencies through the Chief of USRO. It was also provided that: "The staff of USRO will be integrated in the sense that the Chief of USRO will be responsible for providing it with general direction, leadership and coordination and that he has authority to utilize it as he deems necessary for the effective conduct of the operations of the mission."

The importance of the regional factor in West European affairs was such that, even with its greatly reduced authority, the Paris office continued to serve as a center for regional conferences of American officials and as a focus for considerable informal coopera-tion among them. But this is clearly voluntary cooperation, and in no sense one of command.

This history must be carefully weighed in any future considera-tion of overseas regional theater commands led by "super-ambassa-dors." The major points of action tend to be national capitals, where governmental decisions are taken, although these decisions can be strongly influenced by effective regional organizations. In any case, what can be done is to ensure, through organization and otherwise, that regional factors are given full weight in policy-making and program operations. This suggests at a minimum more systematic cooperation among embassies in each region, more frequent and better organized regional conferences at both the ambassadorial and lower levels, and more systematic communication between the delegations to regional organizations and the country missions in the region. It may also suggest very small staffs at regional centers, normally associated with delegations to regional organizations and charged with studying and reporting on regional developments, traveling between the country missions to keep them informed on and thinking about regional problems, and helping to develop policy recommendations on region-wide problems.

COORDINATION IN WASHINGTON

Whether the ambassador is a country theater-commander or simply a coordinator, his effectiveness in serving the entire range of United States governmental interests in a foreign country will depend largely on the kind of direction he gets from home. The problem of organizing the central government at Washington for effective formulation and direction of foreign affairs raises many issues that far transcend the scope of this volume—the appropriate roles and relationships of the Congress and the Executive Branch, the proper limits of Executive discretion, basic relations between the military and civilian arms of the government, bipartisanship in foreign-policy making, and the development of public interest in foreign affairs and public support for foreign policy. The discussion here is confined to the much narrower topic of coordination as it bears on our overseas representation.

Previous chapters have described the range of postwar experiments in overseas organization, at both the country and the regional level, and have emphasized the broad alternatives of full integration, coordination under ambassadors, and division into general-purpose embassies and special-purpose missions. The choice among them will largely determine the harmony of operations abroad, and the balance of information and policy recommendations available in Washington from the field. But no amount of integration abroad can create harmony if there is none in the instructions from home. If it is a sound philosophy that missions overseas are to serve in proper balance the totality of American interests in relation to each country, and that all foreign policies and programs intercept and interact upon one another, the guidance and instructions flowing abroad must reflect that basic unity of relationship.

This does not happen automatically. Among the agencies with foreign interests or employees overseas, only the Department of State is concerned solely with foreign policy. Each of the others has a major, if not preponderant, interest in domestic affairs, and each has its own special committees or friends in the Congress and its own organized interest groups in the American public. This is obviously true of such departments as Agriculture, Commerce, Labor, and the Treasury. It is perhaps less true of the Department of Defense, but even in this instance, the preoccupations with interservice rivalries, budgetary provisions, and procurement from home industry, to say nothing of the special problems of overseas bases and military personnel, may cut across or run counter to the main lines of foreign policy.

Until fairly recently, little systematic attention was given to foreign-policy coordination. The dominant role of the Department of State was taken for granted. The military services sometimes had their own foreign policies, and the other civilian departments were guided in such few foreign activities as they had by their essentially domestic interests. But the conditions of cold war and of world leadership for the United States make this no longer possible. In the postwar period, foreign-policy coordination has become a central focus of attention in Washington. The efforts to deal with it center around three major points: the role of the Department of State; the use of informal coordinating devices; and the systematic organization of the Presidency to this end.

The Role of the State Department

The State Department performs a dual function. It is the President's principal source of advice on foreign policy, and it has the operating responsibility for the central corps of civilian representation abroad in the embassies. Since it is the major foreign-policy department in any case, the question naturally arises: why not broaden it to include the whole range of foreign affairs? Could not the problem of coordination thus be simply swept up in a grand process of consolidation?

Serious thought has been given to this approach in various postwar studies, but it rapidly runs afoul of major obstacles. It obviously could not be applied to the military services; yet there is no way of divorcing the Department of Defense from its foreign-policy interests and foreign operating responsibilities. Nor could consolidation work as a practical matter in relation to the major domestic departments with foreign interests, notably the Treasury, Agriculture, Commerce, and Labor.

To be sure, some of the borderline responsibilities of these departments might conceivably be transferred to the Department of State. This would doubtless be feasible, for example, with the Commerce Department's export controls and the Treasury Department's customs service. But many of the major foreign interests of these departments flow directly from their domestic interests. For example, the promotion of agricultural markets abroad and the disposal of agricultural surpluses are integral parts of the work of the Agriculture Department. The technical knowledge lies there; the contacts with agricultural interests and farm organizations are there; and a strong Congressional interest is allied with the work of that Department. The same could be said of the Treasury's interest in international financial transactions and of the corresponding concerns of the Departments of Commerce and Labor. From their viewpoint, the foreign and domestic aspects of their activities are as inseparably linked as are the various facets of foreign policy in the eyes of the Department of State. Any effort to transfer these responsibilities *en masse* to a single department of foreign affairs not only would create an administrative monstrosity, but would lead to new problems of coordination more numerous than the ones it had eliminated.

Mention must also be made of the chronic susceptibility of the Department of State to a degree of public and Congressional mistrust. This may be partly a result of purely ephemeral factors, but it is to some extent inherent in the position of an agency lacking any organized domestic constituency or corresponding strong Congressional interest, and often thought of as "representing foreigners."

It might be possible, of course, to include in a single department all units now concerned exclusively with foreign affairs. This would mean adding to the Department of State, in addition to the foreign-aid responsibilities placed there in 1955, the intelligence and foreign information functions now in separate agencies. In this connection, mention has already been made of the 1951 proposals for a super-Department of Foreign Affairs, organized on lines parallel to the Defense Department, with subordinate departments in political, economic, and information and cultural fields.*

There is certainly much merit in the view that the distinction between policy guidance, organized in a small State Department, and operational responsibilities, organized wholly in other agencies, is untenable. Policy and action merge in practice. Yet, if one begins to think through the tripartite scheme, certain serious difficulties soon are manifest. There is little real analogy with the symmetry of the Defense Department. Only a very small class of problems is strictly "political," without economic, psychological, or military dimensions. Where overlaps exist—and that is almost everywhere —would the political subdepartment have overriding authority, or would there be the same problems of interdepartmental coordination that now exist on an inter-agency basis? The first Hoover Commission was impressed with the difficulties of lateral coordina-

* In 1959, a similar proposal, worked out in much greater detail, was submitted by the Brookings Institution to the Senate Committee on Foreign Relations in a report entitled *The Formulation and Administration of United States Foreign Policy.*

tion between equally strong functional and geographical offices within the Department of State; its recommended reorganization, which gave primary weight to the geographical bureaus, has substantially improved the internal working arrangements. Would not the tripartite-agency scheme recreate these issues of internal coordination on a greatly magnified scale? It is doubts such as these that have led consistently to the rejection of a "Foreign Affairs Department."

Inter-Agency Cooperation

If consolidation is not feasible, can satisfactory coordination be achieved through inter-agency cooperation under State Department leadership, if not authority? Much of the day-to-day business of Washington is in fact conducted on just this basis. Within the Department of State, there is an elaborate lateral clearance system, with the initiating office securing approval of a proposed instruction or communication from other interested offices. This simple, informal, and usually fairly prompt device can be and is frequently extended to matters of inter-agency interest as well. But it tends to break down whenever there is no clear locus of primary responsibility or wherever there are stubborn conflicts of agency opinion. Moreover, there may be cases where the problem obviously is of interest to a number of agencies at the outset.

To these situations, the normal response is to organize inter-agency committees. Countless committees of this type have been established, some to deal *ad hoc* with particular problems, some to handle a given range of problems on a standing basis, some informal and at low level, others highly formalized at Cabinet or sub-Cabinet level. Committee meetings absorb a remarkably large share of the Washington executive's time, and they are often criticized as inconclusive, frustrating, and tending to the lowest common denominators of agreement rather than clear-cut decisions.

Much depends on how they are led, and on the presence or absence of a center of responsibility within them. Where an inter-agency committee chairman has clear action responsibility, and the committee essentially serves to inform him of other agency views, to criticize and to recommend but not to obstruct, they can work smoothly and constructively. Even if the chairman's decision is subject to appeal, there is at least a single focus of decision. But where inter-agency committees operate on the *liberum veto* principle, frustration is at least as likely as decision.

Could the State Department be given the role of authoritative leadership in all inter-agency coordination concerned with foreign affairs? In many of the postwar inter-agency committees, it has effectively carried such a role. But where there have been really strong military, agricultural, or other non-foreign-policy interests at stake, it has not always been able to assert its primacy.

The only statutory Cabinet-level committee in the foreign-affairs field, except for the Presidentially-chaired National Security Council, is the National Advisory Council on International Monetary and Financial Problems (NAC), established by the Bretton Woods Agreement Act of 1945. This group meets under the chairmanship of the Secretary of the Treasury and contains representatives of the State and Commerce departments, the Federal Reserve System, and the Export-Import Bank. The NAC has fulfilled effectively its primary functions of determining the positions of American representatives to the International Bank and Monetary Fund. Its statutory charter also included coordination of the "policies and operations of . . . all other agencies of the Government to the extent that they make or participate in the making of foreign loans or engage in foreign financial, exchange or monetary transactions." In this broader area, the committee has been less successful, because other departments have been unwilling to accept Treasury primacy on matters that have indeed a financial aspect but that also have other aspects of major concern to them.

The same limitations have often made it difficult for inter-agency committees under State Department chairmanship to secure general agreement on issues cutting across multiple-agency interests. In short, despite the senior Cabinet rank of the Secretary of State and the Department's role as principal foreign-policy adviser to the President, other agencies have often been unwilling to accept it as an authoritative coordinator. This role is necessarily reserved for the ultimate source of Executive authority in the American system, the President himself.

Organizing the Presidency

As inter-agency relations have become more complex, an ever-increasing number of issues are thrust upward for Presidential decision. Both to prevent the President's time from being taken up wholly with them, and to ensure that decisions of cardinal importance are not made casually or in ignorance of essential factors bearing on them, it has become necessary to organize the Presidency to deal with them. During the postwar period, a variety of experiments have been made in the organization of the Presidency on the foreign-affairs side.

The one constant in these experiments has been the National Security Council (NSC). As originally conceived in the Eberstadt Report to the Secretary of the Navy and incorporated into the National Security Act of 1947, this body was to be composed of the President and three Cabinet officers concerned with national-security matters. The Secretary of State was to represent foreign-policy considerations in all their aspects; the Secretary of Defense was to do likewise for the military factors; and the chairman of the National Security Resources Board (now the director of the Office of Defense Mobilization) was to represent the domestic-resource base and to coordinate all the departments and agencies concerned with it. Today, as the developments of the cold war have made security considerations paramount over the broad range of foreign affairs, and because the NSC is the sole inter-agency committee except for the Cabinet in which the President is himself in the chair, it has become the center of formal foreign-policy–making. But the statutory members do not serve as coordinators of subordinate departments, and in fact a number of other agencies are regularly present or invited to appear when their agency interests are involved.

Under the NSC is a Planning Board at the Assistant Secretary level, charged with preparing draft policy papers and giving preliminary consideration to NSC matters. The Eisenhower Administration also established an Operations Coordinating Board designed to oversee action to carry out the established policies, but this was abolished by President Kennedy, who believed that implementation of policy should be handled directly by the departments concerned. In the foreign economic field, the Eisenhower Administration also established a Council on Foreign Economic Policy under a Special Assistant to the President, and other *ad hoc* committees under White House staff chairmanship operated in such fields as agricultural surplus disposal. With his intense personal interest in foreign policy, President Kennedy tended to rely less on formal machinery than on *ad hoc* meetings of his principal advisers. He did add to the White House staff itself, however, several officers primarily concerned with foreign policy.

Because of the particular community of interests between the departments of State and Defense in the national-security field, close working links have also been forged directly between them, including on the Defense side not only the civilian department heads but also the Joint Chiefs of Staff.

With its unquestioned and unquestionable authority, the Presidency has been able to infuse a common stream of policy direction into the work of the many agencies concerned with foreign affairs. Many conflicts of foreign and domestic interests have been frankly faced and decisions taken under the aegis of true authority.

There can be large gaps, of course, between high-level decisions in the National Security Council and day-to-day instructions to or actions in the field. In the sometimes long process of translation from one to the other, harmony may prove to be more apparent than real, and conscious or subconscious administrative sabotage may occur. It is at this point again that the organization and personnel systems for overseas representation may determine whether the operating policy is genuinely coordinated. This is likewise the point at which a unified civilian foreign-affairs service would appear to offer some of its greatest advantages.

COORDINATION, CENTRALIZATION, AND COMPETITION

I remarked at the outset of this chapter that coordination, however important, is not an end in itself. Effective coordination is no matter of mere mechanical procedure, and it is meaningless without clarity in the making and communicating of policy. Moreover, its virtues must be set alongside those of creative initiative, resourcefulness, and flexibility, virtues often stimulated most by a degree of competition. This is the characteristic experience of large business organizations. Despite all the costs of inter-service rivalries, competition in the military field has also produced substantial benefits in such areas as research and development. While a common stream of policy and a means promptly to resolve conflicts are indispensable, it would be a sad day for United States foreign policy if all thought and action were confined on a totalitarian pattern to rigid party-line channels.

Moreover, coordination is not to be confused with centralization. Nothing can be more deadening to working morale and enthusiasm than not being able to carry out a well-defined assignment without having always to glance over one's shoulder at a higher authority or clearing every move with an inter-agency committee. Both in Washington and overseas, a primary task of organizational reform is to draw clean administrative lines wherever it can be done, and to combat relentlessly the chronic tendency toward unnecessary centralization. Maintenance of dispersed centers of initiative and drive is undoubtedly worth a considerable risk of friction and even some duplication. No office or agency is likely to have a monopoly on wisdom and experience. But unless policy is clearly defined and understood up and down the line, delegation and decentralization become almost impossible.

At the same time, in its position of free-world leadership, the United States can hardly afford the luxury of multiple foreign policies or of overseas officials seeking to advance particularistic interests of a dozen different agencies without regard to their interaction, their combined effect, or their possible mutual frustration. Totalitarian centralization is neither the necessary nor the most effective means of coordination, and harmony in purpose and in action can be achieved without destroying vitality and resourcefulness. The true measure of success in any arrangement for coordination of overseas representation will be its ability to meet simultaneously these several tests.

Notes on the Contributors

VINCENT M. BARNETT, JR. is President of Colgate University. He was Professor of Political Science and Dean of Williams College. His experience in public affairs includes service with the War Production Board, the Mutual Security Agency, and in the Agency for International Development. Mr. Barnett is the author of numerous articles and book reviews on international relations.

JOHN LINDEMAN is Adjunct Professor of Economics at the Maxwell Graduate School of Syracuse University. His overseas experience includes service with UNRRA and ECA. He was also an economic consultant to the government of Burma.

HOWLAND H. SARGEANT, President of the Radio Liberty Committee since 1954, was Deputy and Assistant Secretary of State for Public Affairs from 1946 to 1953. In that capacity, he played an important role in developing the United States Government's international information and educational exchange programs. He served as chairman of the United States delegation to three general conferences of UNESCO and, in 1951, was President of the General Conference of that organization.

WILLIAM T. R. FOX is Professor of International Relations and the Director of the Institute of War and Peace Studies at Columbia University. From 1952 to 1963, he was chairman of the Committee on National Security Policy Research of the Social Science Research Council. Professor Fox is the author of several books, including *Challenge to Traditional Ethics: Government, Politics and Administration* and *The Role of Theory in International Relations.* He is also a frequent contributor to a number of periodicals.

PAUL C. DAVIS is currently with the Center for Naval Analyses of the Franklin Institute, Cambridge, Massachusetts. A professional Army officer, he has served in the Department of State and in the Executive Office of the President as an adviser on propaganda and psychological warfare. A former Associate Professor at the Institute of International Studies at the University of South Carolina, Dr. Davis has written extensively on military affairs.

BEN TILLMAN MOORE, Associate Director of the Twentieth Century Fund, was formerly Deputy Chief of the U.S. ECA Mission, London, and Director of the Office of European Regional Affairs. A member of the U.S. delegation to the American-Soviet Joint Commission on Korea in 1946; the conference to establish OEEC in Paris, 1948; the Economic Commission for Europe, Geneva, 1951; and NATO ministerial meetings, 1952–55, he is also the author of NATO *and the Future of Europe,* as well as of numerous articles on European organizations and NATO.

LINCOLN GORDON has been United States Ambassador to Brazil since 1961. In 1946, he was a member of the U.S. delegation to the United Nations Atomic Energy Commission; in 1947, consultant to the State Department for the European Recovery Program; then Director of the Program Division, ECA European headquarters; Assistant Director for Mutual Security; and Director of the U.S. Operations Mission and Minister for Economic Affairs at the American Embassy in London. From 1955 to 1961, he was Professor of International Economics at the Harvard Graduate School of Business Administration.